Sarah Manns   Jim Hill

RHYMES AND REASONS

Senior Authors
Carl B. Smith
Virginia A. Arnold

Linguistics Consultant
Ronald Wardhaugh

Macmillan Publishing Co., Inc.
New York

Collier Macmillan Publishers
London

ACKNOWLEDGMENTS

The publisher gratefully acknowledges permission to reprint the following copyrighted material:

"All Stories Are Anansi's," from *The Hat-Shaking Dance and Other Ashanti Tales from Ghana* by Harold Courlander. Copyright © 1957 by Harold Courlander. Reprinted by permission of Harcourt Brace Jovanovich, Inc.

"All Upon a Stone," from *All Upon a Stone* by Jean Craighead George. Copyright © 1971 by Jean Craighead George. By permission of Thomas Y. Crowell and Curtis Brown, Ltd.

"Annie and the Old One," from *Annie and the Old One* by Miska Miles. Copyright © 1971 by Miska Miles. Reprinted by permission of Atlantic-Little, Brown and Co.

"Anteater," from *Boy Blue's Book of Beasts* by William Jay Smith. Copyright © 1957 by William Jay Smith. Reprinted by permission of the author.

"Bells," from *Bells: A Book to Begin On* by Elizabeth Starr Hill. Copyright © 1970 by Elizabeth Starr Hill. Reprinted by permission of Holt, Rinehart and Winston, Inc.

"Billy Wentworth and the Buried Treasure," by Joan Cipolla, for Educreative Systems, Inc. Copyrighted by D.C. Heath and Company. Reprinted by permission of the publisher.

"The Broken Lantern," from *The Broken Lantern* by Freeman Hubbard. Copyright © 1952 by Freeman Hubbard. Reprinted by permission of the author and his agent, Lurton Blassingame.

"Broom Balancing" and "Follow the Leader," from *Stilts, Somersaults and Headstands* by Kathleen Fraser. Copyright © 1968 by Kathleen Fraser. Used by permission of Atheneum Publishers and Curtis Brown, Ltd.

"A Button in Her Ear," adapted from *A Button in Her Ear*. Copyright © 1976 by Ada B. Litchfield. Reprinted with permission of Albert Whitman & Company.

"The Carp in the Bathtub," adapted from *The Carp in the Bathtub* by Barbara Cohen. Copyright © 1972 by Barbara Cohen. By permission of Lothrop, Lee and Shepard Company, Inc.

"The City Under the Back Steps," from *The City Under the Back Steps* by Evelyn Lampman. Copyright © 1960 by Evelyn Sibley Lampman. Reprinted by permission of Doubleday & Company, Inc., and Faber and Faber, Ltd.

"Consider the Auk," from *The Private Dining Room and Other New Verses* by Ogden Nash. Copyright © 1949, 1950, 1951, 1952, 1953 by Ogden Nash. Reprinted by permission of Little, Brown and Co. Also published in "A Caution to Everybody," by Ogden Nash. Copyright © 1950 by Ogden Nash. Renewed © 1977 by Frances Nash, Isabelle Nash Eberstadt, and Linell Nash Smith. Reprinted by permission of Curtis Brown, Ltd.

This work is also published in individual volumes under the titles: *Growing, Pastimes, Messages, Cycles, Impressions,* and *Happenings,* copyright © 1983 Macmillan Publishing Co., Inc. Parts of this work were published in earlier editions of SERIES r.

Macmillan Publishing Co., Inc.
866 Third Avenue, New York, New York 10022
Collier Macmillan Canada, Inc.

Printed in the United States of America
ISBN 0-02-131820-4
9 8 7 6 5 4

Contents

5

6

GROWING

Growing is something you do all the time. It's both exciting and a little scary. But it's something everyone does. Learning about new things and meeting new people helps you to grow. Learning to understand your own feelings and the feelings of others helps you to grow, too.

In "Growing," you will read about young people having experiences that help them to learn and to grow. The people you will meet will take you on some exciting adventures. You will visit Boston in the days before the American Revolution. You will meet elephants in the African jungle. You will ride horseback with some Navaho friends. You will be in the woods with a young boy as he struggles to escape from an angry bear.

As you read, think about how different people face the problems and excitement of growing. What does growing mean for each of them? What does it mean for you?

The Medal

Clyde Robert Bulla

Sarah Ida Becker was staying with her Aunt Claudia for the summer and was determined to find a job to earn some spending money. Al Winkler, the owner of a shoeshine stand, was the only person who would hire a young girl without experience. Sarah Ida accepted the job.

Every evening after work, Sarah Ida was tired. But every morning she was ready to go back to Shoeshine Corner. It wasn't that she liked shining shoes, but things happened at the shoeshine stand. Every customer was different. Every day she found out something new.

Some things she learned by herself—like how much polish to use on a shoe. A thin coat gave a better and quicker shine. Some things Al told her. "When a customer comes here, he gets more than a shine," he said. "He gets to rest in a chair. When you rub with the cloth, it feels good on his feet. When you tie his shoelaces a little tighter, it makes his shoes fit better. My customers go away feeling a little better. Anyway, I *hope* they do."

One warm, cloudy afternoon, he said, "We might as well close up."

"Why?" she asked. "It's only three o'clock."

"It's going to rain. Nobody gets a shine on a rainy day."

He began to put away the brushes and shoe polish. She helped him.

"Maybe you can run home before the rain," he said. A few big drops splashed on the sidewalk. "No. Too late now."

They sat under the little roof, out of the rain.

"Hear that sound?" he said. "Every time I hear rain on a tin roof, I get to thinking about when I was a boy. We lived in an old truck

with a tin roof over the back."

"You *lived* in a truck?"

"Most of the time. We slept under the tin roof, and when it rained, the sound put me to sleep. We went all over the South in that truck."

"You and your mother and father?"

"My dad and I."

"What were you doing, driving all over the South?"

"My dad sold medicine."

"What kind?"

"Something to make you strong and keep you from getting sick."

"Did you take it?"

"No. I guess it wasn't any good."

She had never before heard him talk much about himself. She wanted him to go on.

"Was it fun living in a truck?"

"Fun? I wouldn't say so. Riding along was all right. Sometimes my dad and I stopped close to the woods, and that was all right, too. But I never liked it when we were in town selling medicine. Dad would play the mouth harp, and he made me sing. He wanted me to dance a jig, too, but I never could."

She tried to imagine Al as a little boy. She couldn't at all. "Why did he want you to sing and dance?" she asked.

"To draw a crowd. When there was a crowd, he sold medicine. We didn't stay anywhere very long—except once. We stayed in one place six months. My dad did farm work, and I went to school."

He told her about the school. It was just outside a town. The teacher was Miss Miller. The schoolhouse had only one room.

"There was this big stove," he said, "and that winter I kept the fire going. Miss Miller never had to carry coal when I was there."

"Did you like her?" asked Sarah Ida. "Was she a good teacher?"

"Best teacher I ever had. Of course, she was just about the *only* one. I hadn't been to school much, but she took time to show me things. Do teachers still give medals in school?"

"Sometimes. Not very often."

"Miss Miller gave medals. They were all alike. Every one had a star on it. At the end of school you got one

if you were the best in reading or
spelling or writing or whatever it was.
Everybody wanted a medal, but I knew I'd never
get one because I wasn't the best in anything. And
at the end of school, you know what happened?"

"What?"

"She called my name. The others all thought
it was a joke. But she wasn't laughing. She said,
'Al wins a medal for building the best fires.' "

"And it *wasn't* a joke?" asked Sarah Ida.

"No. She gave me a medal. One of the big
boys said, 'You better keep that, Al, because it's
the only one you'll ever get.' "

"And did you keep it?" He held up his watch
chain. Something was hanging from it—something
that looked like a worn, old coin.

"That's what you won?" asked Sarah Ida.

He nodded.

"That's a medal?" she said. "That little old
piece of tin?"

She shouldn't have said it. As soon as the words were out, she was sorry.

Al sat very still. He looked into the street. A moment before, he had been a friend. Now he was a stranger.

He said, "Rain's stopped—for a while anyway."

He slid out of his chair. She got up, too. "I—" she began.

He dragged the folding door across the stand and locked up.

"Go on. Run," he said. "Maybe you can get home before the rain starts again."

She stood there. "I didn't mean what you think I did," she said. "That medal—it doesn't matter if it's tin or silver or gold. It doesn't matter *what* it's made of, if it's something you like. I said the wrong thing, but it wasn't what I *meant*. I—" He had his back to her. She didn't think he was listening. She said, "*Listen* to me!"

He turned around. "You like ice cream?"

"Yes," she said.

"Come on. I'll buy you a cone."

She went with him, around the corner to Pearl's Ice Cream Shack.

"What kind?" he asked.

"Chocolate," she said.

They sat on a bench inside the Shack and ate their chocolate cones.

"It's raining again," he said.

"Yes," she said.

Then they were quiet, while they listened to the rain. And she was happy because the stranger was gone and Al was back.

Later that summer, Sarah Ida faced a problem. Al was hit by a car and had to stay in the hospital. Sarah Ida wanted to keep the stand open by herself, but she was not sure she could do it. To find out what she did and what she learned during that important summer in her life, read The Shoeshine Girl *by Clyde Robert Bulla.*

Who's Afraid?

I went to sleep last night
      And dreamed.
They tell me that I woke
      And screamed.
I was not really scared.
      Not me!
I simply called so they
      Could see
The witch who leaped up from
      The floor
And flew right through my
      Bedroom door.
If she should come again
      Tonight,
I'll scream again with all
      My might
But just so they can come
      And see
And not because I'm scared—
      Not me!

—*Lucia and James L. Hymes, Jr.*

25

DAVY CROCKETT

Aileen Wells Parks

Davy Crockett was lonesome. It was a sunny day in early summer, and Pa had given all the other boys jobs to do.

Ma, Janie, and Polly were working, too. And baby Sarah and little Joe were sound asleep.

Davy wandered up the hill. A big hound was lying half in the shade, half in the sun. Davy called, "Here, Whirlwind, here. Come here, Whirly."

The dog cocked one ear and looked around lazily. He did not get up. He didn't even stretch.

"Best bear dog in all the Great Smoky Mountains," Pa often said. "Give me old Whirlwind, and I can tree any bear that ever grew. He has more sense than most men."

"Come on, Whirlwind. Get up." Davy pulled the dog's ear. "Let's go hunt bear."

Whirlwind growled softly. He might have been dreaming.

Davy poked at him. "Bear, Whirlwind. Bear!" He tried to make his voice deep like his father's voice, but he was not successful.

This time Whirlwind got up and stretched. He did not jump around and bark as he did when Pa said, "Bear!"

Davy started up the path toward the forest. Whirlwind followed. He looked slow and lazy, but he kept up with the boy. Davy talked to him.

"We'll go right up this path. Then we come to the trail. Bill showed me one time. It starts at the big sycamore tree where Pa got the wildcat."

Whirlwind yawned loudly. Davy looked back. The hound seemed ready to stop and finish his nap.

"Come on, Whirlwind. Here, boy, here!" Davy picked up a stick, held it before the dog, and then threw it up the path as hard as he could throw.

Whirlwind looked at him with scorn. That was puppy play.

Then Davy remembered. He would need a stick in case he met a bear. Looking for a good strong stick, he left the path. Soon he found a kind of trail which led like a tunnel through the underbrush.

It was fun to go through the tunnel. It turned first to the right and then to the left. Sometimes sunlight came through the leaves. Sometimes the tunnel was almost dark. Davy forgot he was looking for a stick. He pretended that he was a fox trailing an opossum.

His bare feet made no noise on the path. He brushed the little branches away from his face as quietly as he could. Often the tunnel was so low he had to crawl.

After a long time he came out beside a rocky ledge. Davy climbed up and lay down to rest. He watched the sun on the leaves over his head. Then he fell sound asleep.

When he woke up he thought Wilson was pushing him out of their bed. He kicked back. His foot hit soft fur. Since he slept under a fur covering all winter long, that felt right.

Then something cold touched his face. Davy threw up his hand and hit the rug again, but this time the rug felt different. Davy opened his eyes and looked behind him.

A little bear cub was sitting quietly on the rock beside him.

The bear seemed friendly. It wrinkled up its nose and sniffed at Davy. It looked at him out of bright black eyes. Then it put its nose down on his hand.

It was a cold nose and Davy jumped. When he suddenly sat up, the cub moved back. It was such a cute little thing scuttling away on all fours that Davy laughed.

The cub must have liked the sound of Davy's laugh. It stopped and turned to look back.

Davy held out his hand. "I bet I could make a pet out of you," he said.

The little bear wrinkled its nose at him again. Then it sat down and watched Davy. The boy got to his feet to go over to it.

Just as he moved, Davy heard a snort. It was a scary sort of sound. Davy stood very still. He did not dare even to look around.

There was another snort. This time Davy looked up. A large brown bear was watching him out of little, beady eyes. Its mouth was open. Its big red tongue hung out.

The sight surprised Davy so much that he screamed. He looked around to find a place to run. The only open space he could see was across the rocky ledge. There were big trees on the other side with few bushes under them.

Davy tried to slip away. The big bear started moving, too. Davy was watching so closely he slipped on some loose gravel. He grabbed up a handful of the small pebbles and flung them straight at the two bears.

The mother might have caught him then, but the little bear whimpered. The big bear stopped quickly and went to her baby.

Davy, on one knee, saw the mother nuzzle the little bear. He jumped up and ran. Under the trees he turned to look back. The mother bear was watching him. She was in front of the cub.

Davy did want that cub for a pet. "I could call him Bear Hug," he thought.

The bear must have understood. She glared and growled and then took a step forward. "G-r-r-r," the bear said again. She stretched out a forepaw and raked her claws over the rock. The claws were like a cat's, but they were bigger and longer. The scratch left white gashes on the rock.

Davy kept his eye on the bear but began backing down the hill. That growl had made his heart beat fast. Then he stepped on a branch which crackled loudly.

The sound startled the bear, and she moved toward the boy. Not even her baby's tiny growl stopped her this time. She was headed straight for Davy.

Davy turned and ran as fast as he could go.

The woods were clear, and the way was slightly downhill. But the big bear, growling deep in her throat, ran faster than Davy could.

Davy felt a scream burst from his throat. Then he closed his mouth tight to keep all his breath for running.

He could hear the bear behind him. He fell and rolled over and over down a steep place on the hill.

The bear was running very fast. She went right past where Davy lay. But she did not go far. She turned. And Davy saw her beady eyes, red now with anger, as she came toward him.

Suddenly there was a great barking. The bear turned its head, then its whole body, to face this unexpected sound.

It was Whirlwind. The dog was making enough noise for a whole pack of bearhounds. He jumped from side to side of the angry bear. He barked right in her face but kept out of reach of her powerful paws. Her long claws were bared as she grabbed for the dog.

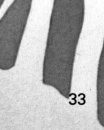

By circling, Whirlwind forced the bear to retreat. When the bear moved toward Davy, the dog dashed forward to nip her.

Davy was too scared to move.

The dog would circle toward one side. And the bear would circle facing him. When he was even with her and threatening to go past, she would growl and attack. As Whirlwind raced around to the other side, she moved back.

Davy looked up the hill. There was the cub, watching with as much interest as Davy.

The mother also saw the cub. She began backing steadily up the hill. Her angry eyes watched Whirlwind. But she did not try to attack him now. The hound kept up a great fury of barking and running. But he was not pressing the attack as hard as he had at first.

Finally the mother bear reached her cub. She and the dog stood growling threats at each other.

Suddenly the two bears were gone in the leafy forest. Davy was amazed that they could disappear so fast.

Whirlwind came back and stood by the boy. He was panting hard.

Just then Mr. Crockett came up the hill. His rifle was ready in his hands. "Davy! Davy!" he was shouting.

"Here I am, Pa!" Davy called.

"You all right, Davy?"

"Pa, you should have seen old Whirlwind drive that bear back up that hill!" Davy forgot he had ever been scared. "Pa, will you give Whirlwind to me for my bearhound?"

Mr. Crockett studied the boy. "When you get big enough to hunt bear, you may have him for your very own," he promised.

TRINA & MAGGIE

Patricia Miles Martin

Words are very important to friends, as you will see when you read this story. Trina is a Mexican-American who has just moved with her parents and older sister, Carla, to a little Wyoming town. More than anything else, Trina wants to be friends with Maggie, a girl at school. Maggie wants to be Trina's friend, too. When Trina speaks Spanish, her words flow out. But when she tries to talk to Maggie in English, nothing comes out right.

Trina went to school. Every night Mama held the reader and listened while she read.

Papa listened, too. Trina spoke words and more words. But she was still shy and unsure of herself with Maggie and the older girls.

In school, she read through the first reader and part of the way through the second. She read slowly. But she read well.

One Friday after school, Maggie spoke to Trina and Carla. "Tomorrow's my birthday. I'm having a party. I'd like it if you two would come."

"It will be at two o'clock tomorrow," Maggie said. "Charlie Wilson is coming and Abner Marshall and all the others."

Trina looked at Maggie. Friendship. She would be a friend to Maggie. She swallowed hard and spoke in English, "I-like-you."

Everyone laughed except Trina. She felt hot with her embarrassment. She could hardly believe that Maggie was laughing at her.

"No voy a tu fiesta," Trina said.

"She says she won't come to your party," Carla said. She shrugged her shoulders. "I guess she doesn't want to go. I'll go, I guess."

Trina told her mother what had happened.

How wonderful it was to tell her troubles to Mama in Spanish. How wonderful to speak Spanish together. It was a beautiful, beautiful language. At the moment, Trina didn't care if she ever spoke English.

"Well," Mama said, "they are at fault. You are not. Sometimes boys and girls do not know how to accept a compliment with grace. Perhaps until they learn this, you will *show* that you like people rather than tell them."

"But I do not like Maggie now," Trina said. "Perhaps I hate her. I am not quite sure."

"You will never have friends if you expect them to be without fault," Mama said.

That evening their mother ironed a red dress for Carla. She reached for a white dress and laid it over the ironing board.

"I am not going to the party, Mama," Trina said.

"You have not yet forgiven Maggie?" her mother asked.

"No, Mama."

"Very well. You need not go, of course. But you may feel differently tomorrow. You will take presents when you go."

"What presents?" Trina asked.

Their mother set the iron on the stove. "Let me think." She lifted the lid of the linen chest. "Perhaps we might make a doll's dress. Maggie will have a doll like your Ana Maria on her birthday.

I was in the store when her father bought it—the doll in the glass counter."

She shook out a short length of red material sprigged with tiny yellow flowers. "See. I have saved this material. Now we will measure your Ana Maria. We will make a dress for Maggie's new doll. We will start at once."

"But if I do not go to the party?"

"You could then have a beautiful dress that will fit Ana Maria. This is for you to decide."

While they talked, Carla said, "I will buy a present for Maggie. I'll stop at the store and get something on the way to the party."

She reached on the shelf for a baking powder can that held coins she had saved. She twisted off the top and emptied the coins on the

table. She brushed half of them into the palm of her left hand and slid them into her pocket. Then she put the rest of the coins back into the can and twisted the top tightly shut.

"What will you buy?" Trina asked.

"A surprise," said Carla.

Mama and Trina measured and cut and sewed to make a dress to fit a doll.

The next afternoon Carla dressed for the party.

Trina looked at her white dress, crisp with Mama's starch. It would be beautiful with her red sash. She remembered Maggie's laughter. "I can't go," she said to her mother.

"Very well," Mama said. "And the present for Maggie? Do you choose to give this?"

"Yes. I choose to give it. I will send it with Carla," Trina said.

She watched the girls and boys going up the hill to Maggie's house.

That afternoon, Mama made hot chocolate, and they each had a sweet roll with it. Even so, the time dragged until Carla came home. The afternoon was so long.

"But I am not sorry I stayed home, Mama. I couldn't have gone."

"I understand," Mama said.

When Carla came home, she took off her red dress and put on her jeans and her blue and yellow shirt.

"Everything happened at that party," Carla said. "It was fun. The birthday cake fell off the table, and if it hadn't been for me, Maggie wouldn't have had any candles to blow out."

'What do you mean?" Mama asked.

"Well, after the cake fell, I picked up the candles and put them on my present," Carla said.

"What was your present?" Trina asked.

"Gumdrops," said Carla. "I put a candle on each gumdrop. It was as good as a cake. Mrs. Tolley lighted them, and Maggie made a wish and blew them out."

"What did Maggie wish?" Trina asked.

"How could I know?" Carla asked. "When you blow out candles and make a wish, you don't tell what it is."

"And the doll's dress?" Trina asked. "What did Maggie say when she saw it?"

"I don't remember," Carla said.

The next day at school, Maggie walked straight to Trina.

"Trina, thank you for the doll's dress. It's the prettiest

dress I ever saw. It fits my doll." She pushed her red braids over her shoulders, and the dimples came in her cheeks. *"Trina, me gusta,"* she said.

Everybody laughed, even Trina. Maggie, too.

"I sound funny," Maggie said. "Spanish words are hard. But if you want to, I can try to speak Spanish while you try to speak English."

"You sound funny, Maggie," Carla said.

"I know. Everybody does at first," Maggie said. "Now, I will say 'thank you,' Trina, and you can say 'you're welcome' in English. Now listen, Trina. Say it after me: You-are-welcome."

Trina repeated the words slowly: "Say it after me, you are welcome."

Maggie bent over with laughter.

Trina felt her own face

crinkling. She blinked to keep back the tears.

"Don't pay any attention to her," Carla said.

"*Ríanse,*" Trina said. "*No me importa.*"

"She says she doesn't care if you laugh," Carla said. "She cares."

"Oh, well," Maggie said. "It's not fun to play with her anyway. If I laugh, she cries. And she won't even try to speak English."

Trina didn't stay to watch Maggie go up the hill. On her way home, she kicked the dirt until the air was thick with yellow-red dust.

"Why you are so dirty?" Mama asked pleasantly in English.

"You have it backward, Mama," Trina said in Spanish. "It should be, 'Why-are-you-so-dirty?'"

"Good," said Mama. "One of us is learning English."

Trina did her homework and thought about Maggie. If she wanted Maggie to be a friend, she would have to do more than learn English. She would have to be a friend. She would have to laugh with Maggie.

She laughed out loud.

"Why do you laugh?" Mama asked.

"I am practicing," Trina said.

And suddenly she and Mama laughed together.

The next day Trina went straight to Maggie.

Trina spoke in English. "You are welcome. That is the lesson for yesterday. And I am sorry. This is my lesson for today."

"All right, Trina," Maggie said. "Now you have to teach me how to say 'I'm sorry,' too."

"So easy," said Trina. "I am sorry. *Lo siento.*"

Maggie repeated the words. *"Lo siento."*

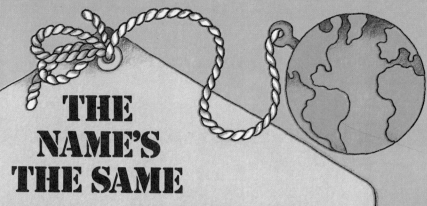

THE NAME'S THE SAME

Did you know that you can read many words in other languages besides English? The reason is that a lot of words are spelled the same or almost the same in many languages.

Here are some examples:

English	German	Spanish	French	Italian
sack	sack	saco	sac	sacco
music	musik	musica	musique	musica
fruit	frucht	fruta	fruit	frutto
school	schule	escuela	ecole	scuola
cat	katze	gato	chat	gatto

Now see if you can match the words below that mean the same thing in these five different languages.

English	German	Spanish	French	Italian
name	naturlich	nariz	nez	nome
nose	name	natural	naturel	naso
natural	nase	nombre	nom	naturale

Next you will read two *Peanuts* comic strips by Charles Schulz. These comic strips are popular all over the world. They have been translated into many different languages. Here is how the name of one main character would look in the five languages.

English
Charlie Brown

German	Spanish	French	Italian
Karl Braun	Carlos Moreno	Charles Brun	Carlo Bruno

THIS WAY, LITTLE FRIEND OF MINE..

IT'S GOOD TO HAVE A FRIEND

8-11

ALTHOUGH I CAN SEE WHERE HAVING TOO MANY FRIENDS COULD BE HARD ON THE STOMACH!

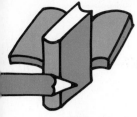

Unlocking New Words

Many words have parts called *prefixes* and *suffixes*. A *prefix* is a word part added to the beginning of a base word. A *suffix* is a word part added to the end of a base word. Knowing the meanings of prefixes and suffixes is very helpful. Sometimes you may see an unfamiliar word. You may not know the meaning of the whole word. But you recognize a prefix or a suffix in the word. Knowing that word part may help you understand the whole word.

Here are some common prefixes and their meanings:

uni-	one, single	**in-**	not
bi-	two, twice	**im-**	not
tri-	three	**non-**	not, without
un-	not	**dis-**	not, the opposite of

ACTIVITY A   Write the answer to each question on your paper.

1. How many colors are there in a <u>tricolor</u> flag?
2. How many wheels does a <u>bicycle</u> have?
3. How many horns does a <u>unicorn</u> have?
4. What are <u>unclean</u> hands?
5. What is <u>impure</u> water?
6. What kind of trip is a <u>nonstop</u> flight?
7. What is <u>invisible</u> ink?

Here are some common suffixes and their meanings:

-or	one whose job is	**-ful**	full of
-er	one whose job is	**-y**	like, full of
-ist	one who works with	**-ly**	like, in the manner of
-less	without		

ACTIVITY B Choose the correct meaning for each word on the left. Write the word and its meaning on your paper.

1. homeless **a.** two homes **b.** without a home
c. one who has a full home

2. artist **a.** without art **b.** full of art
c. one who works in a form of art

3. thankful **a.** full of thanks **b.** no thanks
c. one who has thank-you notes

4. sailor **a.** in full sail **b.** without a sail
c. one whose job is sailing

5. icy **a.** ice cream **b.** full of ice
c. one who works with ice

ACTIVITY C Write the meaning of the underlined word in each sentence.

1. Kim <u>dislikes</u> snowstorms.
2. Andy watched the <u>painter</u> at work.
3. I'll <u>gladly</u> lend you my extra umbrella.
4. Debbie said the job was <u>impossible</u>.
5. The hot summer sun makes me very <u>thirsty</u>.

Growing Up Chinese-American

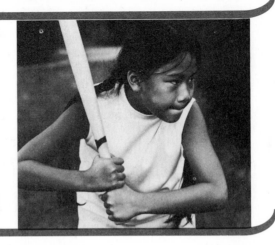

Carol Ann Bales

This selection is from a book called Chinatown Sunday. *The book is about Lilliann Der, a ten-year-old girl who lives near Chicago, Illinois. Lilliann's life is like that of many girls her age. She goes to school, takes piano lessons, and belongs to the Girl Scouts. But Lilliann is also Chinese-American, and with her family, she follows many customs of their Chinese heritage.*

Carol Ann Bales, who wrote this selection, is a friend of Lilliann and her family. Ms. Bales taped an interview with each person in the family. She chose the most interesting parts of the tapes to put in her book. That's why Lilliann Der's own words are used to tell you about herself and some of the customs of her family.

One time last summer some kids started asking me: "Are you from China or Japan?" It's pretty hard to explain. I told them I'm not from China or Japan. I was born in Chicago. But I am a Chinese-American.

I used to be very shy. I didn't know how to answer questions like that. But after kindergarten I started to talk a lot. I'm in the fifth grade this year. I don't talk so much anymore, but I'm not exactly shy—just sometimes.

My name is Lilliann Der—my American name, that is. My Chinese name is Der Wai Lee. Everyone at home calls me *Lee Lee,* which sounds like Lily. *Lee* means a "little jasmine flower" in Chinese.

My father is assistant manager of the Hong Kong Noodle Company in Chinatown, and we live in Wilmette, a suburb of Chicago.

That's me sitting on the end of the sofa. Then there's Caroline, my older sister, and David, my younger brother. Then there's my father and mother. Vivian and Rosalie, my little sisters, are sitting on my grandmother's lap. We were trying to make Vivian and Rosalie laugh.

On the wall is a picture of my grandfather. He died when I was four. His name was Der Chung. I used to get his pipe for him.

My parents and my grandmother were born in China in a place called Toishan. My grandfather's family lived in China, but I think he was born in the United States. He and some other Chinese men founded the Hong Kong Noodle Company.

My grandma lives with us. She grows Chinese vegetables in our backyard. When she gets up in the morning, she reads for an hour or two in her room, and then she goes outside. Some days she stays out all day.

She planted seventeen or eighteen different kinds of vegetables last summer. She planted Chinese broccoli, *bok choy*—that's Chinese cabbage—mustard greens, string beans, peppers, tomatoes, and three kinds of melons. And she planted some other vegetables that I can't remember.

We ask Grandma's opinion before we do anything that's important, and I always say good morning and good night to her. That's how I show that I love and respect her.

When a baby in our family is one month old, we have a special party. I wore my long dress to the month-old party for my little cousin, Aileen Der. The party was held on the top floor of a restaurant in Chinatown. A lot of people came—about three hundred.

I like month-old parties because of all the food. I do like food. They had bird's nest soup, and they had hard-boiled eggs and ginger, both dyed red, which means "good luck." Those foods were special for the month-old party. We had a lot of other food,

too. We ate with chopsticks. At home we usually use a knife and fork. It's hard to use chopsticks with a plate. A bowl is best.

Before the dinner, Mommy helped pin red carnations on the clothes of Aileen's close relatives. Daddy shook hands, and David and I played string games. There were toasts and speeches. One of Aileen's uncles gave a really funny speech. There are mostly boys in Aileen's family, and so everyone was happy that she turned out to be a girl.

Aileen got a lot of presents and lucky money. Lucky money is money someone gives you in a red envelope.

Aileen wore a special outfit with gold necklaces. Your grandmother on your mother's side always gives you a dress for your month-old party, and both your grandmothers give you necklaces. In China, babies wear an outfit with a hat that has two little ears. The parents hang a little gold figure on the hat. I think that sounds nice.

I have one very good school friend. Camille and I met in the second grade, and we've been friends ever since. A few times we broke our friendship, but we made up. It's hard to keep a friendship that long. You find it hard to keep away from an argument. I have other friends, like Robin, and some of them are my relatives.

Camille, Robin, and I all belong to Girl Scouts. Robin's mother is a leader. We go to a meeting one night a week.

I don't have many chores during the school year. I have to practice my piano lessons, but I like to do that. Sometimes when Grandma and Mommy are busy, I feed

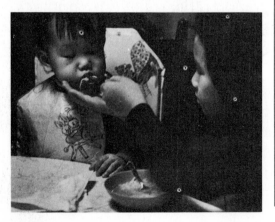

Rosalie. We call her *Moy Moy,* which means "little sister". She eats a lot. She's learning to talk. She says words in Chinese unless they're easier to say in English.

Of all the holidays, Christmas is my favorite. Halloween is my second favorite. I guess I like the Moon Festival—because I like to eat moon cakes —and the Chinese New Year best of the Chinese holidays.

These are the things that remind me of the Chinese New Year. The house smells like flowers because Grandma puts narcissus bulbs in water to bloom for New Year's Day. We each get a new outfit. This year Grandma made Mommy, Caroline, Vivian, and me new pants suits. And we make Chinese pastry.

You have to make pastry because you visit your friends and relatives on the Chinese New Year—or they visit you—and you want to have pastry to give to them. We make egg rolls and pastry called *ham gok, tim gok,* and *lor bok go* in Chinese. We always put two tangerines in boxes of pastry for friends. That's for good luck.

In Chinatown there's always a big celebration on the Sunday closest to the Chinese New Year. It's fun. It's also noisy—and crowded. You hear a lot of firecrackers, and I mean a lot, and people stand in the streets to watch the lion dance.

Chinese New Year comes about a month after the January 1 New Year's Day because the Chinese calendar is different from the calendar used in this country. My grandma says we are a year older not just on our birthdays, but on Chinese New Year's Day, too. She says the Chinese New Year is important because it is the time of the year to make plans for the future.

I made three resolutions for this year: to be more patient, to be less shy, and—I forgot the other one.

The Emperor's Nightingale

Hans Christian Andersen

Many years ago, there was an Emperor who lived in the most splendid palace in the most beautiful city in China. Everything in the palace was made of delicate porcelain. Outside, near the palace, the loveliest flowers grew in a very large garden.

Deep in this very large garden was a forest of tall trees and clear, blue lakes. The forest stretched for many miles, and in it lived a Nightingale. From its home in the forest, the Nightingale sang so sweetly that everyone who heard it would stop what they were doing. They would listen to the song, and all would say the same thing: "What a beautiful song!"

Now the Emperor was very proud of his city, his palace, and his garden, and he was greatly pleased when travelers came from everywhere to admire them. These travelers, when they returned home, wrote many books and poems about the magnificent city, the porcelain palace, the lovely garden, and the Nightingale that sang so beautifully.

People all over the world had read the books and poems, but the Emperor had never read any of them. Then one day it happened that one of the books was brought to his attention. He sat down at once to read the lovely descriptions of his city, his palace, and his garden. As he was reading, he came to this statement: "The song of the Nightingale is the loveliest of all."

The Emperor had never heard of the Nightingale until he read that statement. "What Nightingale?" he cried. "How could there be a Nightingale that sings in my garden when I have never heard it?"

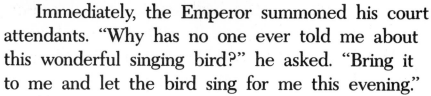

Immediately, the Emperor summoned his court attendants. "Why has no one ever told me about this wonderful singing bird?" he asked. "Bring it to me and let the bird sing for me this evening."

But the court attendants had never seen the bird, and not one of them even knew anything about it. They searched every room in the palace, looking for someone who had heard the Nightingale.

The search was in vain until at last, in the kitchen, they asked a girl who was busily scrubbing pots and pans. "Of course I know the Nightingale!" she exclaimed. "I know it very well."

Gladly, the girl agreed to take the court attendants to the forest. They walked through the lovely flowers in the garden, and just as they entered the tall trees, the Nightingale began to sing. The attendants listened in amazement. Never before had they heard such music.

"Little Nightingale," called the kitchen maid, "our most gracious Emperor would like very much for you to sing for him."

"With the greatest pleasure," answered the Nightingale. "My song sounds best in the forest, but I shall willingly follow you to the palace."

The whole court was present in the great hall of the palace. The Emperor nodded, and the Nightingale began to sing. It sang so sweetly and beautifully that tears came into the Emperor's eyes.

"Stay with us, little Nightingale," the Emperor cried, "and you shall have everything you desire."

"I will stay," said the Nightingale, "but I am rewarded enough. I have seen tears in the Emperor's eyes."

So the Nightingale stayed at the palace. It lived in a splendid cage and was given everything it desired. Then, one day, a package marked "The Nightingale" arrived. When it was opened, it was found to contain a beautifully made mechanical bird, covered with diamonds and precious stones. When it was wound up, the mechanical bird sang one of the songs that the real Nightingale sang.

"Oh, this is splendid!" cried the ladies and gentlemen of the court. The Emperor was also delighted and called for the mechanical bird to sing again and again. No one noticed the real Nightingale as it flew out through an open window and started on its way back to the forest.

Five years passed, and the mechanical bird sang every day. Each time it was wound up, it sang the same song in exactly the same way.

Then suddenly, a great sorrow came to the city. The Emperor became seriously ill, and the court doctors said he was close to death. As they leaned over the dying Emperor, the doctors heard him whisper, "Music! Music! Make the mechanical golden bird sing."

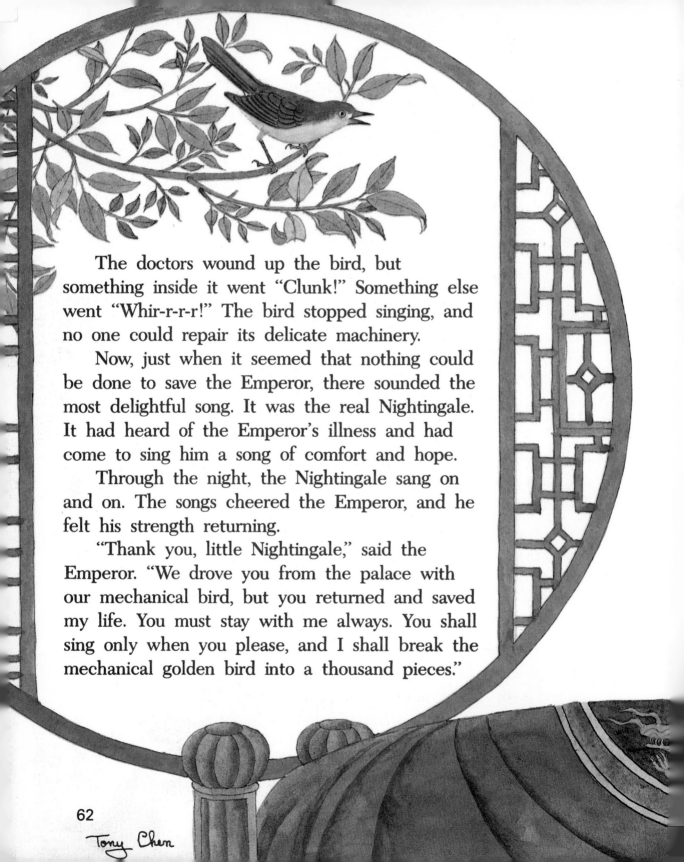

The doctors wound up the bird, but something inside it went "Clunk!" Something else went "Whir-r-r-r!" The bird stopped singing, and no one could repair its delicate machinery.

Now, just when it seemed that nothing could be done to save the Emperor, there sounded the most delightful song. It was the real Nightingale. It had heard of the Emperor's illness and had come to sing him a song of comfort and hope.

Through the night, the Nightingale sang on and on. The songs cheered the Emperor, and he felt his strength returning.

"Thank you, little Nightingale," said the Emperor. "We drove you from the palace with our mechanical bird, but you returned and saved my life. You must stay with me always. You shall sing only when you please, and I shall break the mechanical golden bird into a thousand pieces."

Tony Chen

"No," said the Nightingale. "Don't destroy the mechanical bird. It sang the best it could for as long as it could. As for me, I cannot live in a palace, but I will come to visit you every night. I will sit on a bough outside your window and sing.

With that, the Nightingale flew away, and the Emperor fell into a deep sleep.

The next morning, the sorrowing servants and court attendants came to mourn their Emperor, for they had expected him to die during the night. When they opened the door, however, there stood the Emperor at a window. He turned around and startled them with a strong and cheery "Good morning!"

There followed great rejoicing in the land, for the Emperor was well and strong again. And every evening, he threw open the windows of his room to hear the lovely songs of the Nightingale.

THE TUESDAY ELEPHANT

Nancy Garfield

There once was a boy of ten named Kwani. He lived in a tribe called the Kamba. It was in the country of Kenya on the eastern side of the continent of Africa.

Kwani was one of the youngest boys in his family. There were ten brothers and sisters in all. After school, he was often free to walk about the countryside.

Sometimes he wandered down a hill and sat under the shade of the Mchungwa tree. He peered out at the green field ahead, dreaming. Thinking and dreaming. Watching the sun set in the lazy afternoon.

One day he heard a sound in the bush. He jumped up. Staring straight at him was a baby elephant.

Kwani stood still. He tried not to make a sound. Then the tiny elephant walked up to him and tickled his shoulder with his trunk. Kwani laughed. "Hello, mtoto tembo—hello, little elephant," he said. And then he patted him on the neck.

Suddenly there was a great noise. Kwani saw the mother elephant approaching. She was making all kinds of sounds. He hid at the side of the tree. Then the little elephant ran off to its mother.

From that day on, Kwani often visited that spot. He was hoping to see his friend the baby elephant. And the elephant often came to see Kwani. Kwani named him "Jumanne tembo," or Tuesday Elephant, because that was the day they met.

Over many months Kwani and the Tuesday Elephant became good friends. Kwani often brought berries for the elephant to eat. And sometimes they would get into the shallow part of the river and get wet. Jumanne always sprayed Kwani's back. And they laughed and laughed and laughed.

They could never stay very long in the water. They had to watch out for crocodiles.

Kwani would often go to the forest and play with Jumanne. He would climb on Jumanne's fuzzy-haired back. For baby elephants are covered with soft, black fuzz. They would walk along the banks of the river.

Kwani would run into the forest after school was out. Every day, he would part the bush and whisper, "Jumanne, I am here. Miye, Kwani—it is I, Kwani." And slowly, quietly, Jumanne would come and tap Kwani with his trunk.

They would both run to the path by the river's edge. Often they would see wild geese or ducks drinking. Sometimes the deer and gazelles stood gracefully against the other shore in the sunlight.

Sometimes Kwani took his littlest brother Maliki to meet the elephant. But he made him swear to keep this a secret. And his littlest brother swore. So the secret was kept.

Always Kwani had looked forward to the annual elephant hunt. It was a big event.

The hunters of the tribe tried to catch an elephant. All the children of the village waited to hear of the news that an elephant had been caught.

But this year Kwani did not look forward to the elephant hunt. It was with sadness that he greeted the morning of the hunt. Kwani's eyes were wet with tears. Only his littlest brother knew why he had cried all night. Only his littlest brother knew of his friend Jumanne.

Kwani had tried to warn Jumanne in the weeks before the hunt. "Ficha," he said. "Hide, Jumanne, hide from the wicked hunters—ficha, ficha, ficha."

But Jumanne just ran his trunk along Kwani's back and tickled him. Kwani did not think Jumanne understood him.

The sun came up the day of the hunt. Kwani once more stole out in the early dawn. The forest was filled with a white, spidery morning mist. Some of the leaves shone like wax in the early morning sunlight. Heavy, dark green shadows fell beneath the brush and under the trees.

Kwani was running and running to warn Jumanne. Then he heard the hunters shouting. The hunting scouts had brought back word of a herd down the hill.

The hunters shouted, "Kwani, ondoka rudi, ondoka rudi—go away, go back." And so Kwani did.

He sat on the steps of his hut with his littlest brother. And they cried for the little elephant.

69

The hunters had set the trap, after digging a deep hole in the elephant path. They laid sharp poison-tipped sticks inside it. And they all waited. It was an ugly day for Kwani.

For to Kwani, the elephant was the gentle king of the forest. He and Maliki played behind the hut. They covered a mound of hay with a white cloth. And they cried for Kwani's beloved elephant.

Kwani wore a red cape made of his mother's kerchief. She wondered why he borrowed it. And she wondered why he and Maliki were weeping so loudly. So did everyone. But no one asked. They knew they would get no answer.

Finally the day was ending. All was quiet. The hunters returned. They were all chattering away.

The herd had disappeared magically. It was as if someone had told them to run. A great smile came across Kwani's face. "Littlest brother," he whispered, "have you heard? They have spared my baby elephant Jumanne."

And Kwani thanked the moon and the stars and all the gods for saving Jumanne.

Often now Kwani returned to the forest. He sat under the Mchungwa tree. There he waited for Jumanne to come back. Kwani waited and waited many, many months. Jumanne did not come back.

Sometimes his littlest brother came and sat with him. They stared together out across the clearing. Kwani carved many, many elephants. And the people of his tribe never understood why he called them Jumanne elephants. Only his littlest brother understood.

Kwani waited many afternoons as the sun set. The sky would darken from its fiery orange until it turned hot pink and then red. Finally it turned dark into a deep, deep blue. And Kwani would wander home as the first star appeared.

Kwani had all but given up hope. Then one day he saw a tall, handsome elephant. He was standing in the clearing.

Kwani looked at him. "Jumanne," he said, "Jumanne." And the elephant approached him. He rubbed his trunk along Kwani's back. And Kwani knew it was his Jumanne.

They laughed for a while. Kwani realized that Jumanne had grown very big and handsome. He was no longer a baby elephant. He had left his herd to travel many miles just to visit Kwani. And then Kwani knew it was time to say good-bye.

"Kwa heri," he whispered. "Kwa heri—good-bye. For I know you must get back to your herd." And Kwani watched Jumanne leave the clearing. He was going off through the bush to find his herd again.

Kwani waved good-bye. Then the sun gave a golden glow to the entire forest. And Kwani turned to go back home.

What Does It Mean?

What do you do when you come to a word that you don't know in a sentence? You can use a dictionary to find its pronunciation and meaning. But there is another way to figure out the meaning of an unknown word. You can use other words in the sentence that you do know.

When you are using other words to figure out the meaning of a word, you are using context clues. The words in the sentence that surround your new word are the context clues.

Here is an example of the way you can use context clues to figure out the meanings of unknown words. The unknown words below are from the story "The Tuesday Elephant." They are words in the Swahili language which is spoken in Kenya.

> Kwani laughed. "Hello, mtoto tembo—hello, little elephant," he said.

From the other words in the sentence, you can figure out that *mtoto tembo* means "little elephant." But do you know which Swahili word means "little" and which means "elephant"? The following sentence may give you the clues you need.

> Kwani named him "Jumanne tembo," or Tuesday elephant, because that was the day they met.

If you study the sentences, you can figure out that *tembo* means "elephant," because it is in both Swahili phrases. What word means "little"? What word means "Tuesday"?

There are other Swahili words in "The Tuesday Elephant." Find these words and try to figure out their meanings by using context clues.

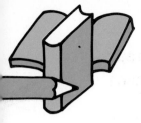

What Is a Paragraph?

A *paragraph* is a group of sentences telling about one subject. The *main-idea sentence* states the most important idea of the paragraph. The *detail sentences* tell about the main idea. Read the following paragraph.

> Desert animals stay cool in different ways. Some find shade under rocks. Others stay near trees and bushes. Some desert animals even dig into the cool ground.

The paragraph tells how desert animals stay cool. The first sentence is the main-idea sentence. The other sentences are detail sentences.

ACTIVITY A   Read the detail sentences below. Then read the three main-idea sentences. Decide which main-idea sentence goes with the detail sentences. Write the best main-idea sentence.

Detail sentences:
In early days, everyone traveled by foot. Later, people used boats. Then the car was invented. Today, people fly in jet planes.

Main-idea sentences:
1. Walking is the best way to travel.
2. Travel has changed over the years.
3. Jet planes are faster than cars.

ACTIVITY B Read the main-idea sentence. Then read the detail sentences. Write the three detail sentences that belong with the main-idea sentence.

Main-idea sentence:
Astronauts walked on the moon in 1969.
Detail sentences:
1. The walk lasted about two hours.
2. The astronauts collected moon rocks.
3. Astronauts can be men or women.
4. They put an American flag on the moon.
5. Some rockets have landed on Mars.

ACTIVITY C Read the two main-idea sentences. Then read the four detail sentences. Write each main-idea sentence with its detail sentences.

Main-idea sentences:
1. An encyclopedia volume is a book of information.
2. Sets of encyclopedia are found in many places.
Detail sentences:
a. Libraries keep sets of encyclopedia.
b. It tells of famous people.
c. It describes important events.
d. Some people have them at home.

ACTIVITY D Read the detail sentences. Then write a main-idea sentence for the detail sentences.

Detail sentences:
The sun provides light for us to see. It gives us warmth, too. The sun also helps plants grow.

STATE HOUSE

SAMUEL ADAMS

PHILLIS WHEATLEY

Kathryn Kilby Borland and Helen Ross Speicher

The American colonies began to rebel against British rule when the British passed the Stamp Act in 1765. According to this law, the colonists had to pay a small tax on all legal papers.

Groups formed to protest the Stamp Act. One group was called the Sons of Liberty. Soon they forced the British to repeal the law. The colonists were very happy. At this time, Phillis Wheatley was a young slave. She lived in Boston with the Wheatley family. Even under the cruel system of slavery some slave owners were kind to their slaves. The Wheatley's son, Nat, taught Phillis and his sister, Mary, many of the things he was learning in school. When the Stamp Act was repealed, Phillis wanted the British king to know just how happy the American colonists were. So she wrote a poem to King George that had interesting results.

Phillis sat up in bed. It wasn't daylight. Some sound must have awakened her. But now the night was quiet again. She lay back and closed her eyes, wondering whether she was mistaken. Then she heard a bell ringing. It rang again and again, louder and louder.

Phillis ran and opened her window. She leaned out into the May darkness. Far down the street, she could hear a horse's hoofbeats. Then a man on horseback came riding down the street. He was shouting. But Phillis could not understand what he said.

Now she could hear Mr. Wheatley's window being thrown up with an angry sound. "What's all this?" he called out.

"Good news! Good news!" the horseman shouted. But he didn't slow down.

Phillis noticed lighted windows in other houses up and down the street. One or two men had come out on the front steps. They were wearing dressing gowns over their nightshirts.

"What is it?" they called to one another. Nobody seemed to know.

Before long, a group of young men came running down the street with lighted torches. They were throwing their hats in the air.

"Three cheers for King George! Three cheers for the Sons of Liberty!" they shouted. Finally, Mr. Wheatley got the attention of one of the young men.

"We have good news about the Stamp Act, sir," the man called. "Word just came. The Stamp Act has been repealed!"

Phillis could hear Nat's shout from his room. "We did it! We did it!"

No one in the Wheatley house, or probably in all of Boston, went back to sleep that night. The bells went on ringing. Soon drums were beating steadily. And once in a while the boom of a cannon could be heard.

The celebration lasted all day. Bands wandered through the crowds, playing loudly if not well. The bells kept ringing.

That night, there was a fireworks display on the Commons. There had never been such fireworks in Boston. The air was filled with rockets, bright serpents, and spinning pinwheels. At eleven o'clock, twenty-one rockets and sixteen dozen serpents were sent up all at once for a glorious finish.

A loud cheer went up for King George. Phillis wished that King George could know how happy the people were about what had been done. She wished someone would tell him.

After Phillis went to bed that night, she tossed and turned. Some idea was trying to form in her brain. But she was too tired to think about it.

In the middle of the night, the idea suddenly came to her.

She would write King George about how the colonists felt. Perhaps she could even write it in verse. She had written a poem not long before, but had not shown it to anyone.

She crept quietly out of bed. Her candle burned for hours while she wrote. When she woke up in the morning, she looked at what she had written.

"What a silly idea," she thought. "How could I ever have imagined that the king would read anything written by a young slave?" She left the poem on the little table by her bed and almost forgot it.

A few weeks later, Phillis was sick in bed with a cold. One morning, Mrs. Wheatley brought a bowl of porridge for her breakfast. As she set the bowl on the little table, she noticed a scrap of paper there. She picked up the paper and asked, "What is this, Phillis?"

Phillis was embarrassed. "Oh, it's nothing, Mrs. Wheatley, nothing at all."

"But it is, Phillis. These are beautiful words. Did you copy this poem from a book?"

"Oh, no, Mrs. Wheatley. I wrote it myself, but it really isn't very good."

"You wrote it yourself? Phillis, this is remarkable. Why didn't you show it to us?"

"I was ashamed to show it to you, Mrs. Wheatley. I actually wrote it to send to the king. And then I decided that would be silly. Besides, the poem isn't any good."

"May I show it to Mr. Wheatley?"

Phillis hesitated. Probably Mr. Wheatley would think the poem was foolish. But she said, "Yes, of course." Mrs. Wheatley did not seem to notice her lack of enthusiasm.

That evening after supper, the whole family came up to her room. Mr. Wheatley was holding the poem in his hand. He looked very solemn. Phillis feared he was angry. Then he cleared his throat and said, "Mrs. Wheatley tells me you wrote this poem."

"Yes, sir," Phillis answered.

"Now are you sure you really wrote it yourself? Sometimes we read something and don't remember it. Later we remember it but don't remember where we saw it. Then we may think we thought of it ourselves. Do you see what I mean, Phillis?"

"Yes, sir, I do," Phillis said, "But that isn't the way it was this time. I wanted somehow to make King George see how grateful we were. This was the only way I could think of. I know it was foolish of me, sir. I guess I was just excited over the celebration."

"I told you, Father," Mary said. "Phillis reads and reads and reads. She uses words I don't even know how to use."

Mr. Wheatley cleared his throat again. "Well, then," he said, "in that case, it's remarkable. Have you written any other poems?"

"Yes, sir. I wrote one about Harvard College. Would you like to see it?"

A few minutes later, Mr. Wheatley left the room with both poems in his hand. Then one evening several days later, he told Phillis that she was to go to the State House with him the next morning. "A few gentlemen there would like to ask you about your poems."

"They'll be angry," Phillis thought. "Mr. Wheatley shouldn't have told them."

Usually Phillis enjoyed looking at the lion over the State House door. Today, she had too many things on her mind even to think about it. Mr. Wheatley had told her that the most important men in Boston would talk with her.

Mr. Wheatley led her into the Council Chamber. Several stern-looking men who were seated at a long table looked up at her. Others looked down from gold frames on the wall.

"Stand at this end of the table where we can see you," one of the men said. He was holding her poems in his hand.

"Yes, sir," Phillis said in a low voice. She folded her hands in front of her. That stopped them from shaking.

"Mr. Wheatley tells us you wrote these poems," said one of the men.

"Yes, sir."

"Did anyone give you any help?"

"No, sir."

"Why did you write about Harvard College?"

"Because, sir, Mr. Nat brought back so much from there for Miss Mary and me to study and talk about. He even taught Latin to Miss Mary. And she taught it to me."

"Latin, eh?" a man said with interest. "Can you tell me what *E pluribus unum* means?"

Phillis smiled. "Yes, sir. It means 'one from many,'" she said.

Some of the other gentlemen asked questions in Latin which she was able to answer. They also asked her what books she liked to read. Then they began asking about her poems.

"Tell us what you meant by these lines, 'May every clime with equal gladness see/A monarch's smile can set his subjects free.'"

The speaker was Mr. Samuel Adams. Phillis had often seen him at the Wheatley's house. "I meant that we were glad the king used his power to make us happy. I'm sorry the meaning wasn't clear, sir," she said.

"I think it was quite clear."

The other gentlemen nodded. They asked her questions almost all morning. She was so tired before they were through that she hardly knew what she answered.

At the end of the questioning, Mr. Adams smiled and said, "We shall send your poem to the king. And we hope that you will write many more. You have a great gift, young woman, a very great gift, and it must be used."

THE SHOESHINE CHAIR

Janice May Udry

One of Angie's favorite places was the secondhand store. The sign in front said "Antiques and Junk for Sale." The old store had three rooms. The front room contained expensive furniture and dishes. But items in the second room cost less. In the third room was the junk. Some things in the junk room cost less than a dollar. The junk room overflowed out into a weedy fenced-in junkyard in the back.

Angie went to the secondhand store. She hoped to find an unusual but inexpensive present for her father's birthday.

"Have you got any really good junk today, Mr. Whitaker?" asked Angie.

"Sure I have, Angie. Just look around. There's a little bit of everything out there in back," said Mr. Whitaker from behind his messy, dusty old desk.

Mr. Whitaker told Angie he had been collecting stuff since he was six years old. Angie looked around his store.

"That's not hard to believe," she said.

"If you think I've got a lot here," he chuckled, "you ought to see my house."

Angie poked around the store for a long time. But she didn't see anything that seemed just right for her father's birthday. Before she left, she decided to take one last turn around the junkyard.

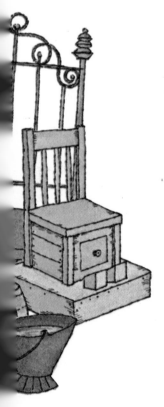

There, lying on its side, she found something that really interested her. It was an old, homemade wooden shoeshine chair. A thin straight chair had been nailed to a large box with a drawer in it. The drawer pulled open with a spool. The chair and the box were nailed to a platform with two wooden footrests on it. The whole thing had been painted sky-blue. It was all loose and rickety now.

"But some nails will fix it up fine," thought Angie.

"How much for the shoeshine chair?" Angie asked Mr. Whitaker.

"You found one of my best pieces of junk," said Mr. Whitaker. "How much money have you got?"

"Fifty cents," said Angie.

"It's a deal," said Mr. Whitaker. "The shoe-shine chair is yours. I'll tell Joe to deliver it to your house when he's taking that sofa over to the Bensons'."

That afternoon Mrs. Brinker answered the doorbell.

"Where do you want this, ma'am?"

"What is it?" asked Mrs. Brinker.

"It's your shoeshine chair, ma'am," said Joe.

"I think you have the wrong address. Wait a minute. Angie!"

Angie came to the hall. "That's mine, Mother. Just leave it on the porch, please."

Joe put the chair down and went back to his truck.

"Angie! Is that what you got your father for his birthday?" asked Mrs. Brinker.

"No," said Angie, "I didn't find anything yet. I bought this for myself. I know it looks

rickety right now, but I'll work on it. All it
needs are some new nails, here and there."

"It makes our front porch look really different," said Mrs. Brinker.

"It has a lot of possibilities," said Angie.

Angie was very pleased when she had
made the old chair sturdy again with nails. It
made a wonderful throne.

When her friend Molly came over with her
skates, Angie had an idea.

"Hey, Molly, let's put this throne on wheels."

In a little while, Angie and Molly were
pushing each other up and down the street in
a strange-looking, high wheelchair. They had
nailed their skates to the bottom of the shoeshine chair.

"That was one of my best ideas," said
Angie later, when they sat resting on the front
steps. "But I still haven't bought a present for
my father. His birthday is day after tomorrow.

I spent all the money I had on the shoeshine
chair. I know what I'd like to buy him."

"What?" asked Molly.

"Have you ever been in the new gourmet
shop?" asked Angie. "Do you know that they
have jars of fried grasshoppers there? That's
what I'd like to buy. He's never had that. And
he'd never guess what it was. Wouldn't it be
fun to taste a fried grasshopper?"

"Oh, Angie!" Molly made a face.

"But I haven't got two dollars," said Angie.
For awhile she was deep in thought.

"Come on, Angie. Let's take turns riding
in the chair again," said Molly.

"O.K.," said Angie, getting up.

The young twins who lived down the block
ran out when they saw Angie pushing Molly
past their house.

"Angie! Angie! Where did you get that?
Can we have a ride?" they begged.

After Angie and Molly had given each of the twins a ride, they didn't want to get out of the chair.

"Please give us another ride! It's fun."

"No more today," said Angie.

"*Please!*"

Angie's face suddenly brightened. "No more *free* rides. Have you got any money?"

The twins nodded.

"Well," said Angie, "for five cents I'll give you a ride all the way around the block."

"O.K.!" The twins dashed away. "Stay there. We'll be right back!"

Angie grinned at Molly. "Do you know what we're going to do?"

"What?"

"Earn the money for my father's present," said Angie.

"How much money do you think the twins have got?" asked Molly.

"Not just them. We'll give anybody who wants one a ride for five cents," said Angie. "Wait here with the chair. I'll be right back."

Angie ran home. She came back with a small can of paint and a brush. On both sides of the box under the chair she wrote:

"Ride—5¢."

As they pushed the twins around the block, other children appeared. Like magic they ran into their houses and popped out again with nickels in their hands. Some of them rode more than once.

By dinnertime, Angie and Molly were very tired, since some of their riders had demanded fast rides.

"We have to go home now," they told some of the waiting customers. "But we'll be out tomorrow."

Angie and Molly pushed the chair home and into Angie's garage. They counted almost a dollar.

"We'll make another dollar easy," said Angie. "See you tomorrow, Molly. Go to bed early so you won't be tired tomorrow."

"I feel like going to bed right now," said Molly.

Angie grinned. "Remember you're invited to my father's birthday dinner. And you'll get to taste fried grasshoppers, Molly!"

The next morning, Angie and Molly added a parasol and a bell to the chair ride. Many of the small children liked the ride even better now. They could sit up high under the parasol ringing a bell, while being pushed along the sidewalk.

By the middle of the afternoon, they had plenty of money for the present.

Angie's mother drove the girls down to the gourmet shop.

"I always like to go in here," said Angie. "People look as if they are enjoying themselves, and they aren't in any hurry. The ice cream store is like that, too. People in ice cream stores and gourmet shops are usually in a good mood."

Angie led Molly into the store and down one aisle.

"Here it is," said Angie. "See, you get quite a large can of grasshoppers for two dollars."

"I wonder what my father would say if I gave him fried grasshoppers for his birthday," giggled Molly.

"It's a nice change from neckties," said Angie.

"This feels like a new can of pipe tobacco," said Mr. Brinker that night, after they had all had a piece of cake.

He untied the ribbon and took off the paper. "Grasshoppers! *Fried* grasshoppers," cried Mr. Brinker with delight. "I have always wanted to taste them." He selected a grasshopper and passed the can. "Help yourselves," he said. "This is a very special treat."

There was a moment of silence. They held their grasshoppers between thumb and forefinger.

They all waited for someone to take the first bite.

"Don't they look yummy?" said Mrs. Brinker.

"Oh, they certainly do," said Mr. Brinker, looking at his grasshopper.

Molly giggled nervously.

"O.K., everybody, one, two, three," said Angie. She popped her grasshopper into her mouth. So did Mr. and Mrs. Brinker. And after taking a deep breath, so did Molly.

They munched in silence, watching each other's faces.

"They are very crunchy," said Mr. Brinker. He ate another one.

"I believe I prefer potato chips," said Mrs. Brinker.

"We're just not used to the idea of eating grasshoppers," said Angie. "In some countries, it's just a plain, ordinary everyday thing to eat grasshoppers."

"My brother will never believe me when I tell him that I ate a grasshopper," said Molly. "May I take one to him?"

"Help yourself," said Mr. Brinker.

"Take several," said Mrs. Brinker. "There's plenty."

"Thank you for such an unusual present, Angie," said Mr. Brinker.

"You're welcome," grinned Angie.

WORDS THAT GO TOGETHER

Read and think about these words from the story "The Shoeshine Chair": *shoeshine, doorbell, snowman, birthday.* Can you tell how these words are alike? If you can, then you know that words like these are called *compound words.* Compound words are two words that go together to form a new word with a meaning all its own.

shoe + shine = shoeshine

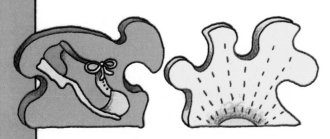

Sometimes you can figure out the meaning of the compound word by thinking about the meaning of each separate word and seeing how the two words fit together.

Look at the word *shoeshine.* You know what a shoe is. Think about what the word *shine* means. These two meanings fit together in this way:

A shoeshine is a shine
for a shoe.

Use this same idea to find the meaning of the word *doorbell.*

A doorbell is a ____ for a ____.

Meanings of other compound words can be figured out in another way. Look at the word *snowman.* Think about what snow is. You know the meaning of *man.* These meanings fit together in this way:

A man of snow is a snowman.

Use this same idea to find the meaning of the word *birthday.*

The ____ of your ____
is your birthday.

Now look at the compound words below. Can you find the meaning of each compound word?

mailbox   junkyard
raindrops   handshake

99

A NEW SONG

Laura Adams Armer

Younger Brother and Uncle had finally rounded up all the horses. The Big Man from the trading post was expected in a few days. He would look them over and choose what he wanted. The next task was to find the steers. The little Navaho boy had been excused from herding the sheep so that he could help Uncle. They were riding their ponies up a narrow gorge. They were keeping a sharp lookout for the red-and-white yearling that was missing. Tracks led to the water hole. There in the damp sand beside the water they found new tracks. They were the tracks of the mountain lion.

"The Soft-footed Chief has been hunting," Uncle said. "He is a good hunter and grows fat on our cattle."

Younger Brother hoped his yearling had not helped to fatten the Soft-footed Chief. Uncle had given the yearling to him when it was just a little calf. He had watched it grow and was very proud of it. He asked Uncle if they would hunt the mountain lion.

"No, my child. He is one of the pets the Turquoise Woman gave to our people. It is better that we leave him to follow his own trail of beauty."

"Uncle, where does the Turquoise Woman live?"

"On an island in the wide water of the west. There she lives in her turquoise house with her husband. He carries the sun."

"And when the Sun Bearer reaches his home in the west, what does he do with the sun, Uncle?"

"He hangs it up on the turquoise peg on the turquoise wall of the turquoise house of the Turquoise Woman. It goes *tla, tla, tla, tla,* as it sways on the wall. When the sun is still, the Sun Bearer lights his pipe from its fire. But he cannot rest too long. Every morning he must start across the sky from the east, bearing the sun on his left shoulder."

"I should like to go to the wide water of the west, Uncle. I should like to see the turquoise house and the Turquoise Woman."

The two talked as they rode.

They were following a narrow stream of water that traced its way under the tall, tender green trees. The trail their ponies followed was narrow and overgrown. Sometimes Younger Brother wondered if it were a trail, it was so full of loose rocks.

He was glad Uncle had let him ride with him. Uncle was a medicine man who knew the stories of the Holy People. The Holy People had lived in the land before the Navahos came. They were the people who built their homes in caves high up in the cliffs. They must have been a busy people. Many broken bits of their pottery could be found lying about the country. The designs on the old pots were painted in black on white or red backgrounds. The designs were strange to the Navahos. Sometimes the Navaho people copied the designs in their weavings.

Uncle had told Younger Brother many stories of the ancient people. He had told him about the boy who wanted to find a new song. And he had told

Younger Brother how the boy had traveled on a rainbow to reach the House of Dawn. Younger Brother had seen the House of Dawn and the House of Evening Twilight, high in a canyon wall. They were so high that everyone knew they could be reached only by a rainbow trail.

Younger Brother wondered if there were any stone houses of the ancient ones near where they were riding. Uncle said he had never before been so far up the canyon wall. Maybe no one had. It was very wild. The trail had given out. They were forced to ride uphill through brush and over loose rocks. They were still looking for the lost yearling.

Breaking through the brush, they came into a clear space. There, at the foot of a cliff, they found a spring of water. It fed the stream they had been following. Younger Brother could hardly believe his eyes when he saw his own red-and-white yearling drinking at the spring.

"Uncle," he whispered, "the Soft-footed Chief did not kill my yearling."

"It is well, my child. I will rope him and we will lead him home."

While Uncle roped the yearling, Younger Brother rode around the end of the cliff. He liked this country with its rocks and mountains and trees. He felt happy. He thought again about the story of the boy who wanted to find a new song. He thought that he, too, would like to make a new song.

Suddenly, the stillness of the mountains was broken by a queer sound like the rattling of hoofs on stone. Younger Brother looked in the direction of the sound. He saw a huge round cave in the mountainside. It was filled with many little stone houses. A blue shadow partly hid them.

Younger Brother could still hear the clattering, rattling noise. Then, into a streak of sunshine on the floor of the cave, leaped seven slender deer. Just for a moment they paused in the light. Then they leaped and danced on the stone floor and were lost to sight in the bushes in front of the cave.

Everything was again still except Younger Brother's heart.

That was beating wildly and words were pounding in his head to be let out. He knew he had found a new song and the words poured out of him like the song of the bluebirds. This is what he sang:

In the yellow sun they danced,
Slender Horns and Slender
*   Feet.*
Near their shadowed homes
*   they danced.*
Slender Horns and Slender
*   Feet.*

Then he rode back to Uncle and whispered, "The Deer People! I saw them enter their houses."

Uncle looked at the child. His big brown eyes were opened wide. He was breathing fast and trembling. Uncle knew something had happened. Probably the boy had been blessed with a vision. That was good. He would make a powerful medicine man if he had visions. He spoke to him.

"It is well, my child. We will

return home. Tonight you may tell us all about the Deer People."

Riding back and leading the red-and-white yearling, Younger Brother was very quiet. He knew he had seen the homes of the ancients. That night in the hogan by the fire he sang his new song for Uncle.

Uncle was pleased. "It is a new song. Never have I heard it before," he said. "Now you must have a new name. I shall call you Little Singer. Because the Deer People danced for you, I shall teach you their songs. It will take many years to learn them. Not until you are a man will you know them all, but we shall begin in four days."

Nobody believed that Younger Brother had seen a real cave with real houses. Only the Big Man believed because he knew that anything magic or wonderful could exist and did exist in Navaho land. Besides, he had a photograph of the big cave with all the houses. He had never shown it to anyone because he too liked to watch the Deer People dance in the sunlight. He knew they never would if noisy people went to their homes with guns and canned goods. So he and Younger Brother kept the secret together.

No One Else

Now, someone else can tell you how
To multiply by three
And someone else can tell you how
To spell Schenectady
And someone else can tell you how
To ride a two-wheeled bike
But no one else, no, no one else
Can tell you what to like.

An engineer can tell you how
To run a railroad train
A map can tell you where to find
The capital of Spain
A book can tell you all the names
Of every star above
But no one else, no, no one else
Can tell you who to love.

Your aunt Louise can tell you how
To plant a pumpkin seed
Your cousin Frank can tell you how
To catch a centipede
Your Mom and Dad can tell you how
To brush between each meal
But no one else, no, no one else
Can tell you how to feel.

For how you feel is how you feel
And all the whole world through
No one else, no, no one else
Knows that as well as YOU!

—*Elaine Laron*

Forms of Literature

Imagine that you have just finished your homework. You turn on the TV. You see a news reporter. She says:

> "It's five o'clock. The temperature is forty-five degrees. The wind is five miles an hour. Rain is expected later tonight ... The President greeted the Prime Minister of India on the White House lawn this afternoon. Stay tuned to Channel 37 for all the latest news."

Now you switch to another channel. There you see three colorful dragons. They are plotting the take-over of a castle in the clouds. You hear:

> "Let's dry up the moat with a wave of the magic wand. Then we'll catch the king in a dragon's dragnet!"
> "Stay tuned to Channel 80 for more adventures of the dangerous dragons."

Which program do you think is about real people and real events? Which is about imaginary people, animals, and events? Stories about real people and real events are called *nonfiction*. Stories about imaginary people, animals, and events are called *fiction*. The news program on the first channel was nonfiction. The dragon story on the second channel was fiction.

Books may be described as fiction or nonfiction, too. Some examples of fiction are books that have fairy tales, legends, myths, and mysteries. Some examples of nonfiction are biographies, histories, science books, and "Do-It-Yourself" books.

Let's see how well you know the difference between fiction and nonfiction. Make two columns on your paper. Label one column, <u>Fiction</u>. Label the other column, <u>Nonfiction</u>. Write your answers to the questions below in the correct column.

1. These selections might be found in a book or a magazine. Which are nonfiction? Which are fiction?
   a. a report on storms
   b. a scary ghost story
   c. a fable about a horse that talks
   d. a short history of Australia

2. These selections may be found in this book. Which are fiction? Which are nonfiction?
   a. "The Medal"
   b. "A New Song"
   c. "Growing Up Chinese-American"
   d. "The Emperor's Nightingale"

3. These books might be found in a library. Which would be fiction? Which would be nonfiction?
   a. *Fish of the Pacific Ocean*
   b. *Aesop's Fables*
   c. *The Chicken Who Visited the Queen*
   d. *George Washington: The First President*

GROWING

The selections you read in "Growing" were about real people and make-believe characters from many different times and places. Some of the people and characters learned how to be brave. Some learned how to develop their talents. Some learned to understand other people's feelings. But they all had one thing in common. They were learning about themselves and others. That's what growing is all about!

Thinking About "Growing"

1. What did Sarah Ida learn about friendship after almost losing Al as a friend?
2. How did Trina and Maggie each have to change and grow in order to keep being friends?
3. Why did Kwani know it was time to say "good-by" to Jumanne?
4. What did Phillis Wheatley and Younger Brother show about themselves when their special talents were discovered?
5. After reading "Growing Up Chinese-American," why do you think that learning about the customs of others helps you to understand other people?
6. Some people think growing means getting older. What do you think it means?
7. Write a paragraph describing what King George might have done after he read Phillis Wheatley's poem.

PASTIMES

Throughout history, people have developed pastimes to help them relax and have fun. Playing games and taking part in sports activities are pastimes that people have always enjoyed. Some games have not changed since they were invented thousands of years ago. Others have changed as people have thought of new ways to play or have developed new rules.

In "Pastimes," you will read the histories of some pastimes that people enjoy today. You will learn about kite-flying in Japan 2000 years ago. You will learn that you and your friends could have played soccer in China long ago. If you had grown up in ancient Greece, you might have waited eagerly to see the Olympic Games. You will read about people who are still enjoying these pastimes today.

As you read, think about the many ways people have had fun in the past. Think about how knowing the histories of pastimes helps you understand popular pastimes today.

WELCOME to SOCCER

Edward F. Dolan, Jr.

The white-shirted team comes rushing down the field. The ball whizzes along the ground as the players kick it from one to another. The other team, in red shirts, guards its goal. They are ready to meet the attack, eager to take away the ball. Suddenly, the ball flies low to a white-shirt near the side of the field. From there, it zooms to a teammate who has slipped behind the red-shirts. Without ever putting a hand on the ball, the teammate snares it. This player kicks it hard at the corner of the goal. The goalkeeper dives to stop the ball. Too late—the ball flashes into the goal....

Welcome to soccer! When you play soccer, you're part of a game that is well-known for many reasons.

First, soccer is one of the oldest games in history. About 2,500 years ago, it began in China as *Tsu-chin*, meaning "to kick a leather ball with the feet." Later, the Romans played a game in which two teams tried to kick a ball across a line on a field. They may be the people who brought the game to Great Britain more than 1,800 years ago. The British name for the sport became *Association Football*. The word *soccer* comes from *assoc*, the shortened form of the word *association*.

Second, soccer is the most popular team sport in the world. It is played on five continents, in 150 countries. Its World Cup tournament attracts a television and radio audience of nearly 900 million fans. Since the beginning of this century, soccer has been one of the sports played at the Olympic Games.

Third, soccer is one of the fastest games played on foot. It requires lots and lots of energy and endurance.

There are two teams of eleven players each. They meet on a field that is a little larger than a football field, but there is nothing else about soccer that is similar to football. In football, the playing stops and starts. In soccer, the ball is almost always in play.

The soccer ball scoots up and down the field, zigzagging as it is passed among players. Again and again, it goes from one team to the other. One minute your team may be deep in your opponent's territory. There, you're trying to score a point. Another minute and you may be back upfield in front of your own goal. There, you're trying to keep your opponent from scoring.

Soccer is really a simple game. There are only a few rules, and they are easy to learn. The idea is to score points by making the ball go into the goal at your opponent's end of the field. You score one point each time you make a goal.

Yet simple as it is to learn, soccer is one of the toughest

Use your feet, legs, chest, and head. But only the goalies can use their hands.

games in the world to play. Only the goalie can touch the ball with his or her hands or arms. Unless you are the goalie, you can't catch the ball as it flies through the air. You can't throw it. You can't pick it up and run with it. Instead, you must move the ball along the field and try for points in other ways.

Your feet must do most of the work, but not all of it. You can also use your legs, knees, and thighs, your stomach, your chest, and even your head. This method of playing makes soccer different from any other game.

Nevertheless, in spite of its fascination and speed, soccer has just recently become popular in the United States. Only within the past ten to twenty

years have Americans begun playing soccer seriously; and now, they are also flocking to soccer matches. As players and spectators, Americans by the millions are turning out for the game.

Young people are especially fond of soccer. They like the game because it is full of action and because on every team there is a place for all who want to play. Size doesn't matter. Are you too short for basketball? Too light for football? A little too heavy for track? Then soccer is for you. Anyone can play. There are positions on the team for players of all shapes and sizes.

People have also learned that they can play soccer without great fear of being

hurt. The game is tough, but it is very safe. It is safe because it is not a rough, body-contact sport like football. If you play wisely, there is only a small chance that you will be injured. But if you *are* hurt, the injury will probably be a minor one.

Furthermore, soccer is a game in which both boys and girls can play as equals. There are some all-boy leagues and some all-girl leagues. But in some areas, girls and boys play together on the same team.

Finally, many young Americans have taken up soccer because its equipment is so inexpensive. You don't need helmets, shoulder pads, bats, or mitts. For soccer, all you need is a ball and a field or vacant lot in which to play.

You can wear shorts, a T-shirt, socks, and a pair of shoes that won't slip on the grass. If you wish, you *can* buy special soccer shoes. However, your favorite sneakers will do very well.

As soccer becomes more and more popular in the United States, teams are sprouting up everywhere. Elementary schools, junior and senior high schools, colleges — all are developing soccer teams.

So welcome to soccer! It's time for you, too, to join in the fun.

PELÉ
One of Soccer's Greatest

Pelé is the nickname of Edson Arantes Do Nacimento. He was born into a soccer-loving family in the Brazilian city of Bauru. When he grew up, he became one of the world's greatest soccer stars.

As a child, Pelé watched his father play soccer for a local club in Bauru. Then, he and a group of friends decided to form their own soccer team. They weren't able to buy soccer shoes, or even a soccer ball, so they played barefoot with a ball made of old socks. This

barefoot team won a city tournament, and its young star had his first taste of victory and fame.

By the time he was fifteen, Pelé was playing major-league soccer. At sixteen, he joined the Brazilian soccer club, Santos. Then, one year later, in 1958, Pelé became a member of Brazil's World Cup team.

Like the Olympics, the World Cup games are an international event held every four years. The first year Pelé was on the Brazilian team, his country won the championship. Brazil won again in 1962 and again in 1970. It is the only country that has captured three world championships.

When he retired from Brazilian soccer in 1974, Pelé had scored 1,216 goals in 1,254 games. No wonder his country honored him by declaring him "a national treasure."

Then, in 1975, Pelé came to the United States to play soccer for the New York Cosmos. His spectacular playing helped to double—even triple—the crowds and to make the sport more popular in the United States. In 1977, just before he again retired as a professional player, Pelé led the Cosmos to the championship of the North American Soccer League.

Although he is a man of medium height—under six feet—Pelé has been a model soccer player. He has played the game as it should be played. He has always been aware of or in control of the ball. He has been able to run fast and change directions quickly. To have seen him play is to understand why he has been called "the greatest soccer player ever."

THE KITE

How bright on the blue
Is a kite when it's new!

With a dive and a dip
It snaps its tail

Then soars like a ship
With only a sail

As over tides
Of wind it rides,

Climbs to the crest
Of a gust and pulls,

Then seems to rest
As wind falls.

When string goes slack
You wind it back

And run until
A new breeze blows

And its wings fill
And up it goes!

How bright on the blue
Is a kite when it's new!

But a raggeder thing
You never will see

When it flaps on a string
In the top of a tree.

—HARRY BEHN

120

AT THE END OF A STRING

No one really knows when or where the first kite fluttered in the wind. However, most scholars think that the Chinese people had kites about 2,000 years ago. European explorers who visited the East brought the first kites to the West. They probably brought the brightly colored kites home to their children as gifts.

Kite flying has always been a very important sport in Asia. In China there used to be a great holiday each year on the ninth day of the ninth month. It was called "The Festival of Ascending on High." Thousands of people, young and old, flew their kites on that day. Kites of different shapes and sizes filled the sky. There were kites that looked like dragons and lions and tigers. And there were kites that looked like fish and birds and snakes.

In Japan a special kite day is still held each year on May 5th. All day long, fish-shaped kites are flown from the roof tops. They are flown in honor of a brave Japanese boy named Kintaro. Kintaro once saved a group of fishers by killing a man-eating fish.

Kite fighting is the most popular kite sport in India. There are kite makers who spend their lives making fighter kites. The fighter kites are made of colored paper. It is stretched over bamboo sticks. The kite line has two parts. One part is the regular string. It is usually white. The other part is a brightly colored cutting string. The cutting string is covered with coated glass. In kite fighting, a kite flier tries to maneuver the cutting string of the kite across an opponent's white string. When the white string is cut, the loser's kite flies away.

Kites are not only for fun. They have been very useful throughout history. Ben Franklin's famous kite experiment proved that lightning is really electricity. And the U.S. Weather Bureau has used kites to learn more about weather. They have sent kites up with scientific instruments attached to them.

The most common kites flown in the United States are the Eddy and box kites. The Eddy kite was introduced in our country by a man named William Eddy. It really came from Asia though. Most kids fly the Eddy kite. It is diamond-shaped. And it has two crossed sticks in back. The box kite was invented in the early 1890's by Lawrence Hargrave.

Kites have their place in the past and in the present. And if you have never flown a kite, you ought to. Then you will better understand why people have been flying kites for the past 2,000 years—and probably always will.

A KITE FOR BENNIE

Genevieve Gray

Bennie was a very happy boy the day he finally got the new sneakers he had waited for so long. On the same day, Bennie saw the most beautiful thing he had ever seen—a kite flying in the wind. From that day on, he wanted a kite even more than he had wanted new sneakers. But in Bennie's family there was no money to buy extra things like kites.

So Bennie set out to make one. With the help of friends, his teacher, and his older brother, Arthur, Bennie made a kite of his own. In this story, you will find out what happened when Bennie and Arthur tried to fly the kite.

After supper, Bennie ran some more string from the top of the kite to the bottom and another piece from one side to the other. Moving the kite around, Bennie began to see just how big it really was. He and Robert and Patricia—all three—could hide behind it with room left over. What if it wouldn't fly?

Now was as good a time as any to find out. He raised the kite high off the floor. "Mama," he said, "I'm taking the kite up on the roof."

Mama's big laugh stopped him. "You think you're going to fly it in the dark?" she chuckled. "You'll tear it up for sure. Wait till Arthur can help you. Tomorrow's Saturday. Maybe he'll take you down to the park. You'll need plenty of space to fly that thing."

When Bennie woke up the next morning, Arthur had already left. "Arthur said to tell you he is coming home at noon," Mama said. "He said he'll take you to the park if there's a good enough breeze to get the kite up."

Bennie put on his shirt and pants and spent the morning watching out the front window for Arthur. A gentle wind blew the old lace curtains. It seemed like a year before Arthur came home. Then Bennie counted the bites while Arthur ate his lunch. At last Arthur said, "Let's go, Bennie."

Since the kite was so big, Arthur ended up carrying it. It looked so big and fine that Bennie stopped worrying. A dog followed them, barking. All along the street on the six blocks to the park, people turned around and stared. "Hey, look at that!" Bennie could hear them saying.

Bennie wanted to tell them all proudly, "I made it! I made it!" but that would have been kid stuff, so he didn't.

When they were almost there, Arthur said, "I hope we can fly this thing, Bennie. You know, I never flew a kite before." But Bennie's eyes sparkled as he looked up at his brother. He and Arthur together could do anything in the world!

"We can fly it," said Bennie.

"Are you sure you made it the way the book said?" asked Arthur.

"Yeah," said Bennie.

At the park, Arthur and Bennie found a wide, grassy space. Off to one side stood some people who came along to watch. "Let's see," said Arthur. "Maybe you ought to take the string and run toward the wind while I hold up the kite. Here, take the ball of string and roll it out."

Bennie walked away from Arthur, rolling out string. When he was about a hundred yards away, Arthur cried, "That ought to be enough! Are you ready to start running?"

"Yeah," Bennie called back. He was so excited his hands were shaking. He'd wanted the kite so much. What would he do if he'd made it so big it wouldn't fly?

"Here goes!" Bennie cried. He turned and began to run.

But when Arthur let go of the kite, it didn't rise up in the air the way Bennie thought it should. It seemed to jump out of Arthur's hands. Then it ducked over and hit the ground hard. A cold feeling came up in Bennie's throat. He dropped the roll of string and ran to see if the kite was hurt. Arthur picked it up. "It's all right," Arthur said. "Come on. Let's try again."

Arthur again held the kite up by the end, and Bennie went back to his ball of string. This time when Bennie began to run, the kite went only a few feet in the air. Once more Bennie saw it jump, swing, and bang its big nose into the ground. He was sick with disappointment and worry.

They tried a third time, but once more the kite dug into the ground. Bennie bit his lip to keep back the tears.

Arthur knelt down by the kite. "Bennie," he said. His voice was so kind and gentle Bennie didn't dare look at him for fear he'd cry like a baby. "When you made the kite, Bennie, could there have been something you left out? Think, now. Think hard. What could you have left out?"

Bennie sat down by Arthur and closed his eyes, trying to remember the pictures in the book. But try as he would, all he could think of was the soaring red kite he had seen the day he got his new sneakers.

He saw it again now, with its long tail swimming in the air.

"Arthur!" cried Bennie. "I know! It needs a tail! The kite won't fly because it needs a tail!"

Arthur looked thoughtful. "I guess the tail is what holds the kite straight," he said. "We need something heavy to hold the end of it down."

"What about a rock or a stick?" asked Bennie, looking around.

"Wel-l-l-l," said Arthur. "Maybe."

129

All of a sudden, Bennie shouted. "Arthur! What about my sneakers? Can we tie my new sneakers to the end of the kite?" Arthur looked surprised for a minute before he threw back his head and began to laugh.

"Bennie!" he cried. "You crazy kid!"

While Arthur was still laughing, Bennie took off his shoes. The warm spring grass pushed up between his bare toes, and he did a quick little dance. Still chuckling, Arthur tied the sneakers by the laces to the end of the kite.

"Okay," laughed Arthur. "Let's try again."

Bennie raced across the grass to take his place with the ball of string. It seemed to him that the sun and trees and sky were all so happy they were laughing. Or maybe it was only the people laughing because they saw Bennie and Arthur tie a pair of sneakers to the end of their big kite.

Again Arthur held the kite. Bennie began to run with the ball of string. This time, the kite no longer acted like a thing made of paper and wood. Bennie had never seen anything so beautiful. It climbed the April wind like a great bird opening its wings to the sky. Bennie could feel its strong, steady pull against the string in his hand.

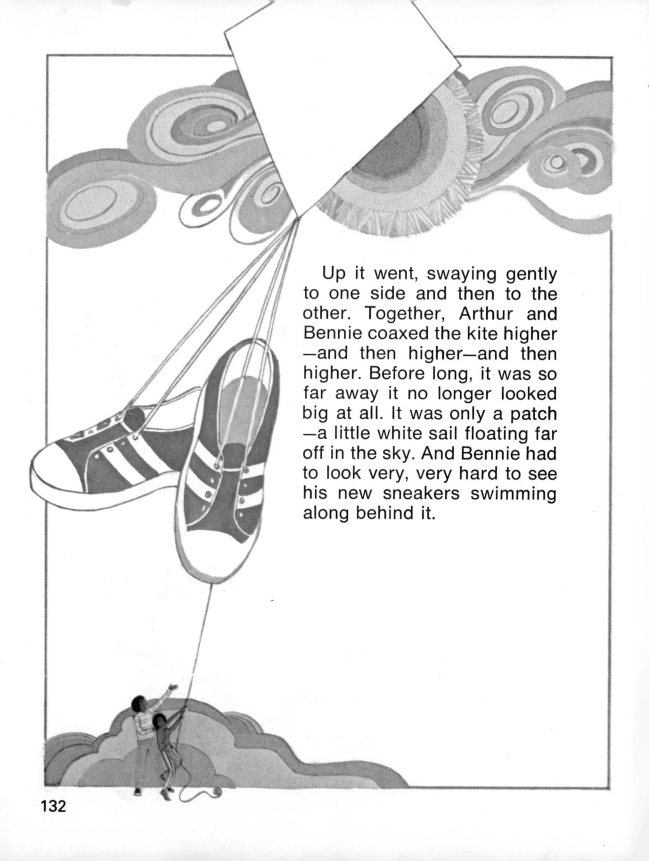

Up it went, swaying gently to one side and then to the other. Together, Arthur and Bennie coaxed the kite higher —and then higher—and then higher. Before long, it was so far away it no longer looked big at all. It was only a patch —a little white sail floating far off in the sky. And Bennie had to look very, very hard to see his new sneakers swimming along behind it.

What Do You Say?

If Bennie had lived in a different part of the United States, he might have gotten a pair of *tennis shoes* or *gym shoes* instead of *sneakers.* Do you know why? The people in the pictures below want the same thing. Would you use one of these sentences? Would you use a different sentence to ask for the same thing?

English is the most common language in our country. But not everyone speaks English in the same way. The different ways we speak are called *dialects,* and different dialects have different names for the same things. What do you call the items below?

Sack?
Bag?
Poke?

Faucet?
Spigot?
Tap?

Frying pan?
Skillet?
Spider?

Do you say *bucket* or *pail?*

Do you say *lightning bug* or *firefly?*

Do you say *skunk* or *polecat?*

Olympic Games–
Past and Present

Laurence Swinburne

This selection is about one of the biggest sports events in the world. If you have ever watched a telecast of the Olympic games, you know how exciting they are! Did you know that more than 120 countries are represented? Did you know that there are summer games as well as winter ones? Did you know that according to the rules of the games, Olympic athletes must be amateurs? That is, they must not earn money at their sports. Here are some interesting facts about the Olympic games.

The first Olympic games began in Greece over 2,700 years ago. They were held in the valley of Olympia. Athletes from many countries came to the games.

All wars stopped during the Olympic games. Soldiers on their way to the games passed in safety through enemy lines. No weapons were allowed at the games.

The Greek Olympics did not have as many events as the modern Olympic games we know today. At first there was only one foot race. It was a short race about the length of the stadium. Then another short race and a race of about three miles were added. Later field events were added to the games. There were jumping and javelin and discus throwing contests. Wrestling and boxing matches were also popular. Later chariot races were added.

An Olympic winner received many honors. He returned home a hero. A parade was held in his honor. His government gave him money. And he did not have to pay taxes for the rest of his life. If he won three contests at the Olympic games, a statue was put up in his honor.

When the Romans conquered Greece, they allowed the games to be held as usual. But they opened the games to everyone, not just the Greeks.

The last Greek Olympics were held in 388 A.D. Then the emperor of Rome decided that they should not be held. So the stadium where the games had been held fell into ruin. The Greek Olympics, which lasted over 1,100 years, were over.

The Modern Games

Baron Pierre de Coubertin was a Frenchman. He was worried about the lack of physical education in his country. Sports were not taught in French schools. De Coubertin believed that sports should go hand in hand with studies.

De Coubertin went to see the ruins of the old Olympic stadium in Greece. This gave him an idea. His idea was to begin the Olympic games all over again. He thought the games would make people more interested in sports. And he also thought they would bring about healthy competition among nations.

Sports directors of other countries liked de Coubertin's idea. So, in 1896, the first modern Olympic games were held in Athens, Greece.

Since that time, the Olympics have been held once every four years, except three times, when there were wars. Unlike the Greek Olympics, war did not stop for the modern games. It was the games that stopped.

The modern games have many foot races and field events. The longest race in the games is called the marathon. Field events include the discus and javelin throwing, the hammer throw, the long jump, and the high jump. There are also wrestling and boxing matches. Basketball and soccer are other games in the modern Olympics.

During the winter Olympic games, skiers glide down steep hills. Skaters race across the ice. Teams of skaters compete in ice hockey games.

Before the start of each Olympics, runners carry a lighted torch through many nations toward the stadium where the games will be held. These athletes are from different countries. Yet they cooperate in carrying the Olympic torch.

The torch is passed from runner to runner. When the final runner enters the stadium, he or she places the torch in a special basin filled with fuel. It catches fire. It is then, and only then, that the Olympic games can begin.

The Olympic flame burns throughout the games. It is right that it should do so. It is the flame of peace.

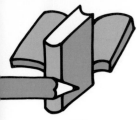

Up, Down, and Across

There are many ways in which writers give information. Some use paragraphs. Some use diagrams. Some use tables or charts. What is important is that the reader understand the information easily. Look at these examples.

In 1977, the National-League player with the most home runs was George Foster. Foster hit fifty-two homers. He was followed by Jeff Burroughs with forty-one, Greg Luzinski with thirty-nine, and Mike Schmidt with thirty-eight.

1977 NATIONAL LEAGUE HOME-RUN RECORDS	
Player	**Home Runs**
George Foster	52
Jeff Burroughs	41
Greg Luzinski	39
Mike Schmidt	38

How many home runs did Greg Luzinski hit? Is it easier to find this information in the first example or in the second? In this case, most people will find the second example—the table—easier to use. A *table* is a special way of showing information in columns and rows.

Look at the table on the next page. Use it to answer the questions. Write the answers on your paper.

1. When and where were the first Olympic Games held?
2. How many events were in the 1920 Olympics?
3. Were there ever more than 200 events?
4. How many athletes were in the 1908 Olympics?
5. In what year did 5,867 athletes compete?
6. How many nations were represented in 1960?
7. When were the games held in Montreal, Canada?
8. In which cities have the Olympic Games been held more than once?

SUMMER OLYMPIC GAMES

Year	Place City, Country	Number of Nations	Number of Events	Number of Athletes
1896	Athens, Greece	13	42	285
1900	Paris, France	20	60	1,066
1904	St. Louis, USA	11	67	496
1908	London, England	22	104	2,059
1912	Stockholm, Sweden	28	106	2,541
1920	Antwerp, Belgium	29	154	2,606
1924	Paris, France	44	137	3,092
1928	Amsterdam, Netherlands	46	120	3,015
1932	Los Angeles, USA	37	124	1,408
1936	Berlin, Germany	49	142	4,069
1948	London, England	59	138	4,468
1952	Helsinki, Finland	69	149	5,867
1956	Melbourne, Australia	67	145	3,184
1960	Rome, Italy	84	150	5,396
1964	Tokyo, Japan	94	163	5,565
1968	Mexico City, Mexico	109	172	6,082
1972	Munich, West Germany	121	194	8,500
1976	Montreal, Canada	89	198	9,564
1980	Moscow, USSR	85	206	6,250

DONNA'S GIFT

Bob Thomas

"Donna's Gift" is a story about a real girl who became a swimming champion. At the age of 13, Donna deVarona won a place on the U.S. Olympic Swimming Team. That made her the youngest athlete in the 1960 Olympic games. In 1964, she won two Gold Medals and broke several world records.

Since that time, Donna deVarona has continued her interest in sports. She has worked on a government committee for improving conditions for amateur athletes. She has also been a sports commentator for television.

Donna climbed into the front seat of the car. As her father drove off, she thought, "I wish that something would happen so I wouldn't have to go to diving practice. Oh, nothing bad! But couldn't we have a flat tire? Or something?"

Anything would do—as long as she didn't have to climb up on that high diving board. She was afraid. But it was a secret fear. She couldn't bear to share it with her father or her diving coach. They were so proud of her. She simply couldn't bear to say "I'm afraid!" out loud. Besides, she was ashamed of her fear. She hated to admit that she was afraid of anything. But...the diving board was so high, and the water was so far, far below!

The deVarona car pulled up in front of the swimming pool. Nothing had happened. She would have to take her diving lesson.

Her coach, Frank McGuigan, was waiting. "Hi, Donna," he said. "How's my prize pupil today?"

"Fine, thanks." But Donna realized as soon as she had spoken that she didn't sound fine. She hoped her father and the coach hadn't caught the tone of her voice.

The coach gave her a sharp look. But all he said was, "Take a few dives off the low board to warm up, Donna."

She walked to the deep end of the pool and began diving off the low board. She didn't mind that. It was the high board that made her breath hard to catch and her knees feel as if they had no bones in them.

Coach McGuigan turned to Mr. deVarona. "What's the matter with Donna?" he asked.

"What do you mean?" said Mr. deVarona.

"She doesn't seem to be as interested in diving as she was at first," said the coach. "She was willing and eager when she started taking lessons. But lately I get the feeling that something is bothering her."

Mr. deVarona nodded. "You may be right. She used to talk my ear off on the way here. But the past few times she's hardly said a word."

"I wonder if we are pushing her too hard."

"But didn't you say that's what we have to do, if she's going to be a champion?" asked Donna's father.

"Yes, I did."

Mr. deVarona's eyes turned to his daughter, then back to the coach.

"Do you think she's got what it takes, coach?"

"Yes, I think she has. She has good toes. That's what we look for in top divers. It means that when she dives, her legs follow a good line, right to the point of her toes. Donna is as natural a diver as I have ever had for a student."

"But you yourself have told me that it takes more than that to become a champion," said Mr. deVarona.

"It takes a lot of hard work," the coach agreed. "Plus one other thing."

"What's that?"

"She has to want it."

Donna was climbing out of the pool after her third practice dive. Coach McGuigan walked toward her to begin the lesson. Mr. deVarona found a seat in the stands.

Donna went to work. She dived over and over again off the low board. She perfected each movement under the coach's instructions. Donna enjoyed this part of the lessons. She liked the all-in-one-piece feeling her body had when her dive was just right.

The hot August sun was beginning to drop toward the west as the coach said, "All right, Donna. Let's have a few dives off the high board. Then we'll call it quits for today."

Donna stood still. This was the bad moment in each of her diving lessons. And this time, she didn't think she could face it. She wasn't at all sure she could make herself walk to the high board and climb the ladder. And that was the easy part. After that came the long dive! "I've got to," she said to herself, but her fear answered, "I can't!"

"I—I don't want to," she heard herself say out loud.

Surprise showed in the coach's eyes. "Oh, come on, Donna. It's nothing to worry about. You've done it before. The water's awfully soft to land on."

Donna couldn't make herself move. "I don't want to," she repeated.

The coach looked toward Mr. de Varona. Donna's father got up and came over. "Now, honey," he said, "you have to do what the coach tells you. That's the only way you are going to be a good diver."

Donna looked at the high board towering above her. She walked slowly toward it. She began climbing the ladder. With each step she felt sicker and sicker. She reached the top and looked down. And her head whirled. She was on the ten-foot board—twelve and a half feet above the water. But it seemed three or four times as high. She tried not to look down.

"All right, Donna," called the coach. "Let's see you do the one-and-a-half flip."

She paused, and he called out: "You can do it. You've done it before. Get a good bounce on the board. And don't forget to point those toes."

There was no turning back, not with her father watching her. To climb back down the ladder would be a defeat for her and a disappointment for him. There was nothing to do but dive. *"Don't think about how you feel— just dive,"* Donna thought.

Donna measured off the steps to the end of the board. Then she stood at perfect attention, arms stiff by her sides. She took the few steps, lifted one leg, and rose into the air. Down she came, and the board dipped beneath her, then rose again. Now she was in the air and ready to do the flip.

At first her form was perfect. Then in a split second something went wrong. Just the slightest arm movement disturbed her balance, and she lost her control. She could not complete the flip. She landed on her back with a great splash.

Donna's father rushed to the edge of the pool. Donna rose to the surface and tried to smile to show that she was all right.

"I think we had better quit for today, Frank," Mr. deVarona said.

"Yes, she's had enough," the coach agreed.

Donna was silent on the drive home. The stinging of her skin had stopped, but her back hurt. Worse than that, she felt she had failed her father, and that hurt more.

Donna's brother, Deet, was full of talk about the Little League game at dinner. But Donna scarcely said a word. Her stomach still felt jumpy, and she picked at her food. Finally her mother said, "Donna, you're not eating. Aren't you feeling well?"

"I'm tired. And I don't feel hungry," Donna replied. "May I be excused, please?"

"Of course, dear," said her mother. "Why don't you go to your room and get into bed? You'll feel better after you rest."

After Donna had left the room, Mrs. deVarona asked her husband, "What's the matter with her? She's usually so gay at the dinner table. It isn't like her to be tired."

"Oh, she had a bad time at diving this afternoon," said Mr. deVarona. "It's nothing. She's bound to have an off day now and then."

But when he passed the door of Donna's bedroom later that evening, he could hear her crying softly. He opened the door and saw her stretched out on the bed with her head buried in her pillow. Her body shook with sobs.

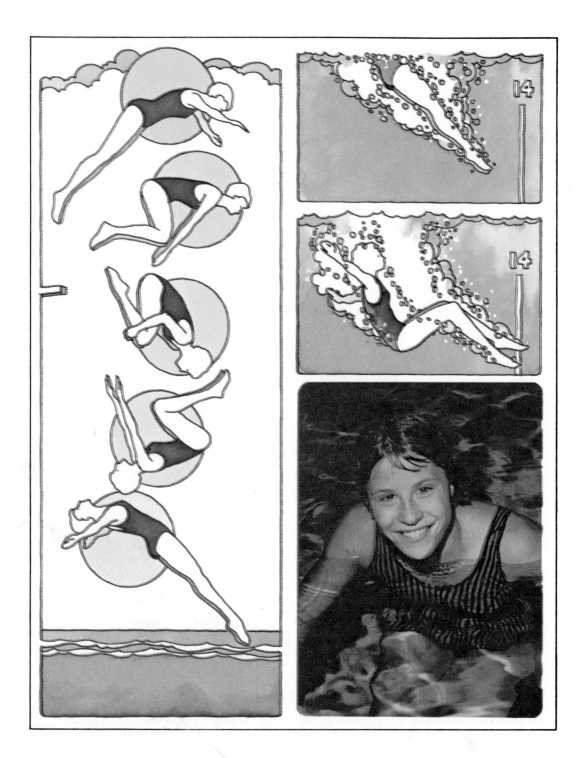

Mr. deVarona hurried to her and wrapped his arms around her. "What's the matter, honey?" he asked.

The answer burst out. "I don't want to dive, Daddy. It scares me."

Her father rocked her back and forth, just as he had done when she was a baby. "There, there," he said. "You don't have to dive if you don't want to. You don't have to do anything you are afraid of."

Finally her sobbing stopped. Her father dried her face and sat beside her on the bed.

"I didn't know you felt that way about diving," he told her. "I certainly wouldn't have encouraged you to do it if I had known. But you see, Donna, you have a certain gift. I recognized it, and so did Coach McGuigan. It's something that very few people have. Do you understand what I'm talking about?"

"No," Donna admitted.

"I'm talking about the natural gift that you have of a fine body and the ability to make it move easily and gracefully. Those who have that gift can become great athletes. Those who don't, can't—no matter how hard they train."

Donna thought about what her father was saying, not understanding all of it.

"That's all I have to say to you," he continued. "We will stop the diving lessons for now.

But think about that gift I told you about. You'll only be able to use it while you are young. It would be terrible to waste it."

He turned out the light on the table beside her bed and tucked the blanket around her shoulders. Kissing her on the forehead, he said, "Good night, honey."

"Good night, Daddy," she said in a solemn voice.

In the darkness, she thought once more about standing on the ten-foot board and looking down at the water far below, and she began to tremble. Then she remembered her father's words—

You don't have to dive if you don't want to — and felt better.

Now she remembered what her father had said about a certain gift. That excited her. Nothing gave her more pleasure than to hit a home run or to kick a football farther than any of her friends could. Yes, there were some things she could do better than most other kids. Not diving. But what about swimming? She liked to swim, even though she had never seriously trained for it.

"Yes, I will think about swimming," she told herself as she slowly drifted off to sleep.

Hobbyhorses, Boneshakers, Highwheelers, and Bikes

Laurence Swinburne

The first bicycle looked like a horse with wheels. It was called a hobbyhorse. It had no pedals. Riders pushed them along with their feet. But the hobbyhorse only traveled in a straight line. If a rider wanted to go around a corner, he or she had to get off, lift up the hobbyhorse, and turn it to face in the new direction.

At first, the hobbyhorse was very popular. There were hobbyhorse races, and many countries had hobbyhorse champions. New riders even went to hobbyhorse schools. They learned how to balance and ride without falling.

Hobbyhorses were forgotten after a few years because they were not easy to ride. Then a machine with iron wheels

was built. This machine had two things that the hobbyhorse did not have. One was the pedal. People no longer had to push the machine along the ground with their feet. The second improvement was the steering. The rider could change direction easily without getting off the machine. However, the machine was not very comfortable. So these iron-wheeled machines were called boneshakers.

Soon every town in England, France, and the United States had a racing club. The races were more exciting than they had been with the hobbyhorses. Champion racers could go as fast as forty miles an hour. They could never have gone this fast on a hobbyhorse.

Tricycles of that time were much more comfortable than boneshakers, but they weren't as fast. They were not like the tricycles children ride today. They had two huge wheels nearly as tall as a person. Another smaller wheel was either in front or in back of the machine. The rider sat on a low seat and pushed the pedals at the front of the tricycle. Pedaling tricycles was hard work, but anybody could learn to ride one.

Then the highwheeler was invented. This strange-looking bicycle had a very tall wheel in front and a small wheel in back. The average highwheeler was about fifty-four inches high.

The highwheeler looked strange, but it was an improvement over the boneshaker. Almost all of the rider's weight was on the front wheel. This made the ride smoother and more comfortable. Soon everyone was riding the highwheelers. Boneshakers were used only by beginners.

Highwheelers were fun to ride. They were fast and light. It was a great thrill to sit as high as six feet in the air and watch the scenery go by. But the highwheeler was dangerous. One bump on a large stone, and a rider could fall. Then the rider had to be careful not to get tangled up in the high wheel.

Around 1880, the safety bicycle was invented. Ten years later, air-filled tires were added to the safety bicycle. These tires were more comfortable to ride on than the iron wheels had been. Also, they made it easier for the riders to keep their balance. It was only a short time before safety bicycles filled the highways. Meanwhile, highwheelers rusted away in junkyards.

Soon there was one more big change. Up to this time, one pedal had been on each side of the front wheel. Sometimes the rider's feet would get tangled in the spokes. So the pedals were moved to a place between the wheels. A chain attached the pedals to the back wheel.

Bicycling started two hundred years ago because somebody tried to figure out a faster way for a person to travel. The bicycle has changed a lot since then. But a rider still needs two wheels and lots of leg power!

The next two selections are about people and their bicycles. The first one, "My Bicycle and Me," was written by a little girl. The second selection was written by a famous writer named William Saroyan. In "Thoughts of a Bicycle Rider," he tells how riding a bicycle helped him to become a writer.

My Bicycle and Me

Stephanie Laidman

I got my bike about one and a half years ago. I remember everything. The store was covered with bikes. They were even hanging from the ceiling! The bike I picked out was big for me then. And the storekeeper told me to use only the first gear until I was experienced enough to use second and third.

The next couple of weeks were filled with bike riding. I didn't do anything else. It was a challenge. We live in the country and have hills all around us. Before I was allowed to go onto the road, I would ride up and down our driveway. I got better

on the bike day by day. I knew that one day I'd be perfect.

Finally I was able to go out of the driveway. I found a hill that kept me pretty busy. I had a lot of trouble making it up that hill. I usually walked.

Dad decided that he wanted a bike. He went to a couple of places. Finally he went to the place my bike came from. He got a big, big black bike. It had big everything. It was twenty-eight inches, the wheel that is.

We went on a lot of bike rides together. One of them was so much fun I have to tell about it. It was about eleven o'clock when we started. We packed bananas and milk. It was a long, long ride, and when we came to a bridge we parked our bikes. Under the bridge we ate our food. It was nice there. When we finished our bananas, we fed the skins to the fish that lived in the stream. The way home was mostly uphill. We walked a lot.

Once my friend Suzanne and I decided to take a long ride. We did. And I finally made it up a hill that I never had made it up before. Suzanne said that if you were a good bike rider, even when you are really tired you would keep on going. I've done that ever since.

Thoughts of a Bicycle Rider

William Saroyan

Before I was sixteen I had many bicycles. I have no idea what became of them. I remember, though, that I rode them so hard they were always breaking down. The spokes of the wheels were always getting loose so that the wheels became crooked. The chains were always breaking. I bore down on the handlebars with so much force in sprinting, in speeding, in making quick getaways, that the handlebars were always getting loose, and I was always tightening them. But the thing about my bicycles that I want to remember is the way I rode them, what I thought while I rode them, and the music that came to me.

First of all, my bikes were always rebuilt second-hand bikes. They were lean, hard, tough, swift, and designed for usage. I rode them with speed and style. I found out a great deal about

style from riding them. Style in writing, I mean. Style in everything. I did not ride for pleasure. I rode to get somewhere, and I don't mean from the house on San Benito Avenue in Fresno to the Public Library there. I mean I rode to get somewhere *myself*. I did not loaf on my bike. I sometimes rested on it after a hard day's riding, on my way home to supper and sleep, sliding off the seat a little to the left, pedaling with the left leg, resting the other on the saddle, and letting the bike weave right and left easily as I moved forward. The style I learned was this: I learned to go and make it fast. I learned to know at one and the same time how my bike was going, how it was holding up, where I was, where I would soon be, and where in all probability I would finally be.

In the end I always went home to supper and sleep.

A man learns style from everything, but I learned mine from things on which I moved, and as writing is a thing which moves, I think I was lucky to learn as I did.

On the way I found out all the things without which I could never be the writer I am. I was not yet sixteen when I understood a great deal, from having ridden bicycles for so long, about style, speed, grace, purpose, value, form, integrity, health, humor, music, breathing, and finally and perhaps best of all, the relationship between the beginning and the end.

The Sidewalk Racer
or On the Skateboard

Skimming
an asphalt sea
I swerve, I curve, I
sway; I speed to whirring
sound an inch above the
ground; I'm the sailor
and the sail, I'm the
driver and the wheel
I'm the one and only
single engine
human auto
mobile.

—*Lillian Morrison*

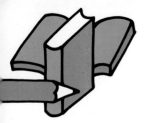

Careful Thinking

A *syllogism* is a way of thinking. It is a way of reaching a conclusion. A syllogism is made up of three sentences. The first two sentences are facts. The third sentence is a conclusion drawn from the facts.

> **Fact 1:** All lizards are reptiles.
> **Fact 2:** Anna's dinosaur is a lizard.
> Conclusion: Anna's dinosaur is a reptile.

When two facts are said in a special way, you can figure out what the conclusion should be. Think about the two facts below. Then see if you can finish the syllogism.

> **Fact 1:** All water contains oxygen.
> **Fact 2:** This glass contains water.
> Conclusion: This glass contains _____.

If you said, *This glass contains oxygen,* you were right.

ACTIVITY A Write the two facts for each syllogism on your paper. Then write the complete conclusion.

1. **Fact 1:** All triangles have three sides.
   Fact 2: This shape is a triangle.
   Conclusion: This shape has _____.

2. **Fact 1:** All oranges contain Vitamin C.
   Fact 2: This fruit is an orange.
   Conclusion: This fruit contains _____.

3. **Fact 1:** All snakes have scales.
   Fact 2: A cobra is a snake.
   Conclusion: A cobra _____.

4. **Fact 1:** All cats are mammals.
   Fact 2: A lion is a cat.
   Conclusion: A lion _____.

Look carefully at the syllogisms you have written. Do you see how each one works? Do you see the pattern it follows? If a syllogism doesn't follow this pattern, the conclusion won't be true.

Look again at Syllogism 4. Now look at this pattern.

All cats are mammals.
My dog is a mammal.
My dog is a cat.

ACTIVITY B Choose the correct syllogism below. Write it on your paper.

1. All nuts contain oil.
   A walnut is a nut.
   A walnut contains oil.

2. All mice eat cheese.
   Joel eats cheese.
   Joel is a mouse.

THE WACKY BIKE

Janet McNeill

Specs' bike gave out on him at the very beginning of the summer. I wasn't surprised really, nor was he. It just fell apart one night, in its place in the bicycle shed. When Specs came to get it, all he found was a heap of rusty spokes and bits of metal and some string and a few old scraps. I think it just gave out from sheer exhaustion.

Honestly, I don't blame it. All the time he'd had it, he never oiled it or cleaned it or anything. He said a bike was for riding, not for messing around with. When anything got loose or jammed, he just hitched it up with string or gave it a kick and went on riding. You could hear him coming for miles—clickety clack. He didn't need a bell, even if he'd had one.

It was a bit of a blow when we found the bike in pieces. I think Specs felt a bit sad about it himself. I was staying with the McCanns for summer vacation. They had taken a nice cabin. It was right at the far end of a

sandy bay. It looked as if we might have enjoyed ourselves. But we found that in a cabin Specs' five sisters seemed to add up to a good many more than five.

"We'll have to get away," Specs said. "We can clear out for whole days with some sandwiches. Maybe we can go exploring on our bikes."

"On our whats?" I said. Then, of course, he remembered.

"Well, we can walk, can't we?" he said. I suppose we could have walked. That is if you like walking. But from the far end of the

bay it was an awfully long way to anywhere. And there were only a few buses on the roads.

At the end of the first week, we were frantic. Specs decided that he simply had to have a bike. There was a bicycle shop up on the main road. We walked up to see if the man who keeps it had any secondhand bikes. Specs told the man he was looking for one with two wheels and some handlebars and something to sit down on. He was desperate, you see.

"There's an old machine at the back there. But maybe you

wouldn't like her," the man told us. Then he wheeled the bike out for us to see.

It was an odd kind of a bike, all right. You couldn't say exactly why it was so odd. Yet you knew that if you saw it among a hundred other bikes you'd recognize it. It had curly handlebars, like the horns of some queer animal you'd see up at the museum. It had two wheels, all right. But when you looked at them, you thought that they weren't quite round. Then you looked again, and of course they were.

"That's a wacky sort of a bike," Specs said. But I could see from the shine on his glasses that he liked it. "A real wacky bike, if you ask me."

"It'll clean up," the man said. "It's been lying there at the back of the shop since the fellow left it with me last summer."

"What sort of a fellow was it?" Specs asked.

The man scratched his head. "The most I remember him for was his nose and the way he set his feet down and the style he had of talking."

"How did he talk?" Specs asked. The man said it was in a sad kind of style, only joking. Specs said oh, like that, as if he understood right away. Then he paid out the money for the bike.

I had my bike with me. So we decided we'd cycle on into Kilkeel and get some ice cream. There's a steep, curvy little hill into Kilkeel. You need all the brakes you've got. I was in front, going carefully, when all of a sudden Specs went swooping past me. He was going full speed. I saw that he didn't even have his hands on the handlebars. He had put them in his pockets and was leaning back, whistling.

He went around the next corner of the road. I went after him as fast as I could. I was shouting and ringing my bell like mad. I expected to find him in bits at the bottom. But no, he was there, all in one piece.

I told him he was an awful silly fool, and what did he mean by going down the hill like that? Then he said, "Curly, it wasn't me, really. It was the bike. The bike took charge." I said it was lucky for him the road had been clear or it would have been the police who'd have been taking charge. He kept on saying, "It wasn't me, it was the bike, the wacky bike."

I was too cross to say anything except, "Come on in and let's have the ice cream." By then I think we both knew that there was something special about this bike. Specs was a little scared, remembering how he'd come down the hill. He was quite willing when I suggested we cycle home along the sand.

It was a good thing we did. The tide was low and the sand was bare and gray and oozy. We had it to ourselves. Have you ever seen a dog that's been shut up for a while and goes crazy with joy when it's let loose? Well, that was the way the bike acted. It had been shut up for a whole year. As soon as it got out on the sand, it gave itself a kind of shake all over. It stood still for a moment. And then it was off. It went around and around. It went in circles and loops and curves. Sometimes it went in figures of

ice cream

KILKEEL

169

eight that got bigger and bigger. Sometimes it leaned from side to side. You never thought it could right itself. But it always did. And all the time Specs sat on the seat, grinning. His hands were on the handlebars. But you knew there was no need for them to be there at all. Specs just sat there, whizzing and swooping on the wacky bike.

He stopped at last—or perhaps it was the bike that stopped. Then he looked at me and grinned. "Quite a bike." And then he took hold of the handlebars very firmly and said, "Home, James." And the bike took him home, very, very quietly.

After that the days were quite a bit brighter. But you had to be careful. You could never be sure how the bike would act. Mostly we stayed along the seashore, where we wouldn't meet anyone.

It seemed a pity to keep the bicycle hidden, if you know what I mean. Then we saw that a slow bicycle race was being held in the local village. We decided we'd risk it. Specs and his wacky bike were quite a sensation. When the gun went off, Specs leaped into the seat. He set off down the track as if he were out to win a race. The other seven riders were wobbling along, trying to go as slowly as they could. Everyone roared with laughter. They stopped laughing, however, when the wacky bike pulled up six inches from the tape. It just stood there. It stood perfectly still, as if it were no trouble at all. Specs sat on the seat grinning his head off. It stayed like that while the seven other bikes crawled past. One by one they went across the tape, passing Specs on their way. He was sitting there as steady as a rock. He even pulled a comic out of his pocket and was reading it! When the last of the other bikes had reached the tape, he folded the comic up and put it back in his pocket. When he went to collect the prize money, the crowd cheered!

The next day Mrs. McCann asked us if we'd like to go over to Kilkeel in the evening to see the circus. "They came to town last night," she said. "Most people didn't think they were coming this summer. Last year was such wonderful weather that they had very bad audiences. Nobody wanted to go into a tent when they could sit in the sun. They say some of the circus people

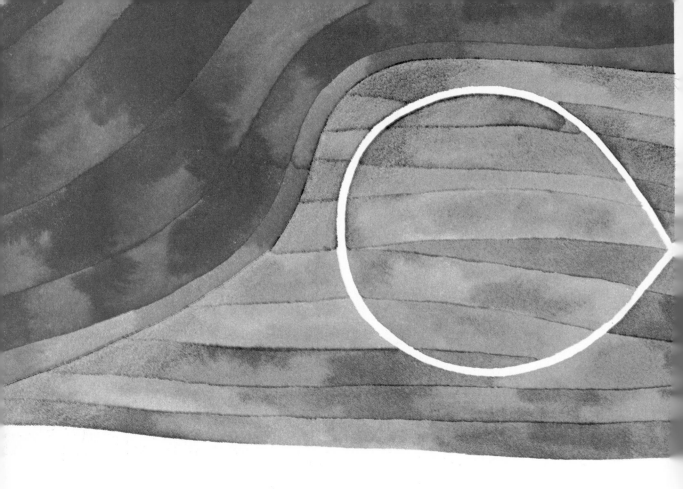

had quite a time raising the money to take them back to their homes. We must all go and see them tonight."

I didn't say anything to Specs. And he didn't say anything either. But after breakfast we found ourselves drifting toward the bicycle shed. I wasn't too surprised to see that my bicycle was there. But the wacky bike was gone. "Stolen," I said. "It's been stolen!"

"Do you think so?" Specs asked.

I said, "What else?" He pointed at the sand.

I told you the cabin was right down on the shore. And out from the bicycle shed ran the track of a bicycle, the wacky bike. It knew for sure where it was heading. The track was straight as if you'd ruled a line with a pencil. We followed it.

Just by looking at the track, you had a feeling of hurry and excitement. We began to run. Specs was in front. Suddenly he said, "Curly, look!"

Footprints had come across the sand from the other direction to meet the bicycle. They were long, thin footprints, set down at an odd sort of angle. They'd been in a hurry, too. You knew that.

Then the footprints and the bicycle track met. The footprints stopped altogether, and the bicycle track went on. Only it was set a little deeper into the sand. And it wasn't going straight any more. It went around and around. We stood looking at the track, watching it disappear over the sand. Then we came back into the house.

The circus was good. Arab horses and trapeze men and a man who juggled plates. Oh yes, and the clown. Just the right face for a clown, a big nose and a sad kind of style of making his jokes and a way of setting down his big long feet. And his bicycle?

Yes, his bicycle was as good as he was. "You'd think it was alive!" someone said. The crowd laughed like anything and gasped and clapped.

We clapped. But we didn't gasp. We'd seen it all before.

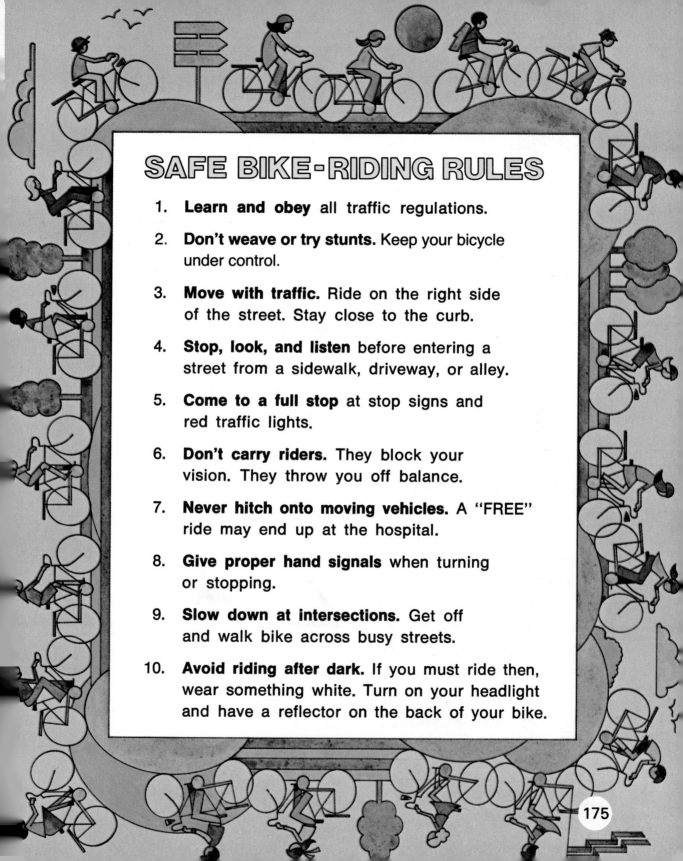

SAFE BIKE-RIDING RULES

1. **Learn and obey** all traffic regulations.

2. **Don't weave or try stunts.** Keep your bicycle under control.

3. **Move with traffic.** Ride on the right side of the street. Stay close to the curb.

4. **Stop, look, and listen** before entering a street from a sidewalk, driveway, or alley.

5. **Come to a full stop** at stop signs and red traffic lights.

6. **Don't carry riders.** They block your vision. They throw you off balance.

7. **Never hitch onto moving vehicles.** A "FREE" ride may end up at the hospital.

8. **Give proper hand signals** when turning or stopping.

9. **Slow down at intersections.** Get off and walk bike across busy streets.

10. **Avoid riding after dark.** If you must ride then, wear something white. Turn on your headlight and have a reflector on the back of your bike.

THE STORY OF

For years these have been magic words all over America. Some people think of a circus on television with dancing elephants and funny clowns. Others remember the high-wire acts way up under the top of the big tent.

The circus we now watch began with the Circus Maximus in ancient Rome. In Latin, *circus* means "circle." *Maximus* means "great."

The Romans built a great circle of seats. Many thousands of people could sit there.

This circus started with a big parade. Then came chariot races. Acrobats and jugglers did stunts. Sometimes men fought other men or wild animals.

For almost a thousand years, people went to the Circus Maximus. Then some countries began to make

THE CIRCUS

Mary
Kay
Phelan

war on Rome. There was no more time for a circus in the great circle.

But still people liked to be amused. The acrobats and jugglers knew that people would pay money to see their stunts.

When they could no longer perform in Rome, they began to wander all over Europe. Two or three performers would travel together. They did tricks on street corners. And people tossed coins to reward them.

In this way, the acrobats and jugglers were keeping the idea of a circus alive. At the same time, fairs were being held all over Europe.

Several hundred years passed. The fairs grew larger and larger. More men came to do their tricks. Some even brought strange animals to show to people.

Then in 1770, an Englishman, Philip Astley, tried something new. He opened a riding ring in London. People sat in seats all around the

ring while Astley did tricks on his horse. Later, he added a clown, a ropewalker, and acrobats.

Philip Astley is often called the "Father of the Circus" because he used a riding ring in his acts.

In 1792, a Scotchman, John Bill Ricketts, arrived in America. Mr. Ricketts had learned trick riding in England. He settled in Philadelphia. He opened the first circus there on April 3, 1793. George Washington, our first president, was watching.

The circus had a clown and a tightrope walker. But the main act was trick riding. On his horse, Cornplanter, Mr. Ricketts made a flying leap over the back of another horse.

To John Bill Ricketts goes the honor of presenting the first complete American circus.

As the pioneers began to move West, the circus followed. There was little to do for fun in the old back-

woods country. Everyone looked forward to Circus Day.

The shows traveled in wagons along rough country roads. Sometimes the mud along the roads was very deep. Because the circus had to travel through so much mud, it was soon nicknamed "the mud show."

Wind or rain could ruin a mud show. But in 1830, a circus manager, Aaron Turner, found the answer to this problem. He invented a round-top tent. No matter what the weather was like, Turner's circus could always perform.

Every outdoor circus since that day has performed under a tent, now called the Big Top.

Another famous name in circus history was Phineas Taylor Barnum. He would do anything to fool people. Sometimes he was called the "Prince of Humbugs."

For thirty years, P.T. Barnum had a museum in New York City. He collected interesting people and things from all over the world. He put them in his museum. People brought lunch baskets and stayed all day, just looking at the odd sights.

In 1870, P.T. Barnum was sixty years old. His museum had burned down. But Barnum had enough money so that he didn't have to work.

Then William Cameron Coup, owner of a big circus, went to Mr. Barnum. He asked him to be his partner in Coup's Circus. Barnum liked the idea.

On April 10, 1871, the Barnum and Coup Circus opened in Brooklyn, New York. It had the largest tent people had ever seen. A year later, the circus was traveling all over the country in more than seventy railroad cars.

Meanwhile, other big circuses were traveling around the country. One of these belonged to James A. Bailey. His show had both circus acts and a wild animal exhibit.

Bailey used the first electric lights in a circus. Thousands of people came to the show just to see this strange new invention.

In 1881, Barnum and Bailey decided to combine their circuses. Instead of one ring or two rings, they now had a three-ring circus. This was the first three-ring circus in America.

The most famous animal in the Barnum & Bailey Circus was Jumbo, the elephant. In 1882, P.T. Barnum bought him from the London Zoo.

Thousands and thousands of children came to the circus just to see the biggest elephant in America. Many of them rode on his back.

In the spring of 1869, the Dan Rice Circus docked at MacGregor, Iowa. Five little boys watched in wide-eyed wonder. They were Al, Otto, Charles, Alf T., and John Ringling.

After seeing the circus, the Ringling boys decided to put on a show in their own back yard. The admission price was one penny.

The five Ringlings were very serious about the circus business. They learned to do tricks. They saved every penny to buy wagons and a tent.

Just thirteen years after seeing their first circus, the Ringlings took their own show out on the road.

During the next few years, the Ringling Brothers kept buying more and more circuses. By 1922, they had bought all the big circuses in America, including Barnum & Bailey. Now they were known as the "Greatest Show on Earth."

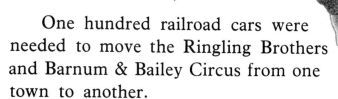

One hundred railroad cars were needed to move the Ringling Brothers and Barnum & Bailey Circus from one town to another.

The circus usually arrived long before dawn. The equipment was unloaded. The tents were set up.

The first tent to go up was called the cook-house. This was where circus people ate. When the meal was ready, a flag was flown from the top of the tent.

Next, the animal tents and the tents for the side shows were put up. Last of all came the Big Top, where the circus was held.

Today, most circuses are held in big buildings.

There are only a few of the tent shows left. But as long as there are boys and girls—and grown ups—to laugh at the clowns, throw peanuts to the elephants, and yell with excitement when the high-wire artists whirl through the air, there will always be a circus!

FROM JESTERS TO JOEYS

The clowns you see here are modern circus clowns. But clowns did not always look like this.

During the Middle Ages, kings had jesters in their courts. The court jesters, as they were called, told jokes. They did tricks for the king and his friends. They wore suits of many colors. They also wore little bells so that they jingled when they walked.

Around the sixteenth century, a new type of clown character appeared in the Italian theater. He was called a *Harlequin* clown. He wore a checkered suit with a ruffled collar and a black mask. The Harlequin clown always tried to spoil the tricks of the other clowns.

Harlequin

Joseph Grimaldi was a pantomime actor in the eighteenth century. He was the first person to use white make-up on his face during his performances. He became very popular. Many clowns copied him. Now white-faced clowns are called "joeys" after Joseph Grimaldi. About this time, there was a clown character in the French theater called *Pierrot*. He wore a special costume. It had a large, loose shirt with a ruffled collar. He also copied Grimaldi's white make-up.

There are four main types of clowns. The *Auguste* clown may have a white or red or blue face. Or he may paint his face many different colors. He may wear any kind of costume he wishes. The *Grotesque* clown usually has a white face and a big red nose. He wears the silliest costume he can think of. It is always exaggerated. The *Character* clown is usually dressed as a tramp. Nothing ever turns out

Grimaldi

Pierrot

Auguste

right for him. The *Midget* clown dresses as an elf, an animal, or sometimes as a baby. All four kinds of clowns call their acts *gags*.

A clown's face is very important. A clown may try several different faces before choosing one to use. But once a clown has decided on a face, no other clown may copy it.

Clowns keep all of their costumes and props in trunks. When they are getting ready for a show, they share a dressing area. It is known as Clown Alley. The rest of the circus performers stay away from here unless they want to have tricks played on them. This doesn't keep the clowns from playing tricks, though. They just play tricks on each other!

Grotesque

Character

Midget

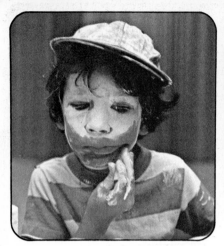

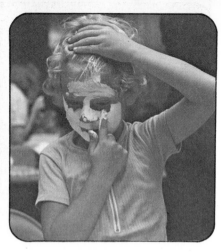

HOW A CLOWN MAKES UP

In the pictures on the opposite page circus clown Peggy Williams shows how she and other clowns put on make-up.

First Peggy covers her face with "clown white." Then she paints on her "clown face" with bright paint of many colors. When her face is finished, she pats white powder on it. The powder "sets" the make-up so it won't come off.

It took Peggy over an hour to put on her make-up when she first became a clown. Now she does it in just half an hour. Now that you see what Peggy's clown face looks like, see if you can find her in the clown picture opposite the beginning of "From Jesters to Joeys."

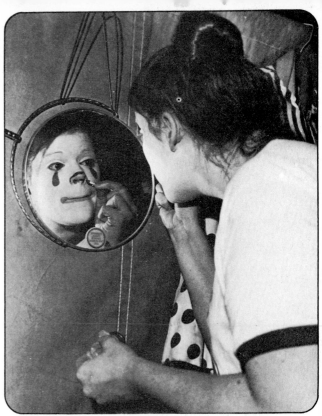

THE CIRCUS IS PEOPLE

A circus is special because the people who work in it are special. On these pages you will meet some of the special people who live and work in the Ringling Brothers and Barnum & Bailey Circus.

190

Meet Bob Welz. He's the ringmaster for the largest circus in the world.

"LADIES AND GENTLEMEN, CHILDREN OF ALL AGES, RINGLING BROTHERS AND BARNUM & BAILEY CIRCUS WELCOMES YOU TO THE GREATEST SHOW ON EARTH!"

With these words, Bob opens each performance of the circus. As a singing ringmaster, he does more than introduce the acts. He sings, too.

Bob must always be alert, because the circus moves at a very fast pace. The moment one act is over, another one starts. And he must always be ready for the unexpected. In a circus with over three hundred people and hundreds of animals, anything can happen.

As a small boy growing up in Texas, Bob was always thrilled by the circus. He says, " Months after the circus had left town and been forgotten by the other school boys, I would be practicing in my backyard, walking the clothesline and teaching myself to juggle."

When Bob grew up, he got a job on a newspaper. But he didn't stop juggling. One day he quit his newspaper job. He had decided to join the circus—as a juggler and a rope walker.

Bob loves working in the circus because it has something for everyone. Perhaps that's why Bob always ends every show with:

"THANK YOU AND MAY ALL YOUR DAYS BE CIRCUS DAYS."

The woman on the elephant is Sarah Chapman. But don't let the elephant fool you. Sarah isn't an elephant trainer. She is an aerial artist.

Sarah does a balancing act on a swinging trapeze high above the circus floor. Standing on the trapeze as it swings back and forth to the music, she looks like a ballet dancer in mid-air.

She makes it look easy. But balancing is very hard to learn. It took many years of practice for Sarah to be able to do the difficult act she does now. She still practices every day.

One reason Sarah likes working in the circus is because she likes to travel. Each year Sarah and her family visit many interesting places throughout the United States and Canada.

Sarah thinks one important reason people come to the circus is to see live entertain-ment. She says, "People want to see people doing things they would like to be able to do themselves." And she may be right. How many of us wish we could swing from a trapeze or ride an elephant? The next time *you* are at the circus, take a close look at the girl on the trapeze. It may be Sarah Chapman.

These aerial artists perform on a flying trapeze.
But it wasn't always so. The first trapezes stayed
in one place and did not move at all. Then a
Frenchman named Jules Leotard came along, and in
1859 he invented the flying trapeze. Aerial performers
and circus-goers alike are glad that he did.

"MAD, MARVELOUS MON-KEYSHINES" reads the circus program. And the chimpanzee acts are just that. There are many kinds of animals in the circus. But the chimps can do things that none of the others can. They ride bicycles and motorcycles, play musical instruments, and do acrobatic stunts. They do things that are usually only done by *people*. This is why chimp trainer Sue Lenz thinks people like to watch chimps.

Sue should know. She and her husband Rudi have been training chimps in the circus for many years. They start training their chimps when the chimps are a year or a year-and-a-half old. The daily training periods are called "school time." In "school" the chimps learn and practice new tricks. When "school" is out, they can play all they want. After

about six months of training, a chimp is usually ready to go into the ring.

Chimps need a lot of affection and care. They get this from Sue and Rudi. The chimps eat and sleep and play in their own trailer. And, like little kids, they sometimes fight. When they fight, the oldest chimp (and baby-sitter) breaks it up.

Sue grew up in a circus family. Her mother and father were animal trainers and performers. Sue has had other animal acts in the circus—dogs and birds. But the chimps are her favorites. For Sue, animals and the circus are a way of life. She loves them both.

Elephants are fairly easy to train, says Gunther. This is because they are smart and can understand what you want them to do. The horses are harder to train, because they are not as bright.

Tigers are dancing and playing leapfrog. An elephant is bouncing a man off a seesaw. And horses are letting tigers ride on their backs. All this can mean only one thing — Gunther Gebel-Williams is in town.

Animals have always been star attractions in the circus. But the animals Gunther has trained are making circus history. And so is Gunther himself.

Why are Gunther and his animals special? There are several reasons. One is the *variety* of animals he trains —tigers, elephants, and horses. Another reason is the *number* of animals he trains —a herd of elephants, a dozen or so tigers, and several horses. And most important, he gets all three kinds of animals to perform together in the same ring.

This is quite a big job. For horses and elephants are

deathly afraid of tigers. Yet two of Gunther's horses and his African elephant, Kongo, don't seem to mind that the riders on their backs are Bengal tigers.

Gunther first became part of the circus world at the age of twelve. Then his mother joined the Circus Williams in Germany. Once he was in the circus, Gunther began to learn everything he could. Now he is a performer as well as an animal trainer. He does acrobatics with elephants. He rides on a tiger's back. He commands a herd of elephants with just his voice, while sitting in the audience.

Gunther is a lot of fun to watch. And the best part is, you can tell that he's having just as much fun as you are.

Gunther's tigers look and act like playful kittens. Even the bulky elephants look playful. This is because Gunther has trained them with love and understanding. They must know that they can trust him. Gunther, on the other hand, knows that he cannot trust them. No matter how well his animals behave or how playful they seem, he must remember that they are wild animals, not pets.

This "joey" is really a Peggy! Clown Peggy Williams learned to put on makeup, make costumes and props, and do juggling and acrobatics at the Circus Clown School. She even learned to ride an elephant.

Peggy was in college when she first heard of the clown school. She was studying to be a teacher of deaf children. She went to the clown school to learn pantomime. She wanted to be able to communicate with the children without using words. At clown school she learned pantomime as well as the other arts of clowning. And by the time she had finished the eight-week course, she knew that she wanted to be a clown.

In the circus, Peggy can communicate with thousands of children. She makes them laugh at her silly costumes and gags. She likes making other people happy—and it doesn't seem like work at all.

Veteran clown Bobby Kay has been in the circus for over 50 years. To him the circus is home. From time to time, Bobby has worked as an actor. But he has always come back to the circus. "For me, the circus is the happiest life there is," he says.

Bobby has seen many changes in the circus over the years. Today the circus moves at a faster pace than ever before. "Everyone in the circus must be on time," Bobby says. "And our clock is the band. It tells us when to go on. And when we have to be finished. And here's a little secret. The horses get some special help from the band. *A horse doesn't dance to the music; the music dances to the horse.*"

Yes, circus people are special. And the next time you go to the circus, remember that you are special, too. For as Bobby Kay will tell you, "When you come to the circus, you're a guest in our home."

Names from People

When P. T. Barnum brought the huge elephant Jumbo to the United States, our language got a new word. Mr. Barnum wanted to be sure that everyone knew about Jumbo. So he did a lot of advertising. Soon people were wearing Jumbo T-shirts and writing with Jumbo pencils. When people heard *Jumbo,* they thought of an elephant. After a while, the word *jumbo* came to mean "large size."

Jules Leotard was a French aerial artist in the 19th century. When he performed, he wore a tight-fitting suit with long sleeves and a high neck. Now suits like his are called *leotards,* and they are worn by both men and women.

Joseph Grimaldi had no idea his white-face makeup would make such a hit. Now clowns are *joeys.* What if his name had been Sam?

Use a dictionary and an encyclopedia to find out about the people whose names these words come from: *braille, watt, pasteurize, diesel.* Now try to think of some things that could be named after you. Perhaps you have made up a game, a song, a dance step, or a recipe for a special dish. What would you call it?

Detail of *Children's Games*.
Kunsthistorisches Museum, Vienna—European Art Color Slide.

The painting you see here is called
<u>Children's Games</u>. It was painted over 400
years ago, in 1560, by the Flemish artist Pieter
Breughel. This painting inspired Kathleen
Fraser to write a book of poems. The poems
she wrote are about the games she saw being
played in the painting. See if you can find
Broom Balancing and Follow the Leader
in the painting.

Broom Balancing

Millicent can play the flute
and Francine can dance a jig,
but I can balance a broom.

Susanna knows how to bake cookies
and Harold can stand on one foot
but I can balance a broom.

Jeffry can climb a ladder backwards
and Andrew can count to five thousand and two,
but I can balance a broom.

Do you think a circus might discover me?

—Kathleen Fraser

Follow the Leader

Whatever he does, you have to do too,
because he is the leader.
When he jumps off the porch, you have to jump
too (even when you're a little bit scared),
because he is the leader.
If he yells "blueberry" very loud
or says "Hello" to a frog,
you have to do all those things
because he is the leader.

But then his turn is over.
And you are next.
And everyone stands behind you
and waits for you to begin
and they have to do whatever silly things
you can think of
because YOU are the leader now.

—Kathleen Fraser

There Isn't Time

There isn't time, there isn't time
To do the things I want to do,
With all the mountain tops to climb,
And all the woods to wander through,
And all the seas to sail upon,
And everywhere there is to go,
And all the people, every one
Who lives upon the earth, to know,
There's only time, there's only time
To know a few, and do a few,
And then sit down and make a rhyme
About the rest I want to do.

—*Eleanor Farjeon*

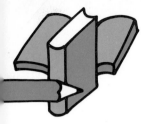

More Than One

A *noun* is a word that names a person, place, or thing. A *singular noun* names only one person, place, or thing. A *plural noun* names more than one person, place, or thing.

Here are some important rules for forming plural nouns:

1. To most singular nouns, add *s* to form the plural.

   boy — boys   odor — odors   age — ages

2. If a singular noun ends in *ch*, *sh*, or *s*, add *es* to form the plural.

   bus — buses   inch — inches   wish — wishes

3. If a singular noun ends in a consonant letter followed by a *y*, change *y* to *i* and add *es* to form the plural.

   spy — spies   try — tries   fly — flies

4. If a singular noun ends in an *f*, form the plural in one of the following ways:
   a. add *s*

      chief — chiefs
   b. change *f* to *v* and add *es*

      shelf — shelves

5. If a singular noun ends in an *o*, form the plural in one of the following ways:

a. add *s*

radio — radios

b. add *es*

hero — heroes

6. Some singular nouns have special plural forms.

deer — deer	moose — moose	mouse — mice
fish — fish	tooth — teeth	man — men

ACTIVITY A Write the plural form of each singular noun.

1. fly	**2.** pony	**3.** part	**4.** house
5. elf	**6.** sash	**7.** itch	**8.** tent
9. sky	**10.** idea	**11.** zero	**12.** half

ACTIVITY B On your paper, write the underlined plural noun in each sentence. Then write its singular form.

1. The rocks rolled down the <u>cliffs.</u>
2. Many <u>puppies</u> played in the park.
3. A small animal hid behind the <u>bushes.</u>
4. We ate <u>potatoes</u> and chicken for dinner.
5. The <u>children</u> went to the zoo yesterday.
6. My <u>feet</u> hurt in those shoes.
7. Paul and his brother have several <u>hobbies.</u>

PASTIMES

People create pastimes for fun and relaxation. The selections you read were all about games and activities that are popular today. You read the histories of some of these games—how they started and how they have changed over the years. You read about how and why people of long ago played soccer, flew kites, watched the Olympic Games, rode bikes, and enjoyed the circus. You also read how people today are keeping these pastimes alive.

Thinking About "Pastimes"

1. What special things about the game of soccer have made it become so popular in this country?
2. Why did both Benny's kite and Spec's bike become almost alive for each boy?
3. How did Donna's father help her to become an Olympic champion?
4. Why do we burn the Olympic flame throughout the games today?
5. Why has the circus always held a fascination for people?
6. What pastimes do you enjoy? Why?
7. Write a story about how your favorite pastime began.

MESSAGES

You send and receive messages every day. Ring a bell. Blow a whistle. Smile. Shake hands. Write a letter. Make a phone call. What do these things have in common? Some are silent. Some use objects instead of words. But all are messages—ways of sharing thoughts and feelings with others.

In "Messages," you will be introduced to some unusual ways of communicating. You will learn about the importance of clear communication. You will learn how messages are sent by drumbeats and bells. You will see how a code was used in secret communication, and you will learn how to send your own secret message. You will read about a brave girl who risks her own life in a raging storm in order to send a message that will save the lives of others.

As you read, think about how and why people send messages. What are some ways you communicate every day?

With the Door Open

Something I want to communicate to you.
I keep my door open between us.
I am unable to say it,
I am happy only
with the door open between us.

— David Ignatow

DANNY'S TWO LANGUAGES

Frank Bonham

Danny Nomura peered through a newspaper rolled into a tube. He looked out his window at the ground below. Slowly he turned and swept the tube over a small Japanese garden. Stone lanterns nestled in clumps of bamboo. A gravel path curved past a little fishpond. A picnic table ringed the trunk of a tree. Danny let the newspaper unroll.

A bell tinkled, announcing breakfast. Danny pulled on a T-shirt and pants. He looked for his socks under the bed. He tingled with excitement. He and his sister Carol were spending two weeks with their grandparents in Little Tokyo. (Little Tokyo is the Japanese business district in Los Angeles.) Their parents were on a business trip.

Grandpa and Grandma Nomura lived above their gift shop, the Far East Trading Company. Hardly anyone else lived in Little Tokyo. The area was snug and ancient. Its old-fashioned buildings housed sukiyaki cafes, bookstores, and gift shops. No one would have guessed that behind the buildings, there was a garden. In the garden, birds sang, goldfish swam, and people barbecued spareribs in the evening.

Danny washed his face. He slicked back his hair with his wet palms, and hurried down the hall. He thumped on his sister's door as he passed. "Hurry up!" he called.

In the kitchen Grandma Nomura was beating waffle batter. She glanced around and smiled.

"Good morning, Danny." Grandma was small and grayhaired, hardly larger than Danny. As she kissed him on the cheek, she exclaimed: "Papa-san, look! He is as tall as I."

Embarrassed, Danny scratched his neck. He grinned at his grandfather who was reading a newspaper in the breakfast nook. Grandpa Nomura glanced over his spectacles. He was a small, formal-looking man who wore black suits and bow ties. He nodded his approval.

Danny sat down across from him. His grandfather folded his newspaper neatly. *"Yoku nemashita ka?"* he asked.

"No, I didn't sleep very well," Danny started to reply. But he knew Grandpa was less interested in how he had slept than in how much Japanese he had learned in language school. He paused and fitted the words together in his mind. Then he replied slowly: *"Yoku nemurare-masen deshita."*

For two years Danny had been going to language school on Saturdays. Just recently, the words had begun to come more easily to his lips. As they talked, he slipped in some of the special polite phrases he knew his grandparents loved. Grandpa nodded approval.

Carol arrived. She was a pretty nine-year-old with black hair cut in a short bob. In her arms she carried her Siamese kitten, Pooh.

"Look," Carol said. "Pooh remembers the garden. She wants to visit it."

Danny gave her a warning scowl. "Only Japanese spoken here, *shojo*," he said quickly.

"*Gomenasai,*" Carol said meekly.

Grandpa tapped the table with a chopstick. "Hanako," he said to Grandma, "I have heard that all things come to one who waits. How long does one have to wait for waffles?"

Batter sizzled in the waffle iron. "Everything is ready," Grandma said hastily.

Everyone ate with chopsticks. Grandpa liked to keep up the old ways. So did Danny and Carol's parents. They were as modern as anyone, but they respected what was good and useful in their Japanese background. So Danny had to go to language school. Carol would start soon. For now, she took lessons in Japanese art and practiced the tea ceremony.

"Daniel," said Grandpa suddenly. He patted his lips with a napkin. "I am very pleased with your progress in language."

"Thank you, Grandpa," Danny said.

"But do you know why you go to school?" Grandpa Nomura asked.

"Sure," he said. "To learn the language and stuff."

Grandpa sighed. "The language and art of a nation are not stuff, Daniel," he said. "Look." From his pocket he drew a black stone. He placed it on the table. It had been polished and glued upon a base. "I found this on the beach," he said. "Does it make you think of anything?"

"An egg," Danny said at once. "A black turkey egg."

"No—a rabbit!" Carol cried. "See its ears—where it's cracked? And the little spot is its eye. It's darling."

Danny's mouth turned down. It did look like a rabbit. Carol could see visions in stones, clouds, and campfires. He never saw them until they were pointed out to him.

"You will certainly be an artist," Grandpa praised Carol. "You may have it as a prize."

Carol cupped the stone in her hands as though it

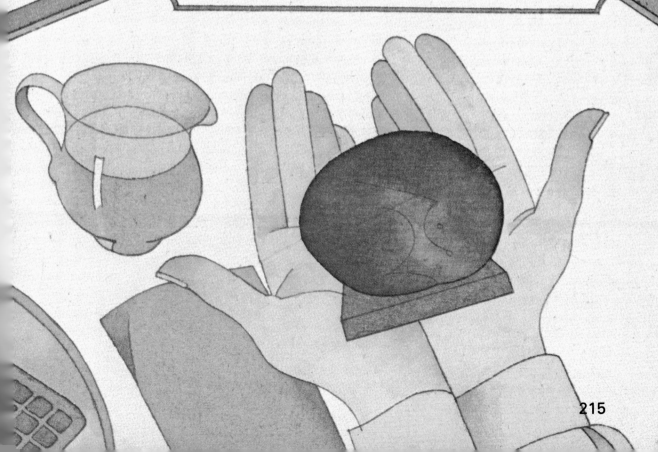

were a live rabbit. She showed it to Pooh. Danny wondered gloomily: What do I get for speaking all that Japanese?

Grandpa said, "I am afraid Daniel will never be an artist. In rocks he sees rocks. In dried tree roots he sees fuel instead of snakes and running horses. Perhaps that is why he grasps the rules of Japanese grammar so quickly and remembers them so well." He gave Danny a smile.

Danny waited. A knife? A Boy Scout compass? He waited eagerly to see what would come out of Grandpa's pocket. But his grandfather left the table without a word. He walked to the hall door where he turned back.

"Before you leave," he told Danny, "please come to my office."

"All right, Grandpa," Danny said. Not even a kite, he thought, disappointed.

With a sparkle in his eye, Grandpa said, *"Office ni kitara go hoobi o agemasu."*

Word by word, Danny broke the sentence down:

"When you come to the office, I will have a . . . a *something* . . . for you." A reward! "A reward for you!"

"Daniel," Grandpa said when Danny entered his office. "The Nisei Festival parade is this weekend, is it not?"

Danny bobbed his head. Tourists had crowded Little Tokyo for a week. They attended the tournaments, contests, and arts and crafts displays that made up the yearly Nisei Festival. Sunday would bring the festival to its glorious climax. The whole week built up to the two-hour parade. Carol would march with the girls in the Ondo Parade, wearing her new kimono. Danny would march with the Scouts.

"Yes, sir," Danny said. "It's this Sunday."

"Would you like to carry one of my old samurai swords again?"

Danny had, in fact, been counting on it. "Yes, sir, if—if it's all right."

Grandpa picked up a samurai sword from the desk. Danny did not recall ever seeing it before. He noticed its fine hilt, the glints of gold and silver in the

mountings, and its plain scabbard. It was not the one he carried in last year's parade.

It was a much finer sword than the other. More skillful hands had shaped it. It looked very old, but it was in perfect condition.

Grandpa drew the blade. Sparks of light slipped along the edge. The steel showed a faint wave pattern like a watermark in fine paper.

Balancing the sword across one finger, Grandpa motioned Danny closer.

"Notice the balance point—like a fine scale. Observe the unusual wave pattern in the steel. There are few swords in the world better than this one, Daniel. This blade is six hundred years old. It is the work of Master Masamune of Sagami. Sagami was my own birthplace. Perfection was never too much trouble for Masamune. Once a knight came to pick up a sword he had ordered. Before his eyes, Masamune broke it over his knee. 'The balance is wrong,' he explained."

Grandpa slipped the blade back into the scabbard

and handed it to Danny. Danny held his breath. Did Grandpa mean he was to carry *this* sword in the parade? He looked up. Grandpa smiled and nodded.

"You will carry a wooden sword in practice, of course," he said. "But on the night of the parade, I shall let you carry the Masamune blade as a reward for your good work in learning Japanese."

Danny laid it back on the desk. He shook his head. "No, thanks. I'd be afraid of losing it."

"I know you too well for that. I also want the spirit of Masamune to go into you through familiarity with his work. We must preserve the diligence we Japanese brought to this country. We must carry it on and foster it in our young people."

"What's diligence?" Danny asked.

"Heart and mind working together—the pride of workmanship. One day, when I am gone, you will own this sword. Already I think you understand what I am talking about."

Danny took a deep breath and nodded. He understood.

Symbols as Messages

Long ago, many people could not read. Shopkeepers used picture signs to show what was sold inside their shops. Today, most people can read. But picture signs are still used. They help travelers who do not understand the language of a country.

International signs are picture signs used by countries around the world. These signs give information without using words. International traffic signs have three different shapes.

A sign in the shape of a triangle warns travelers of possible danger and the need to take care.

| RAILROAD
CROSSING | PEDESTRIAN
CROSSING | SLIPPERY
ROAD |

A sign in the shape of a circle gives instructions.

| SPEED
LIMIT | NO
MOTORCYCLES | NO LEFT
TURN |

A sign in the shape of a square or a rectangle gives information.

HOSPITAL

TELEPHONE

BUS STOP

ACTIVITY A   Read each message below. Decide the shape of the traffic sign that is needed. On your paper, write the words *triangle, circle,* or *square* to identify the shape of the sign.

1. Rocks may have fallen on the road ahead.
2. A garage for repairs is ahead.
3. No bicycles are allowed on this road.
4. There is a dangerous curve ahead.
5. Parking is allowed on both sides of the road.

ACTIVITY B   Look at the messages and signs below. On your paper, write the correct message next to the numeral for each sign.

Restaurant

No passing

Watch out for children

Road being repaired

1.

2.

3.

4.

KNOTS, BEADS, AND BEATS

Mary Lee Johansen

When you write, you communicate with special signs. These signs are the letters of our alphabet. You put the letters of the alphabet into groups called words. Each word sends a special message. But what if we didn't have an alphabet? How could we communicate?

What if one day in the mail you got a piece of knotted string? You might think someone was playing a trick on you. But the Incan Indians of Peru used knotted strings to keep records and to send messages.

These knotted strings were called **quipus**. The knots stood for numbers. The Inca used quipus to keep records of how many sacks of grain they had to sell. They also used quipus to keep track of how many children were born in a village. The Inca also sent quipus messages to other villages. The knots could tell how many days there were until a feast. They could also tell how many people were invited.

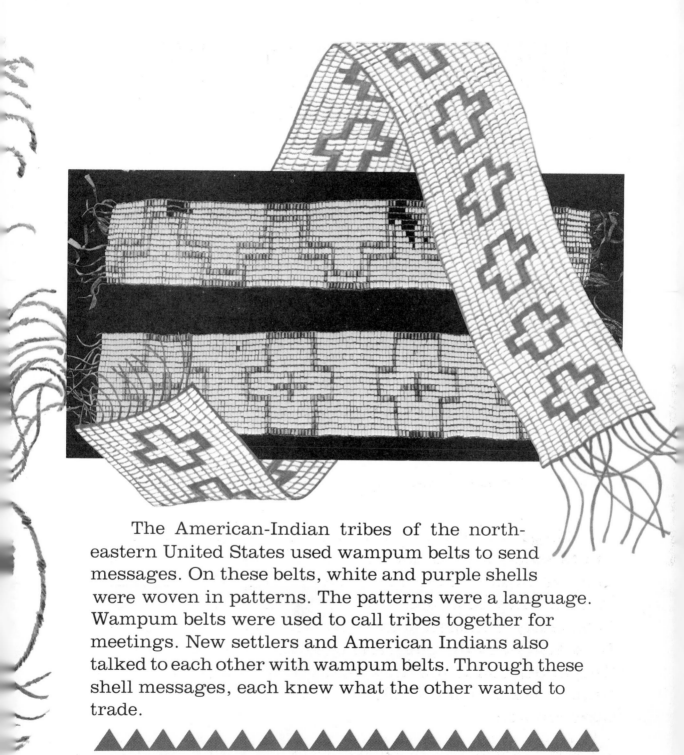

The American-Indian tribes of the north-eastern United States used wampum belts to send messages. On these belts, white and purple shells were woven in patterns. The patterns were a language. Wampum belts were used to call tribes together for meetings. New settlers and American Indians also talked to each other with wampum belts. Through these shell messages, each knew what the other wanted to trade.

Some African tribes used beads on cords to send messages. For messages about food or work, they used black and white beads. They saved their brightly colored beads for love letters.

Today, in parts of Africa, drums are an important way of sending messages. Drums announce the arrival of visitors. Drums are often the fastest way to send news.

People who live on islands near China and Japan also use drums to send messages. Scientists who work on these islands find drums very useful. Once a doctor in a hurry needed someone to take him across a river. But all the people of the village were working some distance away. The doctor quickly beat out this message on a drum: "I need someone with a boat to take me across the river." In a short time, several men came paddling down the river in their boats.

Scientists studying the birds and plants of these islands use drums, too. They beat out messages to tell people far away what kinds of birds or plants they want for their studies. They always tell how much they will pay for what they need.

Quipus and wampum belts are two of the ways people communicated years ago. Drums are one way in which people still send messages today. But one thing is sure. No matter what system people use for communicating, a person has to know what the drumbeats, the knots, or the shell or bead patterns mean in order to get the message.

BELLS

Elizabeth Starr Hill

One of the oldest ways to send a message is by ringing a bell. People began to make bells about 5,000 years ago. Before then, they made rattles with pebbles and shells or hollow pieces of wood. But later people found out how to mix copper and tin to make bronze. Then they could shape bells that would ring loudly. The sound would carry for long distances.

Bells have often helped soldiers in battle. Many years ago, soldiers would string bells on nets. Then they would stretch the nets across a path or a river. If anyone tried to sneak up on the soldiers, the bells sounded an alarm.

Sometimes army uniforms were decorated with bells. Enemy troops climbing over a castle wall would listen for the bells on the uniforms of the guards. As the guards walked along the wall, the enemy would hear the bells. When the noise passed, the enemy troops would quickly climb over the wall. They could start an attack before anyone knew they were there.

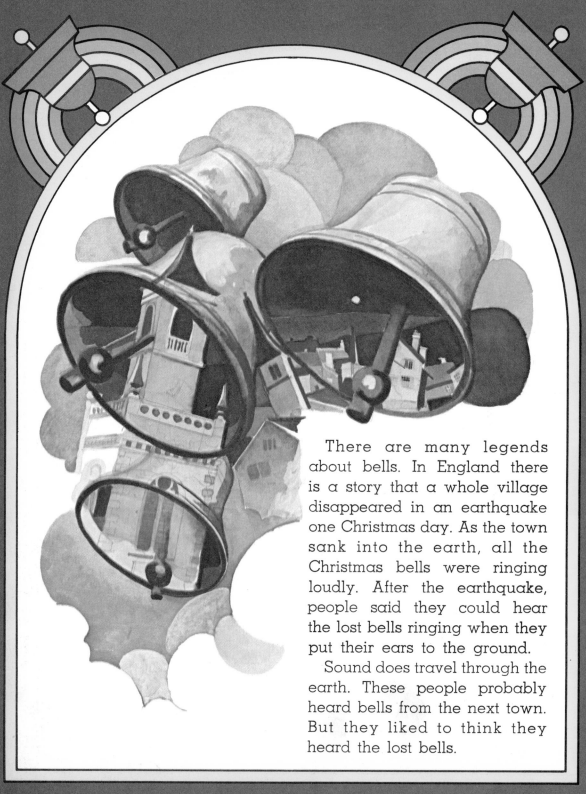

There are many legends about bells. In England there is a story that a whole village disappeared in an earthquake one Christmas day. As the town sank into the earth, all the Christmas bells were ringing loudly. After the earthquake, people said they could hear the lost bells ringing when they put their ears to the ground.

Sound does travel through the earth. These people probably heard bells from the next town. But they liked to think they heard the lost bells.

Often fishermen have reported hearing bells ringing under the sea. Sailors say that mermaids ring the bells to warn sailors of rocks hidden under the waves.

Bells still send us messages. Doorbells tell you someone is waiting outside. A bell can tell you when an elevator is coming. A bell begins and ends your day at school. And on a bus, the bell tells the driver when you want to get off.

Will we ever be able to do without bells?

THE BROKEN LANTERN

Freeman Hubbard

It isn't usual for a train to stop right at someone's front door. But that's what the Chicago and Northwestern Railway did for Kate Shelley for many years. And no wonder! Read the story of Kate Shelley. Then you will understand why.

On a wild night in 1881, Kate Shelley looked out of a window of her family's house. Never in all her life had she seen a storm like this one. It had been raining for a whole week. Thunder and lightning cut through the night sky. Wind rattled the windows. Sometimes it felt as though the old Iowa farmhouse might be picked up and blown away.

The Shelleys lived between the railroad tracks and Honey Creek. Kate's father was dead. He had been a railroad section boss. And Kate had been brought up in a farmhouse near the edge of the tracks that overlooked the bridge. She knew all about the trains. And she knew the creek.

The night of the storm, Kate watched the dark water rush down on its way to the Des Moines River. The river was rising. Kate wondered whether any bridges would be washed away. The clock in the kitchen ticked noisily. The storm kept sweeping down the valley. And Honey Creek rose higher and higher.

Suddenly Kate heard a friendly and familiar sound. An engine was rumbling onto the wooden bridge that crossed the creek. It was coming from the next town.

Kate knew why the engine was coming at this time of night. Some men were testing the bridge to find out if it was still safe. The midnight passenger train would be coming through soon.

Above the roar of the wind and driving rain came the ding-dong of the engine bell. Then ...a splintering crash and a loud splash as the engine fell into the black creek below.

"Mother," Kate screamed. "The bridge has broken. The engine has gone down!"

The family rushed to the window and looked out into the black, wet emptiness. Kate was the first to speak.

"I'm going out! Somebody down there may still be alive." And she turned to get her father's lantern. It hung behind the kitchen door.

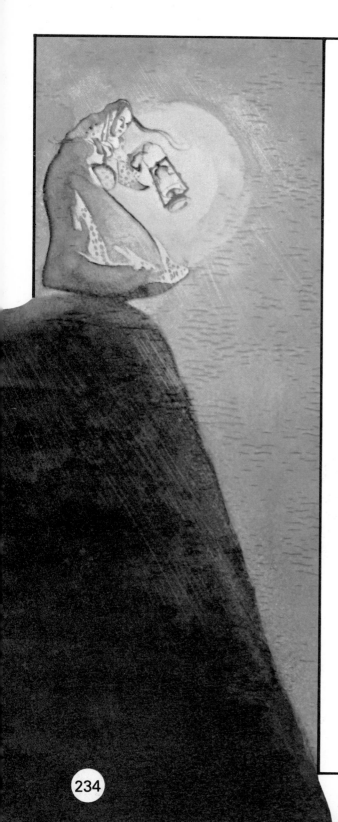

"Kate!" Her mother moved toward her as if to hold her. Then she stopped. "All right," she said. "Do what you can— but be careful."

Kate lit the wick of the lantern, put on her coat, and hurried out into the storm. Making her way through the beating rain, she climbed over the tracks. Then she stood just above the spot where the engine had fallen into the deep black water.

"Hal-loo-oo!" Kate shouted. Her voice was carried into the wet darkness by the wind. "Anyone down there?" All she heard was the wind.

Then a voice came back through the darkness.

"Two of us. We're safe for now. But the midnight train will be wrecked! You've got to warn them somehow!"

"I'll try to get to Moingona and get help. I'll try to flag the train and stop it before it gets here." Kate did not know if the men had heard her. She did not hear them calling. And she did not want to waste any time. She stumbled back to the tracks.

Moingona was only a mile away. But it was on the other side of the raging Des Moines River. To get there, you had to cross the long wooden railroad bridge. Even in daylight, that bridge was dangerous. It had no foot walk. And the sides were open. You had to walk on the railroad ties. And there was enough space between the cross pieces for a person the size of Kate Shelley to slip through and be lost in the river. But somebody had to stop that passenger train—somehow!

Kate stopped when she came to the bridge. Her lantern flickered. Rain beat against her face. The wind howled. She had never seen the river so high. She started across the bridge. But it shook suddenly. Kate stumbled and fell. She smashed her lantern.

"I must get across," she kept thinking to herself. "I must stop that train. I must!"

She started to crawl on her hands and knees from tie to tie across the bridge. Her broken lantern knocked against her with each move. Every minute she was afraid she would see the headlight of the midnight express shining into her face. Then she would be trapped on the bridge— unable to stop the train.

It seemed like hours before she reached the other side and stood safely on solid ground. When she finally opened the door of the one-room station at Moingona, she looked like a crazy person. She was soaking wet. Her hair was in strings around her face. Her eyes were wild. She could barely talk.

The stationmaster hardly recognized her.

"Kate? Is that you? What's wrong?"

"The bridge at Honey Creek!" she gasped. "It's broken...the engine went down...two men ...I...I..." Kate Shelley fell to the floor. She was still clutching her broken lantern.

At that moment, a long whistle signal announced that the midnight express was coming—and coming fast! It had never been scheduled to stop at the small Moingona depot. But it stopped that night. For the stationmaster left Kate lying on the floor. He rushed outside, swinging his own red lantern wildly.

The midnight train ground to a stop. Even in the rain, sparks flew from under the wheels. The engineer swung down from his cab. He walked over to the stationmaster, who was still swinging his lantern. The engineer didn't like being stopped at a small station like Moingona on this kind of night. "What's up?" he demanded angrily.

"Honey Creek bridge is washed out just below here. A girl brought the news. How she got here I don't know." The engineer stood silent.

Suddenly they saw Kate in the lighted doorway of the station. The engineer told his crew to walk through the cars and tell the passengers what had happened.

"But the men," Kate called. "We've got to get back to those men at the Honey Creek bridge."

The engineer ran back to his cab and pulled the whistle cord, giving an alarm signal that woke up people in the village. Then he started the train moving slowly along the tracks, over the bridge that Kate had just crawled across. He stopped just at the edge of Honey Creek. Using a rope, the engineer and his crew hauled the two men up the rocky side of the creek to safety. And they took Kate back to her home.

Kate was famous. Newspapers across the country told her story. Visitors and reporters asked her to describe again and again how she had crawled across the bridge to save the express on that wild night. And the railroad company gave her a lifetime free pass to ride on their trains.

But the thing that Kate liked the best was having the train stop right at her door to deliver her safe at home.

A Little Girl in Old New York
(1849-1850)

from the diary of Catherine Elizabeth Havens

This selection contains parts of a real diary kept by a ten-year-old girl. She lived in New York City over 130 years ago. Life in the city then was very different from what it is today. Cobblestone streets were lined with trees and little two-story brick houses. Horse-drawn carriages moved along those cobblestone streets. At night, the street lamps were lighted by gas, not electricity. Life was much more slow-moving than it is in today's large cities.

As you visit old New York through this diary, think of ways in which it is both similar to and different from the modern cities you have lived in or visited.

August 6, 1849

I am ten years old today, and I am going to begin to keep a diary. My sister says it is a good plan. She says that when I am old, and in a remembering mood, I can take out my diary. Then I will be able to read about what I did when I was a little girl.

I can remember as far back as when I was only four years old, but I was too young then to keep a diary. I will begin mine now by telling what I can recall of that faraway time.

The first thing I remember is going with my sister in a sloop to visit my aunts, Mrs. Dering and Mrs. L'Hommedieu, on Shelter Island. We had to sleep two nights on the sloop. We had to wash in a tin basin, and the water felt gritty.

These aunts live in a very old house. It was built in 1733 and is called the Manor House. Some of the floors and doors in it were in a house built in 1635. The wood was brought from England.

The next thing I remember is going with my nurse to the Vauxhall Gardens and riding in a merry-go-round. These Gardens were in Lafayette Place, near our house. There was a gate on the Lafayette Place side and another on the Bowery side.

Back of our house was an alley that ran through to the Bowery, and there was a livery stable on the Bowery. One time my brother, who was full of fun and mischief, got a pony from the stable and rode it right down into our kitchen. He galloped it around the table and frightened our cook almost to death.

Another time he jumped onto a new barrel of flour and went right in, boots and all.

October 1, 1849

Last year my brother had the scarlet fever. His room was on the top floor of our house. When dear old Dr. Johnston came to see him, my mother felt sorry to take him up so many stairs. But he said, "Oh, doctors and hod-carriers can go anywhere." He lives on Fourteenth Street, and his daughter comes to school with me.

Last week my sister took me to see Helen R., who is very sick with scarlet fever. They thought she would die, but now she is getting well. We went up in her room, and she looked so funny in bed with all her hair cut off. She lives on Tenth Street.

January 2, 1850

Next January we shall be half through the nineteenth century. I hope I shall live to see the next century, but I don't want to be alive when the year 2000 comes. Some people say the world is coming to an end then, and perhaps sooner.

July 15, 1850

I have not written in my diary for ever so long. But now school has just closed for the summer, and I have more time.

Professor Hume teaches us natural science, and every Wednesday he lectures to us. One day he brought the eye of an ox and took it all apart and showed us how it was like our own eyes. And another time he brought an electric battery. We joined our hands—ever so many of us—and the end girl took hold of the handle of the battery. We all felt the shock, and it tingled.

Sometimes he talks on chemistry. Then he brings glass jars and pours different things into them and makes beautiful colors. He told us we could always remember the seven colors of the rainbow by the word *vybgor*.

My mother has read my diary and corrected the spelling. She says it is very good for a little girl. She has also written down her memories of old New York—for me. She was born in 1801 and can remember back to 1805—some things.

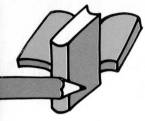

Where Am I Going?

A map usually has two sets of symbols that help you read and understand the map.

1. The *scale* is a bar that shows distances. Each part of the bar stands for a certain number of miles or kilometers.

2. The *key* tells you what the colors and symbols on the map represent.

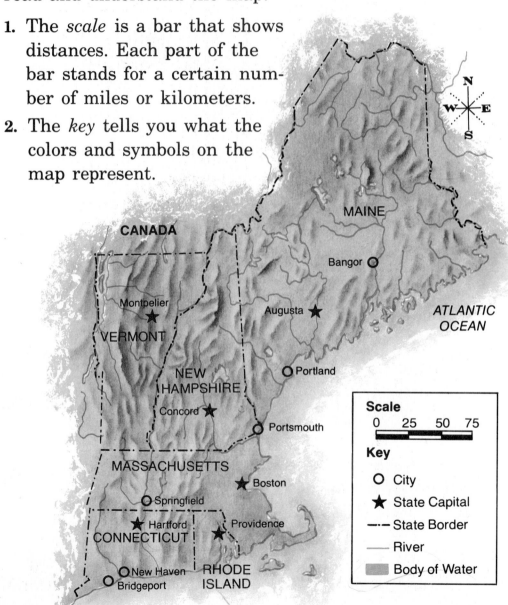

CANADA

MAINE

Bangor O

Montpelier ★

VERMONT

Augusta ★

ATLANTIC OCEAN

O Portland

NEW HAMPSHIRE

Concord ★

Portsmouth O

MASSACHUSETTS

★ Boston

O Springfield

★ Hartford

CONNECTICUT

Providence ★

O New Haven

O Bridgeport

RHODE ISLAND

Scale

0   25   50   75

Key

O City

★ State Capital

-·- State Border

— River

▨ Body of Water

ACTIVITY A   Study the map of the New England states on the opposite page. According to the *scale*, an inch is equal to 75 miles (2.54 centimeters are equal to 120 kilometers). Use a ruler and the scale to answer the questions below. Write the answers on your paper. The answers do not have to be exact.

1. What is the distance in miles between:
   a. Portland and Bangor?
   b. Hartford and Augusta?
   c. Montpelier and Boston?
   d. Bridgeport and Portsmouth?
2. Which two cities on the map are the farthest apart? What is the distance between them?

ACTIVITY B   Now study the *key* on the opposite page. On your paper, write the answers to the questions below.

1. What is the capital of New Hampshire?
2. Which state on the map does not border the Atlantic Ocean?
3. Which state on the map has the most bodies of water?
4. Which is the smallest state on the map?
5. Which of the states on the map shares the longest border with Canada?
6. What is the capital of Vermont?
7. Which Massachusetts city on the map is closest to Connecticut?
8. Which two states share borders with Rhode Island?

SeCRETS

Sam and Beryl Epstein

Suppose you have a secret. You want only your best friend to know about it. Then you must be careful when you write it down. If you write your secret in code, you can be pretty sure it will be safe.

Codes have been used to keep many important secrets. Kings, soldiers, spies, and pirates have used codes for hundreds of years.

Long ago, doctors and scientists used codes. They didn't want people to know about the medicines they had discovered. One of these famous code-makers was Geronimo Cardano. He lived in Italy in the 1500s. He studied the stars and mathematics. And he was also a very fine doctor.

Cardano was very clever. To send a secret message to a friend, he started with two sheets of stiff paper. He cut holes in exactly the same places in each sheet. He would send one of these sheets to his friend.

Then Cardano would put his copy of the pattern over another piece of paper. He would write a secret

message in the holes. He put one word in each hole. Then he would remove the pattern. He would fill the rest of the space with other words. These words fit in with the secret words. They made a friendly letter. Now no one would be able to guess which words in the letter were the secret ones. Only Cardano's friend who had a copy of the pattern would know.

When Cardano's friend put his pattern over the letter, this is what he might have read. The words in the boxes are the ones that showed through the pattern. In this way, Cardano shared his secrets only with his friends. And he never got caught!

YOUR OWN CODING MACHINE

To make your own coding machine, you will need a pen or pencil; a sheet of ruled paper (twelve and one-half inches long by eight inches wide); scissors; ruler; and transparent tape.

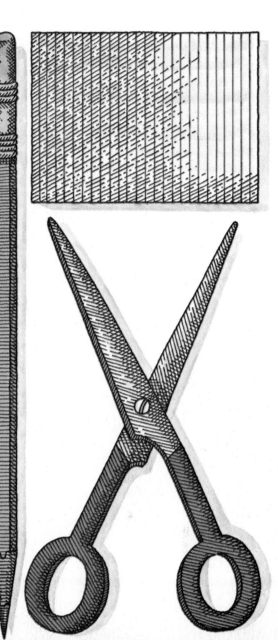

HOW TO MAKE YOUR CODING MACHINE

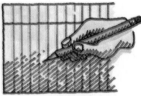

1. Place the paper sideways, so that the lines are running up and down. Draw a line across the paper about two inches from the top.

2. In the spaces above the line you just drew, beginning in the third space, write the letters of the alphabet. Do not skip any spaces.

3. About one-half inch below the line you drew, cut two one-inch slits. Make one between the first and second spaces and one between the last and next-to-last spaces.

4. Cut two one-inch strips from the bottom of the paper. Tape the strips together, end to end. Be sure that the lines match where the strips are taped together.

5. On this long strip, beginning in the first space, write the letters of the alphabet at least twice. Do not skip any spaces.

6. Slip one end of the strip, alphabet side up, into each of the slits. The strip will slide back and forth easily. And the letters on the strip will line up under those on the paper.

Pick a letter which will stand for *A*. As an example, take *D*. Line up the *D* on the strip under the *A* on the paper.

Now, say you want to send the message GAME TODAY. Find the *G* of GAME on the alphabet on the paper. The letter on the strip below *G* is *J*. The letter under *A* is *D*. When you have found all the letters in GAME TODAY, your coded message will read JDPH WRGDB.

Before this can be decoded, the person who receives the message must know which letter stands for *A*. In a circle before the first letter of the message, write the letter *D*. This will tell your friend the *D* on the strip should be below the *A* on the paper.

Let's say you got this message:

Ⓟ BTTI BT APITG

Line up the *P* on the strip with the *A* on the paper. Find *B*, the first letter of the message, on the bottom strip. It is below *M*. Find *T*. It is below *E*. Find all the letters on the bottom strip. Then write down the letters that are on the paper above them. You will find that Ⓟ BTTI BT APITG means MEET ME LATER.

To make sure that no one can read your message, you and your friends can agree on a mixed up alphabet. Write it twice on new strips. Anyone finding the message will know which letter to put under *A*, but no one will know what order your alphabet is in.

Or you and your friends could write the alphabet reversed on your strips. Start with *Z* and end with *A*. Be sure that the person you send messages to knows how the alphabets are written on your strip. Happy coding!

252

WHISPERS

Myra Cohn Livingston

Whispers
  tickle through your ear
  telling things you like to hear.

Whispers
  are as soft as skin
  letting little words curl in.

Whispers
  come so they can blow
  secrets others never know.

WEATHER SYMBOLS

Elizabeth S. Helfman

Meteorology is the study of weather and weather forecasting. It is a science with many symbols. In a newspaper, look at the weather report from the United States Department of Commerce Weather Bureau. At the bottom of the weather map is an explanation of all the symbols used on it. Some of these are just symbols. Some use letters. For example:

- ○ clear weather
- ◐ partly cloudy
- ● cloudy
- ● hurricane
- ⓡ rain
- ⓢ snow
- ⓣ thunderstorm
- ⓕ fog

To show the speed of the wind, a line like an arm is added to the clear weather circle. The number of flags on this arm changes as the speed of the wind changes. Here are just a few of the possibilities:

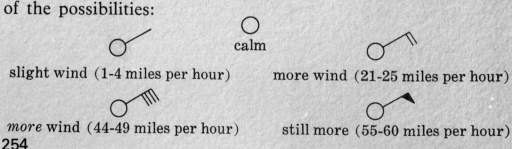

slight wind (1-4 miles per hour)   calm   more wind (21-25 miles per hour)

more wind (44-49 miles per hour)   still more (55-60 miles per hour)

Weather forecasters are called meteorologists. They use the signs you see on daily weather maps. But they also have another weather code. This is not a code just for the United States. Meteorologists all over the world use it. It is an international language. The code makes it possible to send weather reports to all parts of the world. These reports help planes and ships. And they help astronauts who plan to go to outer space. Here are some samples:

dust or sand
raised by wind at
time of observation

continuous rain,
moderate at time
of observation

continuous rain,
heavy at time
of observation

continuous fall of
snowflakes, heavy at
time of observation

ice pellets

moderate or
heavy freezing
rain

heavy thunderstorm with hail
at time of observation

WEATHER WISE

One of the most important languages a pilot uses is the language of weather reports. Pilots must be able to read and understand the symbols on a weather map. They must also be able to read the weather messages from a teletypewriter. Here are a few things a pilot might see on a weather map for St. Louis, Missouri.

23 This is the temperature.

Ⓢ This means snow.

This means wind speed and direction. Each feather means 10 knots per hour. Each half feather is 5 knots. So this wind speed is 25 knots per hour. (A knot is 1.15 miles.)

This means the sky is cloudy.

The information above is also on this sample message from a tele-typewriter. Can you find it?

STL E50①120①1S — 088/23/20/2925/979

Now look at the weather map below. See if you can tell what kind of weather the pilot might find in Indianapolis, Columbus, and Pittsburgh. The symbols below the map will help you.

SKY		WEATHER	
cloudy	●	Ⓢ snow
partly cloudy	◐	® rain
clear	○	ⓕ fog

Painting with Sand

Sand paintings are made by Navajo medicine men in ceremonies to heal the sick. The paints are tiny bits, ground from colored earth and rock. The "canvas" is a bed of sand on a floor. The medicine man sprinkles the sand without sketching the picture first. By the end of the ceremony, the dry painting has been brushed away. The designs in the painting stand for things in the Navajo religion. For example, in the first painting below, the curved design circling the whole is a Rainbow Girl. Try to imagine what some of the other designs might stand for.

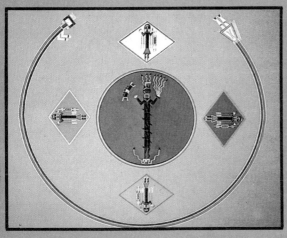

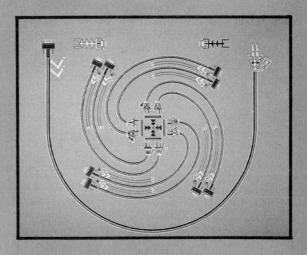

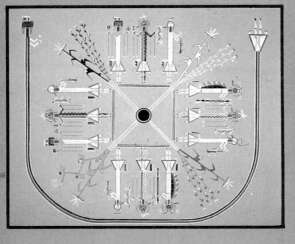

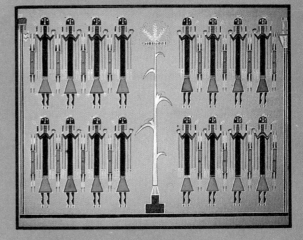

Billy Wentworth and the Buried Treasure

Joan Cipolla

It was an evening in the year 1723. Only a few men had come to my father's inn for supper. I was clearing off one of the empty tables. But I wasn't thinking about what I was doing. Instead I was thinking about the man who had come to the inn earlier that afternoon. He had come to deliver a letter to my father from Mr. Williams. As I wiped off the table, I kept seeing the last sentence of the letter–

...and should you not start the Digging of the Foundation for my Home within Five Days, I shall give this Work to Another.

Mr. Williams must know my father was not yet strong after his illness. How could my father start work in five days? But he would have to, or he would lose the job. And we needed the money that Mr. Williams had promised to pay for the job.

Suddenly the door of the inn opened. A boy about seventeen years old stood in the doorway. He was poorly dressed, but tall and good looking.

"Can I help you?" I asked.

"I'd like some supper," the boy answered. "That is, if it's not too much money." He smiled.

"Supper's only two shillings," I said.

The boy moved to a table and sat down. "Well, no meat," he said quietly. "I'll just take some vegetables and bread."

And that was what the young man got—and double of everything. He ate as though he hadn't eaten in weeks. I wondered who he was and where he had come from. From the little he had said, I knew he wasn't from around these parts. And when he finished, he took a Dutch dollar from his pocket and put it beside the plate. He must have been traveling to have one of those, I thought.

"A fine supper, Mr. Wentworth," said the young man to my father. "I wish I had known about this inn yesterday, when I arrived in your city."

"I thought from your speech you were not from here," my father said. "What is your name? And what is your work?"

"Ben—just call me Ben," he answered. "And I spent today looking for a job as a printer. But perhaps I should leave now, Mr. Wentworth."

"No, Ben, you're welcome to stay the night here. You can pay me when you have a job. Billy can show you upstairs to a room." My father moved away as he heard someone call.

"Billy, do you like to read?" Ben asked me suddenly. I was surprised by this question. But Ben's friendly smile made me feel more comfortable.

"Well, I haven't had much schooling," I said.

"Well, I haven't had much either," Ben answered, "but I can't remember a time when I couldn't read. Read, Billy. There's a whole world of thoughts and places in books."

Next morning, Ben was up bright and early. He had brushed the dust from his jacket. And he must have slept with his trousers under his

261

mattress because they were pressed flat. Ben left as quickly as he had come, saying he'd be back when he'd found work.

I thought of him often. I wondered what he was doing and if we would ever see him again. I thought about Ben so much, I almost forgot about my father and his trouble with Mr. Williams.

The next Saturday, as I was cleaning the sign outside the inn, I saw someone coming down the street. It was Ben,

all smiles. He was dressed in a new suit. He carried a bumpy-looking package under his arm. He tossed me the package. "Books, Billy, books for you. There's a whole new world in those books! Is your father here?" I nodded, and we both went inside.

Father was sitting at his desk. Ben dropped four silver coins beside him. "Just as I promised, Mr. Wentworth. I've found a job with Mr. Samuel Keimer in his printing shop.

I'm helping to fix up his old press. And business is doing well. I hope someday..."

At that moment, our front door blew open. In stamped a fat, red-faced man. It was Mr. Williams.

"Mr. Wentworth, I can't wait any longer. If you do not start work on Monday, I shall give the digging job to someone else." Mr. Williams stormed out.

For a moment, there wasn't a sound. Then I started to tell Ben about my father's trouble with Mr. Williams. When I finished, Ben looked grim. "What can we do?" I asked.

In a minute, Ben chuckled. Then he began to laugh. I could think of nothing to laugh at.

"Don't worry about that man. I have an idea."

Ben said no more. He left at once. But I wanted to know what he was planning. I followed him, keeping out of sight, until he reached Keimer's Printing Shop. Ben went inside.

Looking through the window, I saw him put on an apron. He started to work at a long table. I watched as he chose metal squares from a rack in front of him. He dropped them carefully into a frame on the table. Then he tightened a handle on the frame and rubbed a black, inky rag over it. He placed a piece of paper over the frame. And he put the whole thing under a press.

When he drew the piece of paper out of the press, he held it up to admire it. I could see there was printing on it. But I couldn't read it. Ben nodded and seemed to be laughing. Then he went back to the press and made more copies. Finally I could stand it no longer. I knocked on the windowpane.

Ben looked up. "What are you doing here?" he called. He came over to unlock the door and let me in. "I told you not to worry," he said calmly. But then he smiled. "I've got an idea that will work wonders—if it works at all. Read this."

To all interested People of Philadelphia. Be it known that one Pirate, Captain William Kidd, once visited here. He did bury a large part of his Famous Pirate Treasure on a piece of land at the corner of Fourth and Walnut Streets. The treasure has never been found—nor dug up either.

ONE WHO KNOWS

"Is that really true, Ben?" I asked. "Why, that's the corner where Mr. Williams wants to build his house! I might even get a shovel and dig up the treasure myself." But Ben just went on printing more sheets.

"Here," said Ben at last, "you take hold of these." And he handed me a pile of the sheets. "Put one under the door of each house in the neighborhood. Be careful no one sees you. I'll take the other half. Meet me here at the shop tomorrow night." Then he set off in one direction and I in the other. In an hour, all my sheets were gone. I raced home.

The next night, Ben and I met at the shop. We walked quickly and quietly to the empty lot at Arch and Walnut Streets. We hid behind some bushes and waited. I wasn't quite sure what we waited for. It was cold and damp. And I began to think Ben was just playing a joke on me.

"Look!" Ben grabbed my arm. He pointed across the street. From behind the bush, we saw men arriving at the empty lot.

Soon more men arrived. They were all carrying lamps, picks, shovels, and large empty sacks. Ben could hardly keep from laughing aloud.

The men started to dig. Soon all we could see were the men's heads and shoulders. And piles of dirt. Once in a while someone shouted, "Here's something!" or "I've hit something!" and everyone would rush to that spot. But it was always just a stone or an arrowhead. Disappointed, the man would throw it down.

And the digging would continue. I began to understand Ben's idea.

By morning, the lot had been dug to a depth of about six feet. Tired and angry, the men climbed out of the hole. They had found nothing. No treasure. Nothing. But to Ben and me that hole was beautiful!

"There's your father's job—finished! And ahead of time, too." Ben said proudly. "Now Mr. Williams will have to pay up."

We ran all the way to the inn. Mr. Williams was in the hall. "Mr. Williams, the work is finished," I panted. "And early, too. Now you owe my father the total payment." I kicked some dirt off my shoes.

"It's true," Ben added. "I have just come by Arch and Walnut Streets and have seen the hole with my own eyes. It's the most thoroughly dug up piece of land I have ever seen. Go see for yourself, Mr. Williams."

"I will," declared Mr. Williams angrily.

"And just send your messenger over with the money," Ben called to Mr. Williams as he slammed the door.

Ben explained the mystery to my father.

"You are an amazing fellow, Ben. I thank you for all you have done." And he went off into the kitchen, chuckling. I turned to Ben.

"Ben, will you do something for me?" I asked.

"Whatever you like," Ben said.

"Will you tell me who you are and where you come from?"

"Walk back with me to the shop, Billy, and I'll tell you. I was born in Boston...." Ben closed the door quietly.

What Is an Almanac?

The word **almanac** comes from the Arabic word *al manakh*. It means "the weather" or "the calendar." An almanac is a publication that contains weather information for every day of the year. It tells when the sun and moon rise and set each day. It gives information on the tides. Over the years, almanacs have grown to include all kinds of other useful information.

One of the most famous almanacs was the one Ben Franklin started when he was a printer in Philadelphia. He called it *Poor Richard's Almanack.* It listed the calendar for the year, names of officials in the colonies, local tax laws, and gave general advice on home problems. Franklin wrote most of it himself. His witty sayings and good, commonsense advice made *Poor Richard's Almanack* very popular in the colonies.

Many of the wise or witty sayings from this almanac have stayed in our language to this day. Here are just a few of them.

SAYINGS FROM POOR RICHARD'S ALMANACK

Early to bed and early to rise
makes a man healthy, wealthy, and wise.

Little strokes fell great oaks.

Never leave that till tomorrow
which you can do today.

A penny saved
is a penny earned.

The Railroads Are Coming!

Mary Elting

"The railroads are coming!"

"The railroads are coming!"

The news spread across the United States in 1865. Men and women traveling in wagons brought the news west. They had heard the train whistles. And they had seen the tracks being laid.

The Union Pacific Railroad was laying track from Nebraska toward the Rocky Mountains. The Central Pacific Railroad was laying track eastward from California. Someday the two lines would meet.

The ranchers were excited. They would be able to ship their cattle to the eastern markets by train.

But the American Indians on the prairie were afraid. They watched as the trains rumbled by. They call the railroad the Iron Monster. They feared the railroad companies would take their land. And they were right. The companies did take the land.

Building the railroad was not an easy job. There were no steam shovels or bulldozers in the 1860s. All the digging, carrying, pushing, and pulling had to be done without machines. Men used picks, shovels, and mules. All supplies had to come from the East. Equipment for building the Union Pacific was shipped to the Missouri River by train. Then it went by boat. And then it was shipped on another train. At last it was put onto wagons and hauled to a construction camp.

The builders of the Central Pacific had even bigger problems. They were starting in California. But they, too, had to get their supplies from the East. Everything had to go by ship around the tip of South America and then up the coast to California. It was a trip of 15,000 miles!

For both companies, the hard work didn't stop when the supplies arrived. Rocks had to be cleared away. Tunnels had to be drilled through the high mountains. In winter, snow fell. Sometimes the drifts in California were a hundred feet deep.

But slowly the building went on, mile by mile. The men gave names to some of the places on the way—Devil's Slide, Devil's Gate, Devil's Gulch. You can guess how hard they thought their jobs were.

At last men building tracks from the east could see men building from the west. They would meet on May 10, 1869 in a little settlement called Promontory in Utah. The last two pieces of track were to be joined with gold and silver spikes. And what a celebration there would be!

On the great day, bands played. The crews from both companies gathered around to watch two important men drive in the last spikes. The president of the Central Pacific picked up a huge hammer. He swung it over his head and brought it down hard. He MISSED! The crowd laughed and cheered. Then the vice-president of the Union Pacific swung. He missed, too! There were more cheers—and more laughs! Other men from both companies took their turns. At last the silver and the gold spikes were hammered down.

Then, slowly, a Union Pacific train from the east and a Central Pacific train from the west chugged toward each other. The two engines met. And the crowds roared. Rails now reached across the country from the Atlantic Ocean to the Pacific Ocean. America had a transcontinental railway!

MAKE YOUR MARK

Elizabeth S. Helfman

How do you let people know that something belongs to you or was made by you? One way is to write your name on it. Another way is to make a design or mark that stands for your name. The design or mark can be your initials—the first letters of your first, middle, and last names. In that case, it is called a monogram. It can also be a picture that stands for your name. Many companies have designs, or trademarks, that stand for their names. Often the design shows what the company does or what product it makes. For example, a tree design might stand for a lumber company or a company that makes paper from wood pulp.

Put into words, an identification mark or trademark might say, "This paper was made by the Petersen Paper Company" or "This book belongs to Patricia Ann McCarthy." Like other signs, an identification mark can be understood at a glance by anyone who knows its meaning. Famous marks become known all over the world. They can be read by anyone, no matter what language a person speaks.

Trademarks have been found scratched on tools and weapons from very early times. They were widely used in ancient Egypt. Potters scratched their own marks on the pots they made. Brick makers marked their bricks. Even rulers left behind monuments marked with their identification signs.

Some of these signs were designs, like monograms, made up of some or all the letters in a ruler's name. Here is the monogram of Egypt's Queen Cleopatra:

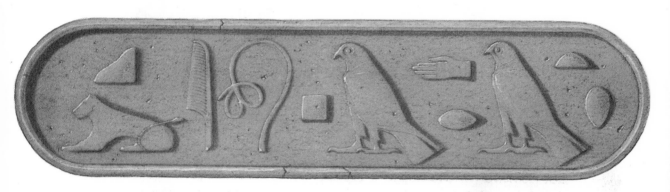

The outside circle is called a *cartouche*. Inside the cartouche are picture-signs that stand for the letters in Cleopatra's name. If you count all the pictures from left to right, you will count eleven pictures—two more than the number of letters in the name *Cleopatra.* The last two signs on the right stand for *Divine Queen,* which was her title.

Royalty and noble families often used coats of arms to identify themselves. The makers of these colorful designs used pictures that had special meanings. A lion was used to show bravery. A leopard was used

to show cleverness. No two families had the same coat of arms.

A coat of arms was necessary in the days of knights in shining armor. One knight, covered in armor from head to foot, looked very much like any other knight. Thus, each knight had a coat of arms on his shield to show who he was.

Ordinary people, too, had their special marks. They designed house-marks to show ownership of property. These marks were clipped out of the hairy coats of horses and painted on the fleece of sheep. They were plowed into the fields, carved on trees, and embroidered on rugs and clothing. A person's tools had house-marks punched into the iron or burned into the wooden handle.

In North America, the American Indian tribes also had identification marks. Each tribe used a picture-sign, or *totem,* as its mark. Families had their own totem animals, too. On the northwest coast of this continent, American Indians decorated the sides of their dwellings and their towering totem poles with these totem animals.

When the European settlers came to American continents, they brought their house-marks and coats of arms with them. One special use of these marks was for the branding of cattle and horses. In branding, the owner's mark is burned into the animal's hide. But branding was not invented here. It has a long history.

Animal branding, like the use of trademarks, was done in Egypt about 4000 years ago. Drawings on the walls of Egyptian tombs show how cattle were branded at that time. Later, in France, horses that were hired out were branded.

Branding was brought to North America by the Spanish. The explorer Cortez brought his brand to Mexico. It had a design of three crosses. Other Spaniards brought their own marks.

Letters turned sideways or upside down in cattle brands take on new meanings. A letter tipped over slightly is "tumbling." Lying down flat, the letter is "lazy." Legs added to a letter make it "walking," and so on. Examples of brands appear on this page.

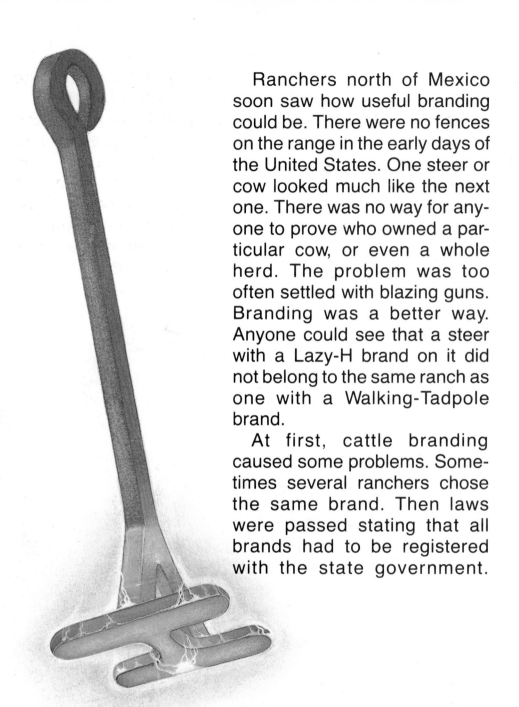

Ranchers north of Mexico soon saw how useful branding could be. There were no fences on the range in the early days of the United States. One steer or cow looked much like the next one. There was no way for anyone to prove who owned a particular cow, or even a whole herd. The problem was too often settled with blazing guns. Branding was a better way. Anyone could see that a steer with a Lazy-H brand on it did not belong to the same ranch as one with a Walking-Tadpole brand.

At first, cattle branding caused some problems. Sometimes several ranchers chose the same brand. Then laws were passed stating that all brands had to be registered with the state government.

Once a brand was registered, no one else could use it. Then the main problem for a new rancher was thinking up a new brand. This resulted in a great variety of brands.

Branding has a language all its own. It is read in a special way. Letters are sometimes used in cattle brands. But they are usually just part of the design, not parts of words.

The age-old use of marking continues to the present day. The trademark, the cartouche, the coat of arms, the totem, the brand—these are some of the many ways in which people have made their marks. How many have you seen?

A VERY BUSY LINE

Norman Borisoff

When you hear someone talking on the telephone, do you ever wonder what the person at the other end is saying? It's like trying to solve a mystery. You have to fill in the missing pieces to make the whole story. When you read Linda's phone conversations, you read only what Linda says. But if you read carefully, you will be able to figure out what trouble Linda's brother Ross and his friend Glenn have gotten into. Each time you see the symbol ◎ it means you have to figure out what is being said on the other end of the line.   *   *   *   *   *

Linda looked out of the living room window for about the tenth time that afternoon. Then she looked at the telephone in the hall. "Why don't they call?" she asked. "They promised to call by noon." But no one answered her. Linda was alone in the house. Her parents wouldn't be back until 3:30. As she walked toward the telephone, it rang. Linda answered it.

"Ross?" she asked without even bothering to say "hello." "Where are you? I . . ." Linda stopped suddenly.

After a few seconds, Linda continued more gently.

"I'm sorry, Margie. I thought . . ." Linda looked annoyed. ◉

"Yes, I know it's after 3:00, Margie. But I can't leave the house. I have to wait here in case Ross calls. He and Glenn left at dawn to hike up Oakwood Hill. Some friends of theirs made the climb last month. It only took them five hours. Glenn and Ross were supposed to call when they got down the hill. That should have been around noon. I still haven't heard from them. Mom and Dad aren't home yet. So I have to stay by the phone. But if we keep talking, our line will be busy . . ." ◎

"Yes, I'll call you back as soon as I hear from him. Bye." ◎

Linda hung up slowly. The room was silent. Suddenly the telephone bell broke the silence once more.

"Hello." ◎

"Yes, this is Linda." ◎

"Oh, Glenn," Linda burst out. "Where are you? And where's Ross?" ◎

"If you're not sure where he is, how do you know he's OK?" ◎

Linda listened to the voice on the other end. But she could not stay quiet for long.

"I'm sure it's a long story. But you don't have to start way back there. Start where you last saw Ross." ◎

Linda, holding the phone, sat down in the chair. She nodded her head slowly several times. "Yes, I know where Oakwood Hill is. But I've never tried to climb it.

I do know the road ends down at the bottom of the hill." ◎

This time Linda sounded a little gentler. "Yes, I understand. Near the top, the trail divides." ◎

"You did what?" ◎

"But didn't you think that the trails might not meet again?" ◎

"I don't care if it was Ross's idea. You're older than he is. You shouldn't have gone along with it. What time did you plan to meet?" ◎

"But that was hours ago." Linda was looking at her watch. ◎

"You're at that gas station now?" Linda's voice had become louder now. But she was worried, not angry. ◎

"But where? . . ." ◎

"No, of course he's not at home! Do you think I'd be asking these questions?" ◎

"I'm not shouting!" Linda said loudly. "I know you were just hoping." ◎

"Well, I'm worried, too." ◎

"What?" ◎

"Do you have another dime, Glenn?" ◎

"Wait a minute operator, this is important! Glenn, give me the number there, and I'll call you right back." ◎

"Yes, just a minute operator, I just want . . ." There

was a click. The phone was silent. Linda slowly put the receiver down.

"I don't even know the name of the gas station to be able to get the number from information," she said in a flat tone of voice. Linda slumped back into the chair.

The clock in the hall ticked loudly. She waited for Glenn to call back. But he didn't.

The sound of the ticking mixed with the scratch of a key in the front door lock. Linda's mother and father came in.

"Oh, Mom, Dad," Linda jumped up. "Glenn called and Ross is lost and . . ." Linda spilled out bits and pieces of her conversation with Glenn. Before she could finish, the telephone rang once more.

Linda picked it up slowly —not knowing what news she might hear on the other end.

"He . . . hello," she stammered.

"Oh, Ross! What's happened?"

"Yes, I know you were supposed to meet Glenn, but where are you?"

"At a gas station on the other side of Oakwood Hill! Then your trail never did meet Glenn's?"

"Yes, I talked to him. He's at the other gas station now. Stay where you are. We'll pick Glenn up and then come and get you. Do you know the name of the gas station where Glenn is?"

"Then you can call Glenn and tell him we're coming. We'll see you in about a half hour, OK?"

Linda hung up.

Then she picked up the phone for what she hoped would be the last time that afternoon. She dialed Margie's number.

"Hello, Margie. This is Linda. They're safe."

What Would We Do Without TELE?

Many of the words we use are taken from other languages. Sometimes we have combined two or more words from another language and made a new English word. The Greek language has given us many words. One of the most useful is the word *tele,* meaning "distant" or "far off."

Watch what happens when *tele* is added to the following word parts: *graph, gram, scope, cast, vision, phone.*

tele + graph ⇒ telegraph   tele + gram ⇒ telegram
tele + scope ⇒ telescope   tele + cast ⇒ telecast
tele + vision ⇒ television   tele + phone ⇒ telephone

Can you pick out the word that goes with each picture?

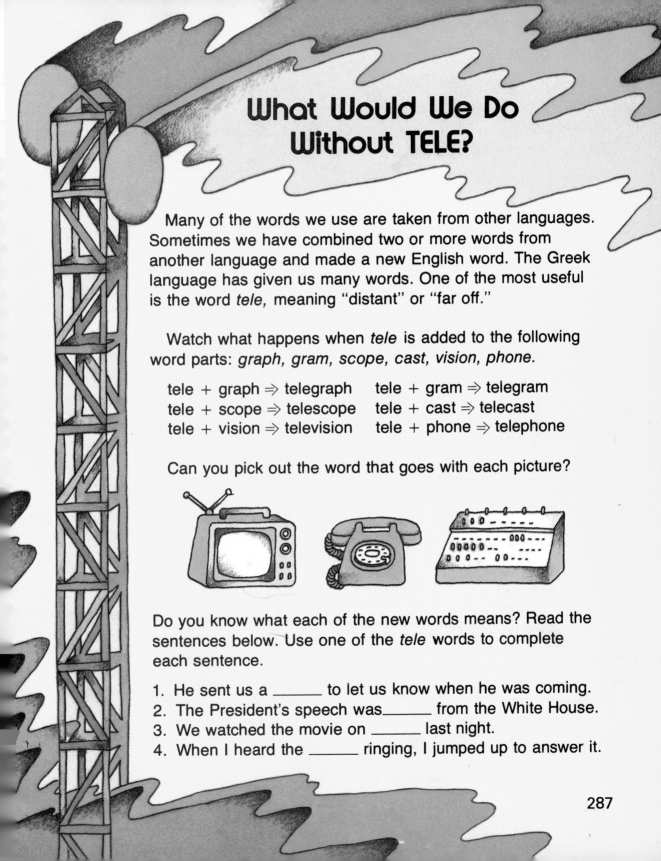

Do you know what each of the new words means? Read the sentences below. Use one of the *tele* words to complete each sentence.

1. He sent us a _____ to let us know when he was coming.
2. The President's speech was_____ from the White House.
3. We watched the movie on _____ last night.
4. When I heard the _____ ringing, I jumped up to answer it.

287

A Button in Her Ear

Ada B. Litchfield

My name is Angela Perkins, and I haven't always had a button in my ear.

Maybe nobody would have discovered that I needed this button if my friend Buzzie hadn't started to mutter. He'd mutter all the time.

One day he shouted, "Throw me the ball! Throw me the ball!" And I did.

What he had really said was "Throw it to Paul!" Because I didn't, we lost the game.

Buzzie was mad at me. But I was even madder at him. I was so mad at him that I threw his bat into the bushes.

Poor Buzzie. He was sort of upset, I guess. But I didn't care. Do you know what he yelled at me then? He yelled, "Just wait. I'll give you a kiss."

A kiss! Aack.

Later I found out what he said was, "Just wait. I'll get you for this."

That did make more sense.

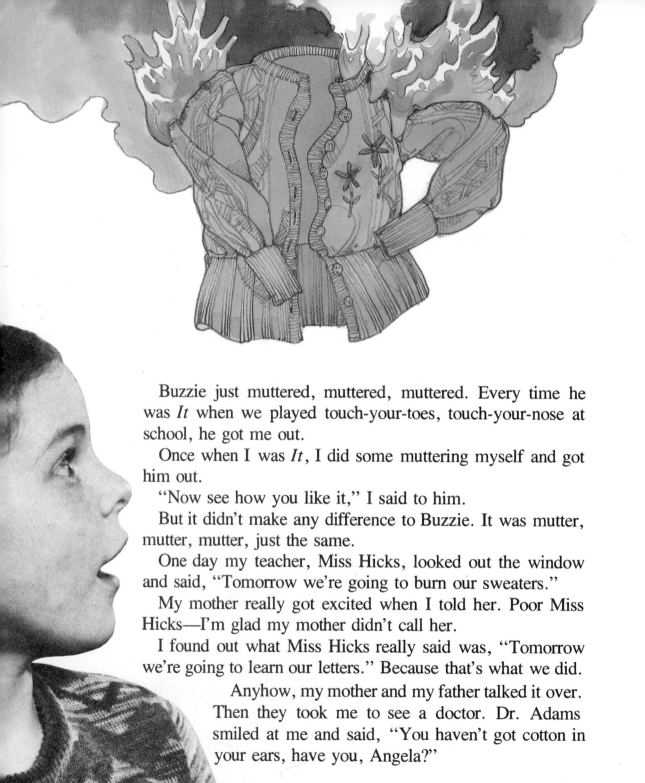

Buzzie just muttered, muttered, muttered. Every time he was *It* when we played touch-your-toes, touch-your-nose at school, he got me out.

Once when I was *It*, I did some muttering myself and got him out.

"Now see how you like it," I said to him.

But it didn't make any difference to Buzzie. It was mutter, mutter, mutter, just the same.

One day my teacher, Miss Hicks, looked out the window and said, "Tomorrow we're going to burn our sweaters."

My mother really got excited when I told her. Poor Miss Hicks—I'm glad my mother didn't call her.

I found out what Miss Hicks really said was, "Tomorrow we're going to learn our letters." Because that's what we did.

Anyhow, my mother and my father talked it over. Then they took me to see a doctor. Dr. Adams smiled at me and said, "You haven't got cotton in your ears, have you, Angela?"

"Of course not," I said. What a silly question!

"Well," he said, "maybe it's earwax." Then he took a silver gizmo with a light on it from a black box and looked into my ears.

"Nope," he said. "No cotton, no earwax, no beans, no marbles . . ."

I laughed. I wouldn't do a dumb thing like that.

"No fooling," he said to my parents. "Sometimes a bean or a marble can get lost in the ear canal and cause all kinds of trouble. But I don't see anything like that in Angela's ears."

Dr. Adams asked my mother questions about me and if I'd ever been very sick. He looked in my ears again and did some other things. Then he wrote something on a paper and gave it to my mother.

"Show her the garden," he muttered.

My parents understood.

What he really said was "Go to Dr. Martin." She was another doctor.

After Dr. Martin had said hello to me, she put me in a little room with one glass wall. She put headphones over my ears. I had to raise my hand every time I heard a beeping sound.

Dr. Martin went into another room and turned some dials. I could see her and my mother through the window.

I raised my hand whenever I heard a beep. Each time, Dr. Martin nodded and drew lines on a chart.

After awhile, I took off the earphones and came out of the little room. I sat down on a stool beside my mother. Dr. Martin gave her the chart and said, "I think Angela needs a hearing aid."

"A hearing aid!" I said. "What's that?"

Dr. Martin took a hearing aid out of a drawer. She opened the box part and put in two tiny batteries. Then she held the earpiece close to my ear. I could hear her clearly when she said, "You can pretend this is a magic button, Angela. With it in your ear, you can usually hear what people say even when you can't see their lips move."

"So, OK," I said. "I guess that will be all right."

To myself I thought, "If it isn't, I'll get rid of it."

The man at the place where I went to get my hearing aid was nice to me, too. He showed me how to change the batteries. Then he told my mother to buy a harness for me to wear that would hold the box part. Mother could make some extra ones, he said.

"Do I have to wear it all the time?" I asked. I was worried about that.

"No," he said. "You won't need your hearing aid when you're asleep or playing rough games outdoors. You can wear it to school, when you go to the movies, or watch TV. It will help you hear some of the things you're missing now."

The next day I wore my hearing aid to school. I wondered if anyone would notice it.

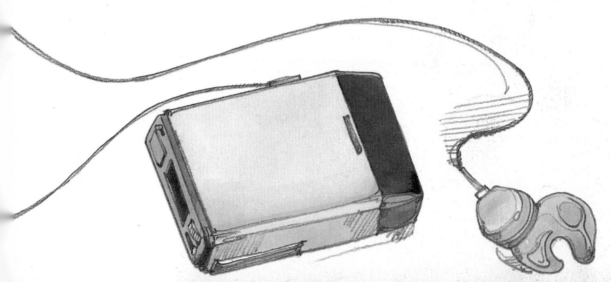

Miss Hicks has sharp eyes, I guess. She noticed my hearing aid right away. She asked very quietly if I would tell the class about it. I said I would.

Then Miss Hicks told everyone, "Angela is wearing something new today." She made it sound like a new locket or something for show-and-tell.

Everybody looked at me, and Miss Hicks said, "Ann and Doug and John and I are wearing glasses to help us see better. Now Angela is wearing a hearing aid to help her hear better."

Then she asked me to take the button out of my ear and my hearing aid out of its harness. I held them up so that everyone could see. I turned the button up, too high at first, and it squealed a little. Then I turned it down and let some of the kids hold the earpiece close to their ears. They could hear what I hear when my hearing aid is working just right.

I opened the case to show the batteries and explained that I have to change them when the batteries go dead.

"Isn't that neat?" Miss Hicks said. All the class agreed. I think some of them even wished a little they could try a hearing aid, too.

Anyhow, here I am with a button in my ear. In a way, it is just like a magic button. I hear nearly everything anyone says to me.

I don't think someone is telling me to wade when I'm supposed to wait. I hear everything Buzzie says when I listen, too.

But here's the special part. If I don't want to hear Buzzie talking, talking, and telling me how smart he is, here's what I do: I press this little gizmo and turn off my magic button. Buzzie fades right out—just like that!

That makes Buzzie hopping-up-and-down-mad, and me winning-grinning glad.

So—a button in your ear is a good thing, if you need it.

Josef

Yuri Korinetz

Sometimes I called my father Josef. I always called my mother Mama, but sometimes I would address my father by his first name, which surprised people. Some of them thought it was rude of me. It seemed to annoy Mrs. Lyapkina especially. When she heard me do it, she would ask, "Aren't you ashamed of yourself? He's not 'Josef' to you, is he? He's your father, not 'Josef'! Have you no manners?"

"Yes, I have!" I assured her.

"It's disgraceful!" said Mrs. Lyapkina. "Such lack of respect! One wonders where a boy like you will end up!"

When Mrs. Lyapkina passed all this on to Mama, Mama just laughed. "Oh, never mind!" she said. "Jura likes it, and Josef doesn't mind. They have a very special relationship."

Mama was quite right. My father and I did have a special relationship. I could depend on him, and he could depend on me. As for calling him Josef, I had a reason for that. It is quite a long story.

The story begins with some poems that Mama used to read aloud to my father. They were written by a famous poet, and the interesting thing was that his name was Josef, too: Josef Utkin. He wrote very good poetry. One of his poems contains the following lines:

A glance she gave him,
From eyes half blind, and said,
Josef, ah, Josef!
I have waited so long!

The poem is about a mother welcoming home her son whom she has not seen for a long time, because he has been fighting as a soldier in the war. But now he is home again, and she says:

Josef, ah, Josef!
I have waited so long!

I had heard these lines only once, when Mama read them aloud, but I memorized them right away. I memorized them because they were full of strong emotion. I also memorized them because they were about someone called Josef, even though this Josef was a son and not a father, the other way 'round from us. Even more important, one day I managed to quote the lines to great effect.

My father was always very late home from work. Mama and I were used to it. But one day Father was to come home early, so that we could

all go to see a movie. We had been wanting to go to a movie for ages, and somehow it never happened. But this time it was all planned—come what might, we were going! So I waited for my father. I waited and waited all day long. Evening came, and time passed by, and soon I would have to go to bed. Then at last he came home, looking tired and feeling low. I went straight up to him and said:

> A glance she gave him,
> From eyes half blind, and said,
> Josef, ah, Josef!
> I have waited so very long!

My quotation was a huge success! Father swung me up in his arms, threw me over his shoulder, and paraded up and down the room with me, laughing. And I laughed, and Mama laughed— none of us could stop laughing! We had made our plan to go to the movie a long time ago, and there was supposed to be a very good film on that evening. But we never got there after all. For one thing, it was too late by then, and for another, we had quite forgotten about the film. We just sat there drinking tea and laughing, and we were still laughing when we went to bed.

It was the poem that did it. Poetry can do wonderful things to people, if you remember it at the right time and in the right place.

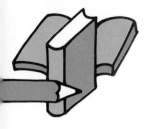

Why Did It Happen?

A *cause* is the reason something happens. An *effect* is the result. Read the following example:

Cause: An elephant sat on the egg.
Effect: The egg broke.

The first sentence describes the cause: too much weight on the egg. The second sentence describes the effect, or result: a broken egg.

ACTIVITY A   Read the list of causes below each effect. Choose the correct cause for each effect. Write the answer on your paper.

1. **Effect:** a sunburn
   Causes:
      a. too much weight
      b. too much sun
      c. too much food

2. **Effect:** a flood
   Causes:
      a. loud noises
      b. heavy rain
      c. dry grass

ACTIVITY B   Read the paragraph below. The last sentence in the paragraph states an effect, or result. Choose the correct cause from the list at the top of the next page. Write the cause on your paper.

   Many penguins live near the South Pole. They stay near the cold sea currents. Penguins won't swim across warm ocean waters. <u>The result is that penguins do not travel to other parts of the world.</u>

1. Penguins can't fly.
2. Penguins are shy.
3. Penguins won't swim across warm ocean waters.

There may be more than one reason why something happens. There may be many causes for one effect. Read the following example:

Effect: being late for school

Causes:
 a. sleeping too long
 b. being caught in a traffic jam
 c. walking slowly to class

In this case, at least three causes resulted in being late for school.

ACTIVITY C   The underlined sentence in the paragraph below states an effect. Choose the correct causes from the list and write them on your paper.

 Chicago had very dry weather in the summer of 1871. Most of the city's buildings were wooden. A fire broke out in a barn. High winds spread the flames quickly. Many alarm boxes were locked. <u>The effect, or result, was that the fire burned most of the city.</u>

Causes:
 a. heavy rains   **b.** noisy barns
 c. locked alarm boxes   **d.** dry weather
 e. wooden buildings   **f.** high winds

MESSAGES

Communication is an important part of your life.
You send messages every day. Sometimes you use words.
Other times you use signs and signals. Passing on a
custom or a tradition is a way of sending a message,
too. All the selections you read in "Messages" sent
you the same message. They all said that the reason
we communicate is because we all have much to learn
from each other.

Thinking About "Messages"

1. What important message about Danny Nomura's culture
   is conveyed by the samurai sword?
2. How do people communicate with drums and bells?
3. How is a young girl's diary an important way of sending a message about life in the past?
4. In what ways was the completion of the first transcontinental railway important?
5. What did you learn from Angela Perkins about the
   importance of one way of communicating?
6. What are some of the many ways in which you send
   messages without speaking?
7. Design a picture symbol for **your school**. Then write a
   paragraph describing your symbol.

CYCLES

Cycles are circular patterns. When a chick hatches from an egg, grows into a chicken, lays its own egg, and a baby chick hatches from that egg, that is a cycle. Most natural things in life happen in cycles. Scientists study the cycles of living things. They are curious. They ask questions. They study and observe and find answers. They learn how to tell fact from opinion.

In "Cycles," you will learn how chicks hatch, and you will read some thoughts on why dinosaurs became extinct. You will find out where ants live and how they work. You will find out how curiosity will help you learn things on your own, just as a scientist learns.

As you read, think about which stories state facts. Which state opinions? Which state both facts and opinions? If you were a scientist, how would you determine what is fact and what is opinion?

All Upon A Stone

Jean Craighead George

In the woods by a stream lies an old, worn stone. It is big as a bear and gray as a rain cloud.

Moss gardens grow on its ridges and humps. Ferns cast shadows of lace on its sides. A puddle of water lies like a lake near its top, and butterflies sit nearby.

A stone by a stream in the woods is like a tiny country. It has its own forests, valleys, and pools. It has its own creatures that live out their lives—hunting, sleeping, and working —all upon a stone.

A summer day dawns.

Deep under the stone a mole cricket moves. Fuzzy hairs cover his back—like fur. His feet are small shovels that dig the soil as he hunts for food.

As he works by himself in the ground under the stone, he breathes through his belly. He hears with his knees, smells with his antennae, and sees through the thousands of parts of his eyes.

Since his hatching in spring, his knees have never heard another mole cricket. His antennae have never smelled one.

Now on this summer day his antennae stretched as he sniffed for the scent of another mole cricket. He peered around roots looking for furry backs, shovels, and knees just like his own.

Tunneling as he searched, he worked himself up to the bottom of the stone.

There he came to a sow bug. He gently touched her with his antenna, but she was no mole cricket. She tucked down her head, pulled in her feet, and rolled herself into a ball.

He crept a little farther, lifting his knees to listen for the crackles of a mole cricket.

He met a ground beetle. She clicked. He went on.

With his shovels he dug up a salamander that was lying under the stone. Its back was not furry but slick and wet.

With his knees he listened to spiders, centipedes, and ants, but he heard no mole-cricket crackles.

He tunneled to the surface and came up beside the edge of the stone.

Thousands of sunbeams spun in his eyes. To shade them he pushed his head between his brown shovels. His two big eyes protected, he entered a path that led up through the moss that covered one side of the stone.

Slowly he climbed.

He heard silken slithers. He followed the sound through the moss. A wood snail was sliding on its big foot. A bright path of silver marked where it had walked.

The mole cricket hurried along.

Under a fern he paused for a rest. A pleasant odor came down his antennae.

He peered through the thousands of parts of his eyes. It was only a firefly asleep in the fern fronds waiting for twilight, his hour to fly and to glow.

The cricket stepped along with all his six feet.

At the edge of a pit filled with stone dust he listened again. He heard crashes, not crackles. Worker ants were stacking sand grains on sand grains. The sound was enormous.

At last he came to the pool in the stone. It smelled like a mole cricket.

He grew excited. He fell in. Plowing the water of the rock pool as if it were soil, he swam.

As he swam he passed fairy shrimp. They darted away upside down, for they live on their backs.

Young mosquitoes flipped to the bottom of the pool. His shovels struck algae and rotifers and freshwater jellyfish. He bumped the tip of a freshwater sponge.

But he did not find a mole cricket.

He beached in a grove of bright bluets and dried off his fur with his second pair of legs.

Silver wings flashed. The mole cricket lifted his knees. The clatter of stone flies was all that he heard. They had hatched in the stream by the stone and were dancing above the bluet grove.

He wedged himself under a starflower. A ground spider leaped to a leaf to pounce on him. He scurried away.

Then, in a jungle of liverwort plants, the tap of his shovels on dry leaves and stone awakened a lizard. He sprang at the cricket. Terrified, the cricket dug himself into a hump of pincushion moss.

The lizard was baffled. He went back to his lair.

The mole cricket continued to dig, and soon came out in the sun. He saw that he had come to the top of the stone. It was scattered with lichens and smoothed by the rain.

He listened and looked.

No mole-cricket crackles came to his knees. No furry backs glowed in the thousands of parts of his eyes.

He set up a wail. Locking one wing into the other, he sawed out his cry.

He crackled his whereabouts. He crackled his need for other mole crickets.

Down on the stone dropped a single mole cricket. Speeding around trees came another.

Up from the bank of the stream flew a third and a fourth, a fifth and a sixth and a seventh.

They gathered together as mole crickets do, not to mate, not to eat, but for reasons no one knows. Solitary creatures all the days of their lives, each leaves its earthen home on one festive night and rushes together with other mole crickets to dance, crackle, and touch.

The mole cricket joined them. His knees heard glorious crackles. He smelled the good scent of other mole crickets. He saw furry backs.

He mingled and met. He bumped, touched, and scrambled. He sang, whirled, and crackled. He danced all night to mole-cricket sounds.

Then he sat still. He was weary. There were too many crackles, too many backs, too many knees, and too many eyes.

Wildly he flew from the stone. He crashed into other crickets flying away.

He zoomed to the ground and plunged into the loam. He tunneled and burrowed and scrambled toward silence. He dug away from the sight of mole-cricket fur. He raced from the scent of their bodies.

He plowed to a quiet spot under the stone.

His senses now told him that he loved his mole-cricket comforts deep in the earth—the silence, the darkness, the black hugging soil.

Back in his home he sighed through his belly, pulled down his antennae, and stretched out to rest under the stone.

HECTOR'S 21st DAY

Alma Whitney

After twenty-one days of being inside, it was time for Hector to get out. Getting out was not going to be easy. Not with a wall all around him. But enough was enough. Hector had to get out!

At first, Hector tried kicking his way out. But he could hardly move his legs. They were curled tightly under him. And he was jammed right up against the wall. He was crowded into a very small space.

The only thing that Hector could move was his head. But how in the world could he use his head to break down a wall? He needed something sharp, something with a point that could make a hole. Why, of course! He could use his tooth, his one and only tooth, as a tool. Hector had never used his tooth before. He hadn't needed it for eating. The food in his big yellow food bag had gotten to him through a tube in his tummy. But now his tooth was going to come in very handy.

Hector pulled his head back a little. Then he pushed his tooth against the wall as hard as he could. Push, push, push . . . nothing. Nothing happened. Hector tried again. Push, push, push . . . still nothing. Hector was not very happy about the way things were working out.

"If only it weren't so crowded in here," he thought, "then maybe I could just stay put." But the more he thought about it, the more he was sure that he could not stay where he was. Not only was it crowded, but his big yellow bag of food was gone. He would starve to death if he didn't make his move pretty soon.

Hector went to work again. He pulled his head back as far as it would go and struck at the wall with his tooth. Again and again he hit the wall. And again and again nothing happened. But just as Hector was about to give up, something exciting happened. As he hit the wall with his tooth, there was a slight sound...

Hector could hardly believe it. Right in the spot where he had been working was the tiniest of cracks. The wall had a crack in it. He was making progress!

Hector was thrilled. But as excited as he was, Hector was also very tired. This was hard work, indeed. Hector closed his eyes and took a nap. Not a long one, though. In a short time, he was at work again, jamming his only tooth in the crack in the wall.

How proud Hector must have been as he went about his job! Just think. Twenty-one days ago he had hardly been anything at all. In fact, he had looked like just a little white spot in the beginning. But by the time he had been around for three days, he had a head and a heart pumping blood. And after six days, he had eyes. In three more days, Hector had the beginnings of legs and the beginnings of wings. Then after ten days, his beak had started to form. And that tooth. Let's see. Oh, yes. That had formed on Hector's beak by the time he had been around for about twelve days.

Hector worked busily at the wall. He rammed his tooth against it again and again. And each time he did, the crack got a little bigger. Suddenly there was a sound much louder than the crack Hector had heard before...

CRUUUUNCH..

There was no longer just a crack in the wall. Now there was a little hole. Little, but big enough for Hector to stick his tooth through. And that is just what Hector did. He stuck his tooth through the hole in the wall and made as much noise as he could.

All that noise-making. All that work. Time for another nap. Hector pulled his tooth back inside. He fell asleep.

A little while later, Hector woke with a start. There was still a lot of work to be done. He pushed his tooth against the crack in the wall. The crack got bigger and bigger with each push. Time passed.

The crack in the wall went almost all the way around Hector now. Seeing this, Hector tried again to kick his way out.

He pushed his feet as hard as he could. Not yet. It wasn't quite time yet. He tried again. Kick, kick, kick . . .

With a loud noise, the wall finally split open.

Hector was so excited that he started making more noise than before. But he was not out yet. Hector still had a little squirming and wiggling to do before he would really be free.

So he squirmed. And he wiggled. And he wiggled and squirmed. And he pushed his feet with all his might against the wall. And then . . .

HECTOR WAS FINALLY OUT!

Did he leap for joy? Did he run around yelling about what a good job he had done? No, he did not. He simply wobbled around a little bit. And then he fell asleep.

It would take a little while before Hector's wet, flattened-out feathers would look dry and fluffy. It would take some time before Hector would be rested enough to walk about properly. But he really didn't care about that now. He was just glad he was out of the shell and on his way to being a lively little chick.

the inside story of the egg

E. A. Schano

All female birds lay eggs. Ostriches lay very big eggs. Hummingbirds lay very small ones. Hens lay up to 350 eggs a year. But some birds lay only one egg a year.

Bird eggs come in all sizes and colors. They may look different on the outside. But on the inside, bird eggs are very much alike.

In all eggs that will hatch, the bird-to-be starts out as only a tiny, whitish spot. All eggs contain a yellow part called the yolk. The yolk and the white of the egg give food to the bird-to-be as it is growing inside the egg. The yolk and the white of the egg are a cushion for the bird-to-be. The shell of the egg protects the bird-to-be until it is ready to hatch.

You have just read about a chick hatching out of its shell. Now let's take a look at how the chick looks as it grows inside the egg.

1

FIRST DAY: Can you see the whitish spot in this picture of the yolk of an egg? This is the beginning of a new chick.

3

THREE DAYS: The chick-to-be now looks like a question mark. It already has a heart. Do you see the little red lines all around the chick-to-be? These are blood vessels that carry blood and food to the chick-to-be.

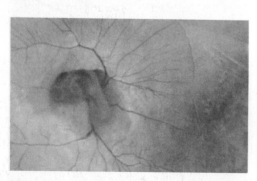

6

SIX DAYS: You can now see the eyes of the chick-to-be.

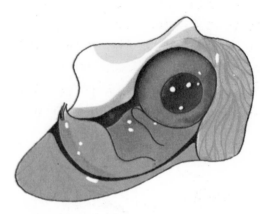

9

NINE DAYS: The wings and the tail are beginning to form. Can you see the little bumps on the body? These bumps are where feathers will grow.

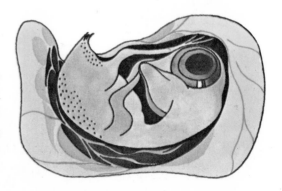

12

TWELVE DAYS: Now the feathers are beginning to come out. The beak has already formed. Look carefully. Find the little tooth. This tooth will help the chick-to-be to hatch. The tooth will fall off soon after the chick is out of the shell.

18

EIGHTEEN DAYS: Now the little chick-to-be almost fills up the egg. The yolk of the egg is getting watery. This is because the chick-to-be has been using it for food. Soon the chick-to-be will use up the whole yolk.

That will give the new chick enough food to last for two or three days after it is hatched.

21

TWENTY-ONE DAYS: And here it comes! The chick-to-be has a strong neck. This helps the chick-to-be to hit its tooth against the shell. The chick-to-be does this for many hours. Finally the shell breaks open.

THE ENORMOUS EGG

Oliver Butterworth

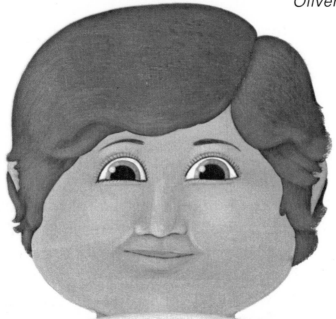

Sometimes
writers like to mix real things with
things that have never happened. For example,
we all know that chickens lay eggs that hatch into
chicks. Now think of all the other creatures that lay eggs.
Suppose things got mixed up and a chicken laid an egg that
hatched into a different animal. And suppose this animal was
believed to be extinct. What do you think would happen?
Oliver Butterworth thought about what it would be like if
this happened. And he wrote all about it in his book
called The Enormous Egg.

The day the egg hatched, I saw Joe Champigny out in his backyard. I went over to talk to him.

"Hey, Joe," I said. "Guess what hatched out of my egg?"

"A duck?" Joe asked.

"Nope."

"A turkey?"

"Nope. I'll give you a hint. It's got four legs."

Joe looked at me and wrinkled his face. "Two ducks?"

I could see that he wasn't going to get anywhere that way. So I told him. "It's a *dinosaur*. A real little live dinosaur. What do you think of *that*?"

"Aw, go on," Joe said. "Who are you kidding?"

"*Honest,* it is. Come on over and look at it. It's got little horns on its face and everything." We went across the street into my backyard. We squatted down by the dinosaur nest. Joe didn't see him at first. But then his eyes got used to the dark. "Jeepers, it's a big lizard!" he said. "Is he poisonous? He sure looks poisonous to me."

"I don't know," I said. I hadn't even thought of that before. I'd have to ask Dr. Ziemer.

"That's no dinosaur," Joe Champigny said. "It's just a big lizard. Where'd you get the idea it was a dinosaur, anyway?"

"Dr. Ziemer said it was one. Dr. Ziemer works in a museum. He knows all about dinosaurs and things like that. He knew the egg was going to hatch out. And he knew what kind of an egg it was, too."

"You know what I think?" Joe said. "This Dr. Ziemer is just making fun of you."

I didn't agree with what Joe said about Dr. Ziemer. He didn't look like the kind of man who'd play a trick like that. And he looked too excited when he first saw what had hatched out of the egg.

That afternoon, Dr. Ziemer drove up in his car. He walked out to the backyard, where I was sitting watching the dinosaur.

"Hello there, Nate," he said. "How is our little freak? Still lively?" He bent down and looked inside the box to make sure for himself. "Yes sir, he looks fine. Probably hungry, too."

"What does he eat?" I said. "Do we have to feed him milk out of a baby's bottle?"

Dr. Ziemer laughed at that. "Oh no, Nate. You see, dinosaurs are reptiles like snakes and turtles. When they hatch out of the egg, they are all ready to eat the same kind of food that grown-up dinosaurs eat. Your dinosaur is a *Triceratops*. The *Triceratops* kind of dinosaur is a grass-eater. So all we have to do is keep him supplied with grass or leaves or lily pads or lettuce—and a few small pebbles now and then."

"Pebbles?" I said. "Does he eat pebbles?"

Dr. Ziemer smiled. "What kind of teeth does a chicken have, Nate?"

"Doesn't have teeth," I said. "It just has little stones in its gizzard. Say, do you mean a dinosaur has a gizzard like a chicken?"

"Some of them do. When scientists dug up dinosaur bones, they sometimes found a pile of smooth stones right in the middle of the dinosaur skeleton. They finally figured out that they were gizzard stones. Some of the stones were as big as a man's fist."

We picked some maple leaves from the tree in the yard. And I got a handful of grass from outside the fence. We put them down in two piles—grass in one and leaves in the other. We put the nest box on its side. The dinosaur could come out if he wanted to. Then we sat down and watched. The little dinosaur saw the piles of food, I guess, because he started right out for them. His legs looked kind of weak at first. And he stumbled around a little. But he kept right on going. The first pile he came to was the grass. He put his head right down into

that green grass. He started swallowing away at it. The little fellow kept right on swallowing until the handful of grass was all gone. All that was left was a blade of grass hanging out of the corner of his mouth. Then he wobbled over to the pile of leaves. He started in on that. I ran over and got some more grass and another pile of leaves.

When it was all gone, he stood on three legs and scratched his neck with a hind foot. Then he walked over to a smooth, sunny place and lay down.

"Well," Dr. Ziemer said, "with that appetite he's going to have us jumping to keep him supplied with food. By the way, we ought to keep a record of his growth. Do you happen to have some scales in the house?"

We did. I brought the scales outside, and we put them on the ground. Then I went over to pick up the animal. He had a bluish skin like a lizard's. And he had a funny kind of a beak, something like a snapping turtle has. I wasn't scared to pick him up. But you see, I'd never handled a dinosaur before. And I didn't know much about how to do it.

Dr. Ziemer was watching me. "What's the matter, Nate? Does he look dangerous?"

"I was just wondering how I ought to get hold of him," I said. "He has a kind of sharp-looking mouth. I'd just as soon not get my hand nipped. What do you think?"

"Well, to tell the truth, I've never had to deal with any of these fellows when they were alive. My dinosaurs have all been just piles of old bones. Let's just see how touchy he is." He put his foot out and gently poked one of the dinosaur's feet. The dinosaur sat up and looked around. He was pretty sleepy.

"He looks rather calm and friendly," the doctor said. "Would you like me to pick him up this first time?"

As a matter of fact, I wasn't too eager to catch hold of him. But I thought I ought to be the one to pick him up first, since he was my dinosaur and all. So I said, "No thanks, I'll pick him up."

"All right, Nate. I'd suggest you hold him just back of the front legs. He has a short neck. I don't think he could reach you that way. Be easy, now. We don't want to frighten him."

I reached down slowly. I slid my hands around his body. He wriggled a little but didn't try to bite. His skin felt all warm and sort of slidy and loose. When he seemed to be used to my hands being there, I picked him up slowly and set him down on the scales.

We looked at the dial on the scales. It said four-and-a-quarter pounds. The doctor wrote that down in a little notebook.

"Of course," he said, "this is not what he weighed before he ate. Let's gather as much grass and leaves as we had before. Then we'll weigh that and see how much he's eaten."

We gathered the grass and leaves, and it weighed just a little over a pound.

"Your baby's got a good appetite," the doctor said. "The food he ate weighed over a third of his own weight. Let's see now, that means that he weighed about three pounds when he hatched." He wrote that down in his notebook. "And now for his length." He took a tape measure out of his pocket.

We stretched out his tail and measured him from tip to tip. He was thirteen-and-a-half inches. The doctor wrote it down. Then he measured his head and the length of his tail and his legs. He wrote the measurements down each time in his notebook.

"Is a *Tricerapops* poisonous, Dr. Ziemer?" I asked him.

"No sir, Nate. These fellows had too much armor to need poison. Do you think I'd ask you to pick him up if I thought he was poisonous?"

"How big does the *Tricerapops* get to be?" I asked.

"Sometimes more than twenty feet, with the tail, of course," said Dr. Zeimer. "And it's Tricera*tops*, not *pops*. They might weigh up to ten tons or so at full size."

"Ten tons!" I almost fell over backward with surprise. "My gosh, think of all the grass it would take to feed him. How long does it take him to get that big?"

"Oh, it would take a long time, I'm sure," said Dr. Ziemer. "The fact is, we don't really know much about how fast these animals grew. We've never had any live ones before. We know how big they were because we've found their skeletons. But we don't know much else about them. That's why we must keep careful records on this little fellow. Science is going to be very interested."

Dr. Ziemer finished writing and said he had to go into the house for a minute.

I sat down under the maple tree in the shade. Pretty soon Joe Champigny came along and sat down with me.

"How's your lizard, Nate?" he said.

"It's no lizard. It's a dinosaur."

"I betcha it isn't. I asked my pop about it. He said there wasn't any such thing as a dinosaur. Some crazy scientist found a lot of old bones and made up all that business about dinosaurs."

"There were too dinosaurs," I said. "Besides, if there weren't dinosaurs, how come I've got one right here?"

"Fooey, that's no dinosaur," Joe said.

"It is too. It's a *Triceraclops*, or something like that. And if a *Triceralcops* isn't a dinosaur, I'd like to know what *is*."

"Fooey," Joe Champigny said.

Sometimes Joe's an awfully hard guy to argue with.

THE LIZARD

The Lizard is a funny thing.
    He has a snaky head,
A snaky tail beside, —and yet
    He is a quad-ru-ped.

He has a little lightning tongue
    With which he snaps the flies,
And yes, —there is a funny look
    About his fiery eyes!

I think he was a Dragon once,
    With great big pointed wings,
And wicked jaws and wicked claws,
    And teeth and scales and things.

I think a Hero sought him out,
    And fought an awful fight,
Then changed the Dragon by a spell
    Into this helpless mite.

I like to watch the Lizard bask.
    But oh! Suppose some day
The Dragon should change back again, —
    How fast I'd run away!

                —Abbie Farwell Brown

MILLY AND FRED

WRITTEN BY ALMA WHITNEY

AND WHATEVER HAPPENED TO THE TERRIBLE LIZARDS

FRED, WHATEVER HAPPENED TO THE TERRIBLE LIZARDS?

THE TERRIBLE WHATS?

THE TERRIBLE LIZARDS! YOU KNOW—DINOSAURS! DINOSAUR MEANS "TERRIBLE LIZARD"!

WHY OF COURSE, I KNOW THAT!

WELL, WHATEVER HAPPENED TO THEM? HOW DID THEY BECOME EXTINCT?

EXTINCT? I'M NOT QUITE SURE I UNDERSTAND.

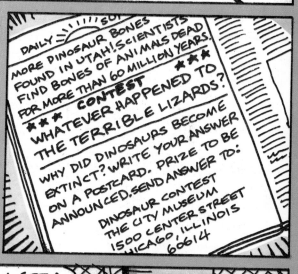

THINK WHAT HAPPENED WHEN THEY WALKED! SOME OF THEM WEIGHED AS MUCH AS NINE ELEPHANTS PUT TOGETHER. CAN YOU IMAGINE WHAT WOULD HAVE HAPPENED IF ONE OF THEM STEPPED ON YOU? I SURE WOULDN'T WANT AN ANIMAL LIKE THAT TO BE MY ENEMY!

LOOK AT THIS, FRED. HERE'S ANOTHER CLUE. THIS BOOK SAYS, "SMALL INTELLIGENT MAMMALS GREW IN NUMBERS AS THE DINOSAURS STARTED DYING OFF...IT IS VERY POSSIBLE THAT THESE SMALL MAMMALS ATE THE DINOSAUR EGGS. THEY MAY HAVE EATEN SO MANY OF THE DINOSAUR EGGS THAT FEWER AND FEWER NEW DINOSAURS WERE HATCHED."

IT ALSO SAYS THAT MAYBE SOMETHING WENT WRONG WITH THE DINOSAUR EGGS, AND THEY STOPPED HATCHING. **WOW!** FRED, DID YOU KNOW THAT THE DINOSAURS LIVED FOR 120 MILLION YEARS BEFORE THEY STARTED DYING OFF?

Dinosaur Contest
The City Museum
1500 Center Street
Chicago, Illinois 60614

Dear Sir/Madam:

Here's our answer to your question "Whatever Happened to the Terrible Lizards?" We can't fit it on a postcard, so we are writing you a letter.

1. Some dinosaurs ate plants. Maybe the plants disappeared and those dinosaurs starved. Some dinosaurs ate the dinosaurs that ate plants. When the plant-eaters died, the meat-eaters also died.

2. The dinosaurs were not very smart. Maybe they could not escape from their enemies or figure out how to take care of themselves as the earth changed.

3. Maybe the dinosaurs became extinct because smaller animals ate their eggs, or because their eggs didn't hatch anymore.

4. Maybe the dinosaurs became extinct because they had just lived long enough.

5. Maybe the dinosaurs all got very sick and died. (That's our own idea.)

In other words, our answer is that no one knows for sure why dinosaurs became extinct.

Yours truly,
Milly and Fred

342

CONSIDER THE
AUK

Consider the auk;
Becoming extinct because he forgot how to fly and could
    only walk.
Consider the man who may well become extinct
Because he forgot how to walk and learned how to fly
    before he thinked.

—Ogden Nash

CATHERINE HUERTA

WHAT'S IN A NAME?

Do you remember when Nate in "The Enormous Egg" had trouble remembering the name for his little dinosaur? If Nate had understood what the name *triceratops* means, he probably would have had less trouble remembering it. *Triceratops* is a name that is based on a special characteristic of the animal. Each part of the name *triceratops* comes from a Greek word. The word part *tri* means "three"; *cerat* means "horn"; and *ops* means "eye or face."

Once you know the meaning of each part, you can figure out the meaning of the name. When you put them all together, you get "three-horned face," which is what a triceratops has.

The words below are names for other animals that existed long ago. Read the meanings of the word parts that make up each name. Then choose the correct animal name to complete each sentence under the pictures.

ptero (wing) + **daktylos** (finger or toe) ⇒ **pterodactyl**

stego (cover) + **saurus** (lizard) ⇒ **stegosaurus**

A _____ was a dinosaur whose body was covered by bony plates along its back, neck, and tail.

A _____ was a reptile whose front legs ended in fingers. The fingers were attached to the hind legs by bat-like wings.

Here are some more Greek words that have been combined to name animals.

cent (hundred) + **pede** (foot) ⇒ **centipede**

platy (broad, flat) + **pus** (foot) ⇒ **platypus**

rhinos (nose) + **ceros** (horn) ⇒ **rhinoceros**

porcus (pig) + **spina** (spines) ⇒ **porcupine**

octo (eight) + **pus** (foot) ⇒ **octopus**

Choose the correct animal name to complete each sentence below. The first one has been done for you.

1. A _platypus_ has a broad, flat, paddle-shaped tail and large webbed feet.

2. A _____ has one or two horns on its nose.

3. A _____ has sharp quills all over its body.

4. A _____ is a worm with many feet.

5. An _____ has eight legs.

345

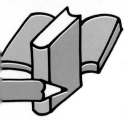

Chart Your Course

A *graph* gives information in picture form. Here are three kinds of graphs. All three show the same information. But they show this information in three different ways.

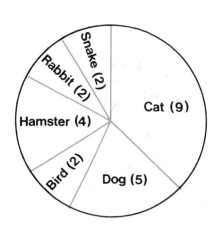

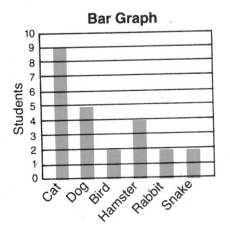

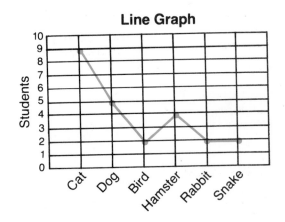

ACTIVITY A   Use the graphs that give information about the pets owned by students to answer the questions below. Write the answers on your paper.

1. Why do you think the first graph is called a *circle graph?* Why is the second called a *bar graph?* Why is the third called a *line graph?*
2. Which pet is owned by the most students?
3. Which pet is owned by only four students?
4. Which pets are owned by only two students?
5. How many students own dogs?
6. How many students own birds?
7. How many more students own dogs than own birds?

ACTIVITY B   Carefully read the information on the table below. Then use the information from the table to make a circle graph, a bar graph, and a line graph. Draw the graphs on your paper.

SANDWICHES FAVORED BY STUDENTS

Sandwich	Number of Students
Tuna Salad	4
Peanut Butter	9
Cheese	2
Egg	1
Chicken Salad	7
Ham	3

The City Under the Back Steps

Evelyn Lampman

Ants live in complete cities that they build under the ground. Each ant in an ant city has a special job to do. The City Under the Back Steps is a book about two children who shrink to the size of ants. They visit an ant city.

Jill, the girl in the book, travels with Nannie. She is the ant in charge of taking care of the baby ants. In the part of the book that you are going to read, Nannie takes Jill on a tour of the nursery.

Jill turned. She looked around the room. She wondered where the baby ants were kept. She could not see any. Along one wall was a stack of tiny white eggs. The eggs were piled in neat rows. The smaller ones were at one end. And the larger ones were at the other end. Some ants moved up and down in front of the row, licking each egg with their quick black tongues.

"Babies have to eat," Nannie said. "They are always hungry."

"That's what I've always heard," Jill agreed. "And they have to be kept clean, too. I guess that's what those nurses are doing over there—washing the eggs."

"Dear me, no," said Nannie. "Those eggs are clean. They are being fed. Come along. I'll show you. These are the newest babies," said Nannie. And she pointed to the smallest eggs. "They were just laid today. And there, at the other end of the wall, are the older babies. They have had many days of feeding and have grown quite fat. They are almost ready to be hatched into little larvae."

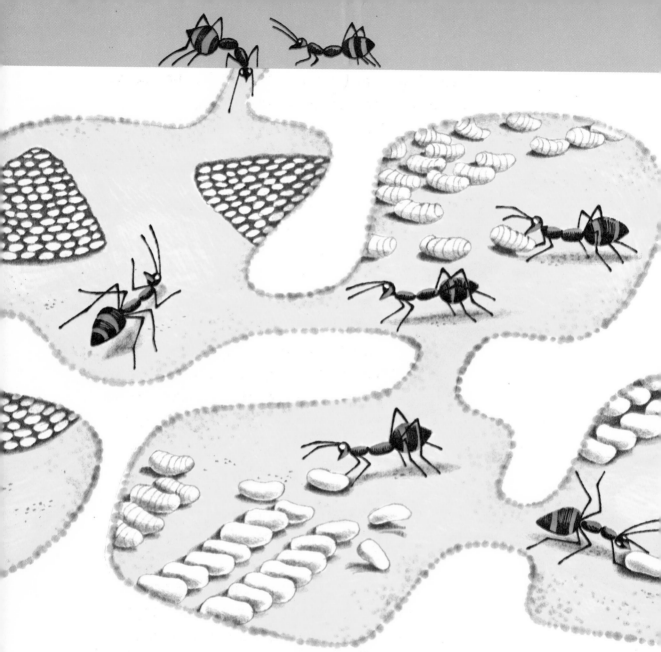

Jill did not want to say that she had
never heard of eggs growing larger once
they were laid or that she had no idea of
what larvae were. So instead she asked,
"What do the babies eat?" She had no

idea about that either. There did not seem to be any bottles or food around.

"The babies have milk," said Nannie. "You really don't know anything about baby ants, do you?"

Nannie stopped talking. She moved her antennae. Then she turned to the other nurses in the room. "This room will soon be too chilly for the eggs. They must be moved to Nursery 7 at once."

"You have more than one nursery?"

"We have many of them," said Nannie. "We move things around all the time. The eggs must be kept at just the right temperature. And we move the eggs for safety, too. If we should be attacked by an enemy, the enemy would have to hunt for the nursery. Now come along. Let's go and see the babies who have already become larvae. They are in the next room."

There were so many larvae in the next room that Jill could not begin to count them. The larvae were also being licked by their nurses. Jill began to realize that the nurses had the baby food in their mouths. And she could see that by licking the eggs and larvae, the nurses were giving the food to the babies.

Jill did not want to say so, but she did not think the larva stage of ant babies was very pretty. The larvae looked like little, white, hairy worms. They were soft and squashy. And they did not have eyes. They had mouths, though. And out of their mouths came threads that looked like the webs a spider might spin. As Jill watched, the threads grew longer and longer. Nannie was excited when she saw them.

"Will you look at that," Nannie said. "Such smart babies. They are already changing into pupae!"

"Pupae," thought Jill. "My goodness. First the babies were eggs. Then the eggs turned to larvae. Then the larvae turned to something else. What a lot of steps there are before an ant becomes an ant!"

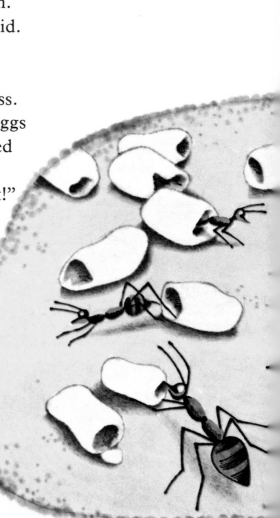

One of the wormlike creatures shook. Then it let out a long strand of thread. It rolled over and over until it was completely wrapped in the thread.

"Be careful," cried Jill. "It may choke."

"Bless your heart," said Nannie. "It's only doing what it's supposed to do. Soon it will spin enough thread so that it's wrapped up as neatly as a little sack. Then it will be a pupa. Come over here. You can see some."

The pupae did not have to be fed. In fact, it would have been impossible to feed them. The pupae were nothing but little cocoons of tightly wrapped thread. They were laid out in neat little rows. They looked like so many white packages. And there was no sign of the pale worm inside.

"Now it's time to go to the delivery room and see the new babies coming out of their pupae," Nannie said.

The delivery room was a busy place. It was not nearly as neat as the other rooms in the nursery. The cocoons were not piled in neat rows. They were lying here and there. The nurses were running about, trying to see everything at once.

Most of the cocoons were moving. Some
only gave a little twitch or jerk. Others
were tossing and jumping like little bits of
popping corn. Here and there lay an empty
pupa. And beside it lay a tiny dark insect.
It looked like the larger ants but had a
strange, soft body.

"Oh, there are the babies," cried Jill
in excitement. "But they shouldn't be left
on the floor. They might get cold."

"Don't touch them!" Nannie yelled.
"They haven't been out of their cocoons
long enough for their skins to harden.
Give them a little while. Then it will be
perfectly safe to hold them. Oh, here's one
that's ready to come out but needs help."

Jill followed Nannie to one of the cocoons that was popping up and down. Nannie bent over the cocoon, holding it still with one of her feet. She opened her mouth and gently tore at the thread until there was room for the little ant to get out.

"Cute, isn't it?" Nannie said proudly. "We have to help them, poor dears. They have such a hard time getting started."

"Are they fed pretty soon?" Jill asked, staring at the newly hatched baby.

"Soon, but not here," said Nannie. "In a little while these babies will be strong enough to walk. Then they will be taken to another nursery to be washed and fed. They must not be touched until then."

"Now it's time to go," said Nannie. "We'll come back later."

"All right," said Jill. "But I hope all the babies won't be hatched by the time I get back."

"Don't worry about that," Nannie told her. "There are new babies every day. Our city must go on, you know."

Your Own Ant City

Lenore Flehinger

Reading about ants is one way to learn about them. Another way to learn about these interesting insects is to watch them. The best way to watch ants is to have your own ant city.

Here is a plan for building and keeping your own ant city.

BUILDING THE CITY

You will need:

Glass jar (at least quart size with a screw-on lid)

Piece of wood (as large as you can find that will fit into the jar)

Moist soil (the kind that holds together when you squeeze it)

Sponge

Black paper (enough to wrap around the jar)

String (two pieces long enough to tie around the jar)

Block of wood (to use as a stand for the jar)

Pan (large enough to hold the jar and the block of wood)

HOW TO PUT THE CITY TOGETHER

1. Stand the piece of wood in the center of the jar.

2. Fill in the space around the piece of wood with enough soil to hold the wood in place. (Ants make tunnels in their cities. If you do not put the wood in the jar, the ants might make their tunnels in the center of the jar. Then you would not be able to see them.)

3. Keep everything else ready until you bring your ants to their new home.

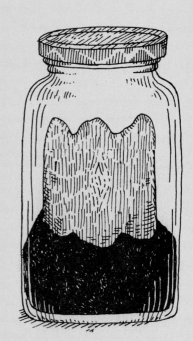

COLLECTING THE ANTS

You will need:

Glass jar
Old sheet or pillowcase
Small shovel or garden trowel

HOW TO FIND THE ANTS

Some ants make their homes under a stone or a rotting piece of wood. If the weather is warm, you may see many ants right under the stone or the wood. If the weather is cool, some ants may be where you can see them. But many others will be in their tunnels under the ground.

The first ants you'll see will be the workers. They gather food, care for the young, and even collect the garbage. Some of the workers will be carrying what look like grains of rice. They are really carrying the larvae, a stage of ant baby that you read about in The City Under the Back Steps. Gently dig out as many of the workers and the larvae as you can. Pile them, along with some of the soil you find them in, on the sheet or pillowcase. Then gently push as many workers as you can into the jar. You

will need about one hundred workers. If the workers drop the larvae, carefully push the larvae into the jar yourself. Be sure to put some of the soil from the nest into the jar also.

Finally, if you want your ant city to last for some time, you must have a queen ant. The queen is important because she lays the eggs from which new ants come. You can recognize the queen because she is bigger than the other ants. You may have to dig a bit and look very carefully to find her.

If you can't find ants under a rock or a piece of wood, look for an ant hill. An ant hill is a little cone of earth built around a tiny hole in the ground. If an ant nest is under an ant hill, you may have to dig quite deep to get the ants. But remember, you will need workers, larvae, and a queen to have a healthy city.

PUTTING THE ANTS IN THEIR NEW HOME

1. Bring the ants to their new home as quickly as you can. Put them, along with the soil you found them in, into the city you built.

2. Wet the sponge and wring it out well. Place it on top of the piece of wood in the jar. (This will keep the air in the jar from getting too dry.)

3. Wrap the black paper around the jar. Tie it with the two pieces of string. (Ants make their tunnels away from the light. If you do not cover the city, the ants will make their tunnels as close to the center of the jar as they can.)

4. Put water in the pan and set the block of wood in it. Then set your ant city on top of the block of wood. The ant city should not sit in the water, or the paper around it will get wet. (Ants will not go into water. If they try to get out of their city, the water will keep them from leaving.)

5. Punch some holes in the screw-on lid of the jar. Stuff the holes with cotton. (The cotton will let air in. But it will keep the ants from getting out.) Screw the cover on the jar.

CARING FOR THE ANT CITY

You will need:

Eyedropper
Tweezers
Bits of food

WHAT TO DO

You must take care of your ant city every day. If it is in school, make sure you take good care of it during the week. Then it should be all right by itself on the weekends. Here are the things you should do to care for your ant city:

1. Check the sponge every day. See that it is moist. Add a drop or two of water from the eyedropper when the sponge starts to get dry.

2. Try to feed your ants at the same time each day. Put the food in the same place in their city. The ants will learn where and when to come and get the food. Ants especially like bread, cake, and sugar. You can also give them honey mixed with water. If you can find some dead insects, feed them to the ants, too. Put small pieces of food into the city every day. Each time you add new food, remove the old food with your tweezers. This keeps the city from getting moldy.

3. Leave the black paper tied around the ant city for the first few days after you put the ants in. After that, you may remove the paper for just a few minutes from time to time to look at your ants. By watching closely, you may be able to see the ants feed each other, care for the larvae, and collect the garbage. You may want to keep a diary of what you see.

My Diary

Ant Cities are easy to make. You can watch the ants move in their cities.

Anteater

— William Jay Smith

The Anteater makes a meal of ants
That run up and down the leaves of plants.
No matter how hungry I ever got,
I wouldn't eat Ants, I would certainly not.
I think that Ants would make me squirm;
I'd rather eat an angleworm;
Or if it really came to that,
A mashed mosquito or a gnat,
But not a big red twitchety ant
That crawls on a fat green tropical plant.

362

Where Would You Look?

Now that you know something about ants, you might like to find out even more about them. Suppose you want to find the answer to this key question:

What are the different kinds of ants?

Where would you look? You would probably start with the encyclopedia. The information in an encyclopedia is arranged in alphabetical order according to *main topics*.

Look at the key question again. Under what main topic would you look to find the answer? The main topic would be Ant, not Ants. To find the main topic Ant, you would first have to find the *A* volume of the encyclopedia.

Like a dictionary, each encyclopedia volume has *guide words* at the top of each page to help you find the main topic you want. In what order would the following guide words appear?

Alaska   Antarctica   Amarillo   Afghanistan

By putting the guide words in alphabetical order, you know that the main topic Ant appears after Amarillo and before Antarctica. Now read the second key question:

Do ants have other enemies besides anteaters?

Under what main topic would you look to find the answer?

You might find the answer under Ant, but sometimes information about a subject appears in more than one place in an encyclopedia. For example, you might find additional information about the enemies of ants under the main topic Anteater.

Here's one more question for you. Use an encyclopedia to help you answer it.

Would an aardvark rather find an affenpinscher or an ant?

The Carp in the Bathtub

Barbara Cohen

When I was a little girl, I lived in an apartment house in New York City with Mama and Papa and my little brother Harry.

It was not very fancy, but Papa said we were lucky. We had our own bathroom. Mrs. Ginzburg, who lived downstairs, was also lucky. She had a bathroom, too. Everyone else had to share the bathrooms in the hall.

Mama was a wonderful cook. It was well known that she made the finest chicken soup in New York City. Everything she made was the best.

But best of all was Mama's gefilte fish. Mama made gefilte fish twice a year. She made it in the fall for the Jewish New Year. And she made it in the spring for the festival of Passover.

Everybody loved Mama's gefilte fish. But I will tell you a secret. I never put a piece of it into my mouth.

Mama made her gefilte fish out of carp. For a day or two before the holidays, carp was hard to find in the stores. All the ladies in the neighborhood had been buying it for their own gefilte fish. Mama liked to buy her carp at least a week early. She wanted to get the nicest, fattest, shiniest one. But Mama knew that a dead fish sitting in the icebox for a week would not be very good when the time came to make it into gefilte fish.

So Mama bought her fish live and carried it home in a pail of water. All the way home the fish flopped and flipped because it was too big for the bucket. It would have died if Mama had left it in there.

As soon as she got home, she would call, "Leah, run the water in the tub."

And I would put the rubber stopper in the drain and run some cold water into the bathtub. Then Mama would dump the carp out of the pail and into the tub.

The carp loved it there. He was always a big fish. But the tub was about four times as long as he was. And there was plenty of room for him to swim around.

Harry and I loved the carp. As long as he was there, we didn't have to take baths.

Most of our friends took baths only once a week. But because we had our own tub, Mama made us bathe twice a week.

"Otherwise," she said, "what is the use of having our own bathroom?"

We didn't think it was fair. And we would gladly have moved into an apartment where the tenants shared the bathrooms in the hall.

Except, of course, when we had a carp living in our bathtub. Harry and I would go into the bathroom and feed the carp a rusty lettuce leaf or a crust of bread.

But the day always came when Mama marched into the bathroom and took the stopper out of the tub. The carp always seemed to know what was coming. He swam away from her as fast as he could, splashing water all over her apron with his strong, flat tail. But he didn't even have a chance. Before all the water was out of the tub, Mama had caught the carp. Then she dumped him right into the bucket and carried him to the kitchen.

We knew what she did with him when she got there, although we would never look. She killed him. Then she scraped off the scales with a huge knife. The head, skin, and bones she boiled, along with some carrots and onions, in a big kettle of water to make broth. She put the meat through a meat grinder with some more onions. After she put in some other things, she made the mixture into balls. She took the broth and put it through a strainer to remove all the skin and bones, which she threw into the garbage.

Mama saved the broth for cooking the fish balls. That took hours. Harry and I would run out into the hall. But even there we could not escape the smell of fish.

Mama once told us that her mama had not thrown away the fish skin. She removed it carefully from the carp. After the fish was cooked, she could put it back in the skin and bring it to the table. That's why the fish is called *gefilte*. Mama said, "*Gefilte* means stuffed." At least Harry and I never had to see that!

You can see why we managed never to eat gefilte fish on the Jewish New Year or Passover. Could *you* eat a friend?

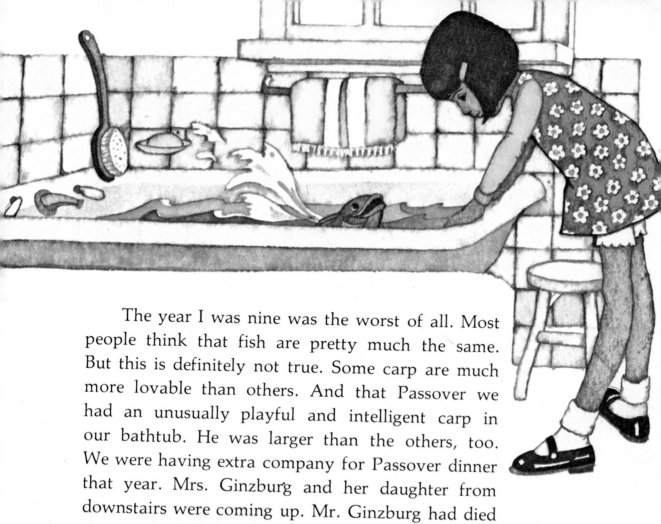

The year I was nine was the worst of all. Most people think that fish are pretty much the same. But this is definitely not true. Some carp are much more lovable than others. And that Passover we had an unusually playful and intelligent carp in our bathtub. He was larger than the others, too. We were having extra company for Passover dinner that year. Mrs. Ginzburg and her daughter from downstairs were coming up. Mr. Ginzburg had died six months before. And Mrs. Ginzburg didn't have the heart to fuss over Passover.

This carp was also shinier than the others. His eyes were brighter. And he seemed much livelier and friendlier. It got so that whenever Harry or I went into the bathroom, he'd swim right over to the end of the tub nearest to us as if he knew we were going to feed him. There was something about his mouth that made him seem to be smiling at us after he had eaten his bread crust or his lettuce.

In those days, people like us did not have pets. Harry and I would have loved owning a dog, a cat, or a bird. But Mama and Papa had never thought of such a thing. And we never thought to ask. I'll tell you one thing, though. After that carp had been in our bathtub for nearly a week, we knew he was not just any old carp. He was our pet. In memory of Mr. Ginzburg, we called him Joe.

Two days before Passover, when I came home from school, Mama said, "You look after Harry, Leah. I have to go out. I'll never get anything done if I have him trailing after me."

As soon as Mama was gone, I looked at Harry, and Harry looked at me.

"We have to save Joe," I told him.

"We'll never have another chance," Harry agreed. "But what'll we do?"

"Mrs. Ginzburg has a bathtub," I reminded him.

Harry nodded. He saw what I meant right away.

I went into the kitchen, got the bucket, and carried it to the bathroom. Harry had already let the water out of the tub. He helped lift Joe into the bucket. It was not easy for us because Joe must have weighed fifteen pounds. But we finally managed. We could add only a little water to the pail because it was already almost too heavy for us.

With both of us holding onto the handle and banging the bucket against every step, we lugged Joe downstairs to Mrs. Ginzburg's door. Then we rang her bell. It took her a long time to get to the door. But she finally opened it.

"Why, Leah, Harry!" she said in surprise. "I'm very glad to see you. Won't you come in? Why are you carrying that bucket?" Mrs. Ginzburg was a very nice lady. She was always kind to us, even when she couldn't understand what we were doing.

We carried our bucket into Mrs. Ginzburg's front room. "May I ask what you have there?" she said politely.

"It's Joe," said Harry.

"Joe!" Mrs. Ginzburg closed her eyes and put her hand over her heart.

"We named him for Mr. Ginzburg," I explained quickly. "He smiles like Mr. Ginzburg."

"Oh..." Mrs. Ginzburg tried to smile, too. Just then Joe twitched. His tail flashed over the top of the bucket. And a few drops of water dripped onto Mrs. Ginzburg's rug. Mrs. Ginzburg glanced into the pail. "My goodness," she said, "he looks like a fish to me."

"He is a fish," I said. "He's the best fish in the world, and Mama can't kill him for Passover. She just can't. Please let him stay in your bathtub. Please. Just for a little while. Until I can figure out where to keep him for good."

"But, Leah," Mrs. Ginzburg said, "I can't do that. Your mama is my dear friend."

"If you don't let us put Joe in your bathtub soon," Harry pleaded, "he'll be dead. He's almost dead now."

Mrs. Ginzburg and I peered into the bucket. Harry was right. Joe didn't look too good. His scales weren't shiny bright anymore, and he had stopped thrashing around. There was not enough water in the bucket for him.

"All right," said Mrs. Ginzburg. "But just for now." She ran some water into her tub, and we dumped our carp in. He no sooner felt all that clear cold water around him than he perked right up and started swimming. I took a few morsels of chopped meat I had stored away in my dress pocket and gave them to him. He smiled at me, just like always.

"This fish can't stay here," Mrs. Ginzburg warned. "I'm afraid I can't help hide him from your mother and father."

"What shall we do?" Harry asked me, blinking his eyes hard to keep back the tears.

"We'll go find Papa," I told him. "Papa doesn't cook, so maybe he'll understand. We'll have to find him before Mama gets home."

Every night, Papa came home on the subway from his job in a factory. That night, Harry and I went down to the corner and waited by the stairs that led up from the station. After a while, we saw a big crowd of people who had just gotten off the train come up the stairs. Papa was with them. He

374

was holding onto the rail and climbing slowly, with his head down.

"Papa, Papa," we called.

He looked up and saw us. He straightened his shoulders, smiled, and ran quickly up the few remaining steps.

"You came to meet me," he said. "That's very nice."

We started home together. I was holding one of Papa's hands, and Harry was holding the other. "Papa," I asked, "do you like gefilte fish?"

"Why, yes," he said, "of course I like gefilte fish. Your mother makes the best gefilte fish in all of New York."

"But would you eat gefilte fish," Harry asked, "if the fish was a friend of yours?"

Papa stood absolutely still right in the middle of the sidewalk. "Harry," he said, "Harry, what have you done to Mama's fish?"

"Leah did it, too," Harry said.

Papa turned to me. Putting his hands on my shoulders, he looked right into my eyes. Papa's brown eyes were not large. But they were very bright. Most of the time his eyes smiled at us, but when he was angry or upset, like now, they could cut us like knives. "Leah," he said, "what did you do to Mama's fish?"

"Please, Papa," I said, "don't let Mama kill our fish. His name is Joe. We love him. And we want to keep him for a pet."

"Where is he now?" Papa asked.

I looked down at my hands and began to pick my fingernail. I didn't want to tell Papa where Joe was. But he put his hand on my chin and forced my face up. "Where's the fish now?" he asked again. His voice was gentle. But those eyes were cutting me up.

"In Mrs. Ginzburg's bathtub," I mumbled.

Papa started walking again, faster now.

We trailed along behind him, not holding his hands anymore. He didn't say anything for a while. But when we got to our front stoop, he stopped to talk to us. "We are going to Mrs. Ginzburg's apartment. And we are getting that fish," he said. "It's your mother's fish. And it cost her a lot of money. She had to save a little out of what I give her each week just so she could buy such a big fish and make an extra nice Passover holiday for all of us." When we got to Mrs. Ginzburg's, Papa said to her, "We've come to take the fish home. I'm sorry for the trouble."

"Oh, he was no trouble," Mrs. Ginzburg said.

"Well, he would have been as soon as you wanted to take a bath," Papa said.

We didn't say anything.

Mrs. Ginzburg let the water out of the tub. Papa used his hands and the bucket to catch Joe.

It was much easier going back upstairs than it had been coming down. Papa carried the bucket. When we got into our apartment, I ran the water, and Papa poured Joe into our bathtub. Joe flitted so gaily through the water you'd think he was happy to be home. Foolish Joe.

"Carp are for eating," Papa said, "just like chicken. You always eat two helpings of chicken."

"We never met the chicken," I said.

Papa shook his head. "That's not the point, Leah," he said. "What was put on this earth to eat, we eat. We don't kill more creatures than we need, and we don't kill them for fun. But we eat what must be eaten. It would break your Mama's heart if she knew you children didn't like to eat her gefilte fish. We won't tell her about any of this. Mrs. Ginzburg won't tell her either."

So nobody told Mama about how we had stolen her carp. Luckily I was at school when she made Joe into gefilte fish. When I got home I asked Harry how he could have stood watching her catch Joe and carry him off into the kitchen.

"I didn't watch," Harry said. "When I saw her go to get Joe, I went right down to Mrs. Ginzburg's. But even there I could smell fish cooking."

Although Mama opened all the windows that afternoon and no one else seemed to notice anything, Harry and I thought we smelled fish cooking for days.

We cried ourselves to sleep that night and the next night, too. Then we made ourselves stop crying. After that, we felt as if we were twelve years older than Mama and Papa.

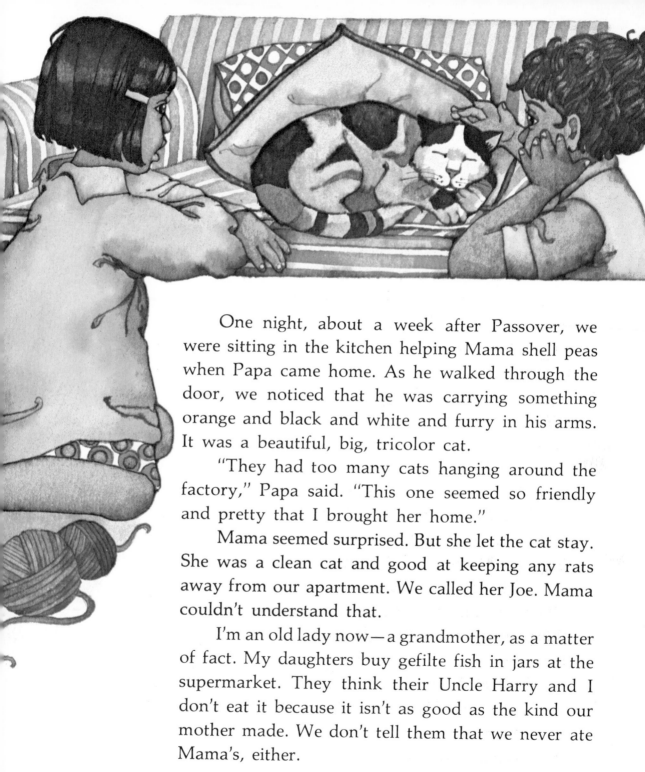

One night, about a week after Passover, we were sitting in the kitchen helping Mama shell peas when Papa came home. As he walked through the door, we noticed that he was carrying something orange and black and white and furry in his arms. It was a beautiful, big, tricolor cat.

"They had too many cats hanging around the factory," Papa said. "This one seemed so friendly and pretty that I brought her home."

Mama seemed surprised. But she let the cat stay. She was a clean cat and good at keeping any rats away from our apartment. We called her Joe. Mama couldn't understand that.

I'm an old lady now—a grandmother, as a matter of fact. My daughters buy gefilte fish in jars at the supermarket. They think their Uncle Harry and I don't eat it because it isn't as good as the kind our mother made. We don't tell them that we never ate Mama's, either.

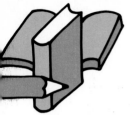

Science Words

Sometimes, in reading about science, you may find a word that you don't know. You could, of course, look up the meaning of the word in a dictionary. But first, you might try another way of finding the word's meaning. You might use *context clues*. To use context clues, begin by noticing how the new word is used in a sentence. Then read the other sentences near the new word or in the same paragraph. The other words and sentences may give clues to the meaning of the new word.

In "The City Under the Back Steps," Nannie talks about ant eggs. She says:

> "There, at the other end of the wall, are the older babies. They have had many days of feeding and have grown quite fat. They are almost ready to be hatched into little *larvae*."

You may not know the meaning of the word *larvae*. To find its meaning, look at the way it is used in a sentence. Then look at the other sentences in the paragraph. The first two sentences say that the eggs have grown older and larger. The last sentence says that the eggs are almost ready to be hatched into larvae. With these clues, you can guess that larvae are early forms of insects. After insect eggs are laid, larvae come from the eggs.

Read each set of sentences. One science word is underlined in each set. Notice how the word is used. On your paper, write what you think is the meaning of the word. Then check your answer in a dictionary.

1. Today was a very cold day. We looked at the thermometer outside. It showed that the temperature was two degrees.

2. Blood must constantly circulate through your body. If something stops the blood from traveling, you are seriously ill and in danger.

3. People cannot see tiny germs with their own eyes. They must use a special instrument. They must look at germs through a microscope.

4. During the summer, many birds live in the northern part of our country. But when winter comes, they migrate south.

5. The scientist heated the liquid. Very quickly, the liquid evaporated. It became a gas in only two minutes.

6. The geologists wanted to know more about the history of Earth. They studied many rocks in different parts of the world. The rocks told them how Earth had changed over thousands of years.

7. The girl's face was a little red and felt very warm. After taking her temperature, the doctor said she had a slight fever.

Spotlight on Scientists

What do you think of when you hear the word scientist? A marine biologist? An astronomer? A chemist? A medical doctor?

All are scientists, but their jobs are different. Then what do scientists have in common? How are they alike? One way in which they are alike is that they all are curious. They are curious about the world around them. They want to know why or how things happen. They want to know what they can do to make life better. Each scientist looks for answers to special questions or problems.

This article is about two people in the field of science. Their interests are different, but each began by asking why.

Ciricao Gonzales

Imagine living on a farm. Picture the black, brown, and white cows grazing in a wide pasture. Beside them are white, woolly sheep. In the distance is a big red barn. Next to the barn, yellow cornstalks dance in the wind. Can you see this farm?

Dr. Ciricao Gonzales probably can. He grew up on a farm in New Mexico. When he was a boy, he worked the farm with his father. As he worked, Ciricao asked his father many questions. He wanted to learn about farming, for he hoped to be a farmer himself someday.

The father answered his son's questions. He explained why certain animals were fed certain foods. He described how different cycles work inside an animal's body. These cycles keep the animal alive.

Everywhere Ciricao looked, something exciting was happening on the farm. The more he watched the animals, the more he wanted to know about them.

To help find answers to his questions, Ciricao joined the 4-H club. The four *H*'s in the club's name stand for Heads, Hearts, Hands, and Health. One purpose of the 4-H club is to train young people who want to learn about farming.

While he was a 4-H club member, Ciricao met
a man from New Mexico State University. This
man, like Ciricao, was a Mexican-American. He
noticed how interested Ciricao was in learning
about animals and plants. So, he helped him get a
4-H club scholarship. Then he helped Ciricao win
a scholarship for Mexican-American students who
want to attend New Mexico State University.

At the university, Ciricao learned more about farming. He also studied biology. On the farm, he had learned about the life cycles of animals. Now, in biology class, he studied the life cycles of humans.

Ciricao studied hard. He continued to go to school. When he graduated, he had earned a doctorate in science. Then he began to think of all the young people across the country who might want to study science. He remembered the man who had helped him, so Dr. Gonzales wanted to help these young people.

Through his job at the National Institutes of Health in Washington, D.C., Dr. Gonzales has found a way to help these students. He directs the Minority Biomedical Support Program. This program helps minority students to pursue careers in science.

Dr. Gonzales continues to seek answers to his own scientific questions. At the same time, he is helping young, future scientists to seek answers to other questions.

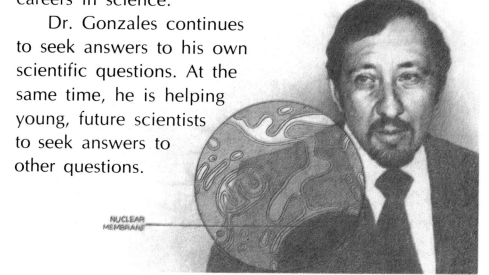

NUCLEAR MEMBRANE

Becky Schroeder

Once, when Becky Schroeder was in the fifth grade, she stayed in the car to do her homework while her mother went shopping. Before long, evening came. The sky grew dark. Becky couldn't see well enough to finish her work.

She wished she had something better than a flashlight that glowed in the dark. A glowing light would help her see her work. She wondered if she could invent something that would help people read and write in the dark. The more Becky thought about it, the more interesting the idea became.

Becky mentioned her idea to her father. She told him about the toys she had that glowed in the dark. She knew they contained special substances that gave off light. She wanted to use some of these substances for her own invention.

Becky's father explained that the substances she described were *phosphorescent chemicals*. He doubted her idea would work. Still, he helped Becky get the chemicals she needed for her project.

Becky worked with the chemicals. Finally, she came up with something. It was a phosphorescent sheet. The sheet had horizontal lines that glowed when she put it under a piece of paper. Using the sheet, one could write in a straight line in the dark.

Now Becky had solved one problem. She had invented a sheet that allowed her to write in the dark. But she still couldn't read in the dark. So Becky kept experimenting. At last, she succeeded. She made it possible to use her phosphorescent sheet for both writing and reading in the dark.

Becky's invention was finished. The next step was to obtain a patent for it. As a patent owner, Becky would be the only person who had the right to make or to sell her invention. But it isn't easy to get a patent.

Thousands of people apply for patents every week. All the requests for patents are sent to the U.S. Patent Office in Washington, D.C. Each invention must be checked. The Patent Office must be sure that a similar invention has not already been patented. This checking process can take a long time. It took two years for Becky to receive a patent.

Many people are interested in Becky's invention. They think the phosphorescent sheet might be used by police officers for writing parking tickets. It might also be used by astronauts to read and write in space capsules. The possibilities are endless!

Becky's curiosity continues to grow. So does her desire to solve problems. She is now working on another invention. It will probably be something very useful. Becky likes to invent things that help people.

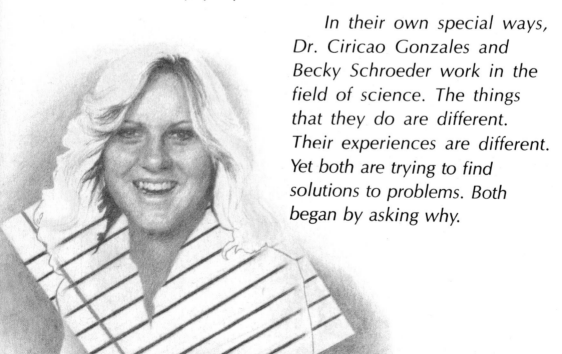

In their own special ways, Dr. Ciricao Gonzales and Becky Schroeder work in the field of science. The things that they do are different. Their experiences are different. Yet both are trying to find solutions to problems. Both began by asking why.

WHAT CAN WE DO?

Alma Whitney

389

Some children in an elementary school in New York wanted to know if they could do anything to help animals that are in danger of becoming extinct.

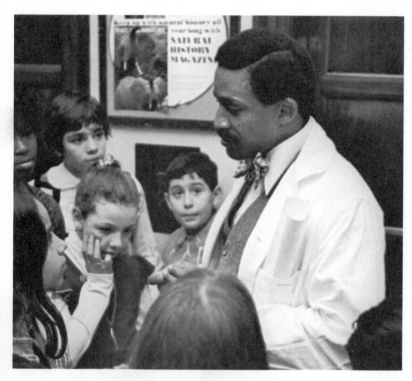

The children went to the American Museum of Natural History to talk to Mr. Gene Agustin. Mr. Agustin is a zoologist, a scientist who studies animals.

"Before we talk about what you can do to help," Mr. Agustin said to the children, "let's try to understand some things about the problem. Do you know why many animals today are in danger of becoming extinct?" Some children said that they had learned DDT has hurt many animals. "You're right," said Mr. Agustin. "DDT and other things that harm animals are sometimes sprayed into the air."

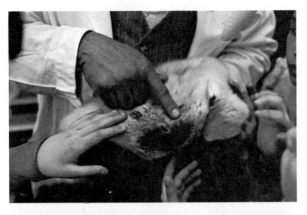

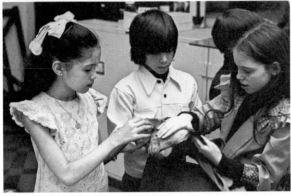

"There are other reasons that many animals are in danger of becoming extinct. Look at this. It's the skin of a baby seal. Can you see this ugly spot where the little seal was hit with a club?"

"Why would anyone want to club a little seal?"

Mr. Agustin explained that hunters club seals to death. Then the seal's fur is used to make coats. So many seals have been killed that now some kinds of seals are in danger of becoming extinct.

"It makes me sad to think about wearing the skin of a baby seal."

391

"Did any of you know that the tiger is also in danger of becoming extinct? People kill tigers for their skins. People will pay a lot of money for a coat or rug made out of tiger's skin."

"What's wrong with people, anyway?"

"I can see you're beginning to understand the problems," said Mr. Agustin. "But there's some good news about tigers. Most tigers live in India. The government of India has made it a crime to hunt tigers. The country has set aside special places where tigers can live safely. We don't know if this will keep the tigers from becoming extinct, but we hope it will. People have *got* to stop killing wild animals for their fur."

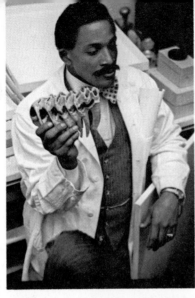

"This tooth comes from another animal in danger of becoming extinct—the Indian elephant."

"But why is the elephant in danger of becoming extinct? Elephants don't have fur."

"No, they don't," explained Mr. Agustin. "But some people kill elephants to get trophies or curios. For example, this is an elephant's foot someone made into an umbrella stand. People also kill elephants for their tusks. Some people feel very proud when they kill a really big animal."

"How could anyone be proud of killing an elephant?"

The children wanted to know if any animals had already been saved from becoming extinct. "We think so," Mr. Agustin told them. "In Ethiopia, for example, there is an animal called the oryx. It's a kind of antelope. People used to kill the oryx for its skin. Then, a few years ago, Ethiopia decided to try to save the oryx. The government sent some of them to the United States to see if a new herd could be formed. Now there is a small herd of oryx in Arizona. It is growing larger each year. So it looks like we may have saved the oryx. We will have to see how well they do in the next few years."

"Well, what can *we* do to save the animals? What *can* we do to help?"

"The first thing to do is learn all you can about the problems facing animals today," Mr. Agustin said. "Tell your families and friends what you learn. Join organizations which are trying to save the world's animals. And write letters to people in the government and tell them how you feel about animals being killed for no good reason."

On the way home,
the children discussed
what they might do
to help save the animals.

When they got back to school
they started telling their
friends about what they had
learned at the museum. They made posters about
animals in danger and hung them in the halls of the
school. They wrote articles for the school newspaper.
Then the children prepared an assembly program
about endangered animals. Here is part of a song
they wrote for the program.
You can sing it to the tune of "The Stars and
Stripes Forever."

We Are All in Danger

**The tigers, the polar bears, too.
And maybe someday even you.
The dodos were here for so long,
But we no longer hear their song.
So let's give a big rousing cheer
For the animals that are still here.
We think that they are very dear,
And we don't want to see them all disappear.**

UNLESS WE GUARD THEM WELL

Perhaps the children of a future day
Between picnics on Venus and the moon
And explorations of the Milky Way
Will come and spend a summer afternoon
Among the quaint old-fashioned people, asking,
"And did you really see a robin, sir?
And even a clover field with cattle basking?
And could you tell us just what daisies were?"
Let us speak carefully of the long ago
Lost days when earth was green, and country air
Was filled with winging song and petaled glow
Lest any yearning listener may declare,
"Oh, I would give the moon if I had heard
A thrush, or ever seen a hummingbird!"

—Jane Merchant

397

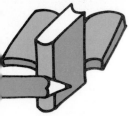

What's the Key?

The *main-idea sentence* states the most important idea of a paragraph. It sums up the other ideas in the paragraph. The main-idea sentence may be at the beginning, middle, or end of a paragraph. Read the following paragraph.

> Spiders come in all sizes and colors. Some spiders are as large as a person's hand. Other spiders fit on the head of a pin. Many spiders are brown or gray. Others have brighter colors.

The paragraph tells how spiders vary in color and size. The first sentence is the main-idea sentence. The other sentences tell about the main idea.

ACTIVITY A   Read each paragraph. Then read the main-idea sentences. On your paper, write the sentence that best states the main idea of the paragraph.

1. Corals are sea animals. They live underwater in colonies. These animals cannot swim or move. They are stuck to the sea floor. The waves and currents bring them food.

Main-idea sentences:
a. They live underwater in colonies.
b. They are stuck to the sea floor.
c. Corals are sea animals.

2. Running does not cost much money. Your whole family can take part. Running is good for your health. It does not take much time to run. Running is popular for many reasons.

Main-idea sentences:
a. Your whole family can take part.
b. Running is popular for many reasons.
c. Running does not cost much money.

ACTIVITY B   Read each paragraph. Find the main-idea sentence and write it on your paper. Then write where the sentence is found in the paragraph: beginning, middle, or end.

1. The United States began with only thirteen states. The number of states grew to thirty by 1849. In 1958, there were forty-eight states. Alaska and Hawaii became the forty-ninth and fiftieth states. The United States has grown in the past two hundred years.

2. Ducks are different from geese or swans. Ducks have shorter necks and wings. Their bills are flatter. Ducks quack or whistle rather than honk.

3. Deep-sea divers often want to study the sea. Recent inventions have helped sea study. New pumps pick things off the sea floor. Underwater lights and cameras help divers. Special boats explore the deep waters.

CYCLES

People learn by being curious and asking questions. They learn to tell what is fact and what is opinion. Scientists study the world around them by being curious. They ask; they observe; they learn. The selections you read were about many different cycles in nature. You followed the cycle of a chick hatching from an egg. You saw a cycle at work in the life of an ant colony. The disappearance of dinosaurs showed you that some cycles can be broken forever.

Thinking About "Cycles"

1. Upon what facts were the stories "All Upon a Stone" and "Hector's 21st Day" based?
2. What facts did you learn about how dinosaurs lived long ago?
3. Why are all the reasons given for the disappearance of dinosaurs merely opinions and not facts?
4. "The City Under the Back Steps" takes you on a trip to an ant city. What are the imaginary events in the story? What are the facts?
5. Why is it important to think carefully about the information you receive and determine whether it is fact or opinion?
6. Write a short report about an ant colony. Use the facts you have learned in "The City Under the Back Steps."

IMPRESSIONS

All of us have feelings and thoughts about ourselves and our worlds. We share these impressions with others in different ways. Language, painting, music, and dance are only a few of the ways we might choose to share our impressions with other people.

In "Impressions," you will read about some of the ways people have chosen to share their impressions with others. Some of the selections are nonfictional—they are about actual people and events. Others are fictional—they are about imaginary people and events. There are selections that will teach you how to build a gocart and how to make a house of cards. You will read about a man whose special talent helps someone to see.

As you read, think about your impressions of the ways people choose to express themselves. Think about the ways in which art, music, and dance can bring about important changes in people's lives. How do you share your impressions with others?

THE WONDERFUL WORDS

Never let a thought shrivel and die
For want of a way to say it,
For English is a wonderful game
And all of you can play it.
All that you do is match the words
To the brightest thoughts in your head
So that they come out clear and true
And handsomely groomed and fed—
For many of the loveliest things
Have never yet been said.
Words are the food and dress of thought,
They give it its body and swing,
And everyone's longing today to hear
Some fresh and beautiful thing.
But only words can free a thought
From its prison behind your eyes.
Maybe your mind is holding now
A marvelous new surprise!

—Mary O'Neill

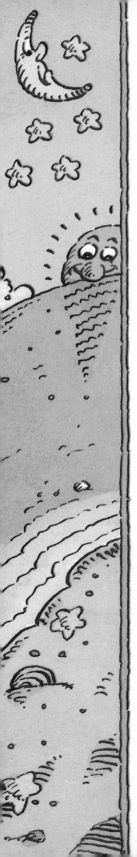

The Walrus and the Carpenter

Lewis Carroll

This is a well-known poem from Lewis Carroll's Alice in Wonderland. Perhaps you have read it yourself or have had someone read it to you. Maybe you have even heard someone say parts of it from memory. It is a poem that can be enjoyed through both silent and oral reading.

After you have read the poem silently, you and your classmates may enjoy assigning roles and reading it aloud. You might also invite other classmates to pantomime some of the roles.

First Reader: The sun was shining on the sea,
    Shining with all his might:
He did his very best to make
    The billows smooth and bright—
And this was odd, because it was
    The middle of the night.

The moon was shining sulkily,
    Because she thought the sun
Had got no business to be there
    After the day was done—

Second Reader: "It's very rude of him," she said,
    "To come and spoil the fun!"

First Reader: The sea was wet as wet could be,
    The sands were dry as dry.
You could not see a cloud, because
    No cloud was in the sky:
No birds were flying overhead—
    There were no birds to fly.

404

The Walrus and the Carpenter
    Were walking close at hand:
They wept like anything to see
    Such quantities of sand:

Third and
Fourth Readers: "If this were only cleared away,"
    They said, "it would be grand!"

Third Reader: "If seven maids with seven mops
    Swept it for half a year,
Do you suppose," the Walrus said,
    "That they could get it clear?"

Fourth Reader: "I doubt it," said the Carpenter,
    And shed a bitter tear.

Third Reader: "O Oysters, come and walk with us!"
    The Walrus did beseech.
"A pleasant walk, a pleasant talk,
    Along the briny beach:
We cannot do with more than four,
    To give a hand to each."

First Reader: The eldest Oyster looked at him,
      But never a word he said:
The eldest Oyster winked his eye,
      And shook his heavy head—
Meaning to say he did not choose
      To leave the oyster bed.

But four young Oysters hurried up,
      All eager for the treat:
Their coats were brushed, their faces washed,
      Their shoes were clean and neat—
And this was odd, because, you know,
      They hadn't any feet.

Four other Oysters followed them,
      And yet another four;
And thick and fast they came at last,
      And more, and more, and more—
All hopping through the frothy waves,
      And scrambling to the shore.

The Walrus and the Carpenter
   Walked on a mile or so,
And then they rested on a rock
   Conveniently low:
And all the little Oysters stood
   And waited in a row.

Third Reader: "The time has come," the Walrus said,
   "To talk of many things
Of shoes—and ships—and sealing wax—
   Of cabbages—and kings—
And why the sea is boiling hot—
   And whether pigs have wings."

Chorus: "But wait a bit," the Oysters cried,
   "Before we have our chat;
For some of us are out of breath,
   And all of us are fat!"
Fourth Reader: "No hurry!" said the Carpenter.
First Reader: They thanked him much for that.

Third Reader: "A loaf of bread," the Walrus said,
   "Is what we chiefly need:
Pepper and vinegar besides
   Are very good indeed—
Now, if you're ready, Oysters dear,
   We can begin to feed."

Chorus: "But not on us!" the Oysters cried,
Turning a little blue.
"After such kindness, that would be
A dismal thing to do!"

Third Reader: "The night is fine," the Walrus said.
"Do you admire the view?"

"It was so kind of you to come!
And you are very nice!"

Fourth Reader: The Carpenter said nothing but
"Cut us another slice.
I wish you were not quite so deaf—
I've had to ask you twice!"

Third Reader: "It seems a shame," the Walrus said,
"To play them such a trick.
After we've brought them out so far,
And made them trot so quick."

Fourth Reader: The Carpenter said nothing but
"The butter's spread too thick!"

Third Reader: "I weep for you," the Walrus said:
"I deeply sympathize."

First Reader: With sobs and tears he sorted out
Those of the largest size,
Holding his pocket-handkerchief
Before his streaming eyes.

Fourth Reader: "O Oysters," said the Carpenter,
"You've had a pleasant run!
Shall we be trotting home again?"

Chorus: But answer came there none—

First Reader: And this was scarcely odd, because
They'd eaten every one.

THE SEEING STICK

Jane Yolen

Once in the ancient walled citadel of Peking,
there lived an emperor.
He had only one daughter,
and her name was Hwei Ming.

Now this daughter wore ivory combs
to smooth back her long black hair.
On her tiny feet, she wore embroidered slippers.
Her robes were woven of the finest silks.

But rather than making her happy,
these possessions made her sad;
for Hwei Ming was blind.
All the beautiful handicrafts in the kingdom
brought her no pleasure at all.

Her father was also sad
that his only daughter was blind.
But he could not cry for her.
He was the emperor, after all,
and had given up weeping
when he came to the throne.

Yet still he had hope
that one day Hwei Ming might be able to see.
So he decided that anyone who could help her
would be rewarded
with a fortune in jewels.
He sent word of his offer
to the Inner and Outer cities of Peking
and to all the towns and villages
for hundreds of miles around.

Monks came, of course,
with their prayers and prayer wheels.
With these things, they thought
they could help Hwei Ming see.
Magicians came, of course,
with their charms and spells.
With these things, they thought
they could help Hwei Ming see.
Physicians came, of course,
with their potions and pins.
With these things, they thought
they could help Hwei Ming see.

But nothing could help.
Hwei Ming had been blind
from the day of her birth,
and no one could cure her.

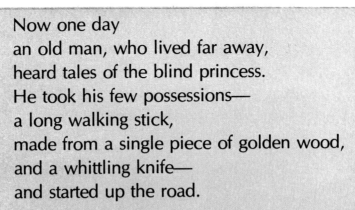

Now one day
an old man, who lived far away,
heard tales of the blind princess.
He took his few possessions—
a long walking stick,
made from a single piece of golden wood,
and a whittling knife—
and started up the road.

At last, the old man,
his clothes tattered by his travels,
stopped by the gate of the Outer City.

The guards at the gate
did not want to let in such a ragged old man.
"Grandfather, go home.
There is nothing here for such as you,"
they said.

The old man
touched each of their faces in turn
with his rough fingers.
"So young," he said,
"and already so old."
He turned as if to go.
Then he propped his walking stick
against his side
and reached into his shirt
for his whittling knife.

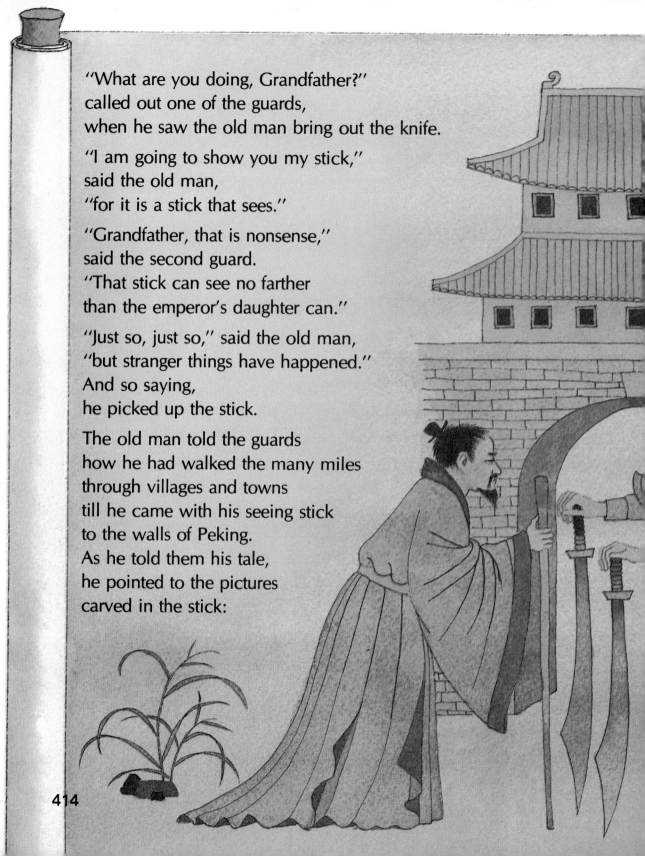

"What are you doing, Grandfather?"
called out one of the guards,
when he saw the old man bring out the knife.

"I am going to show you my stick,"
said the old man,
"for it is a stick that sees."

"Grandfather, that is nonsense,"
said the second guard.
"That stick can see no farther
than the emperor's daughter can."

"Just so, just so," said the old man,
"but stranger things have happened."
And so saying,
he picked up the stick.

The old man told the guards
how he had walked the many miles
through villages and towns
till he came with his seeing stick
to the walls of Peking.
As he told them his tale,
he pointed to the pictures
carved in the stick:

an old man,
his home,
the long walk,
the walls of Peking.
Then as the guards watched,
the old man carved their portraits
into the wood.

The two guards looked at each other
in amazement and delight.
Indeed, they had never seen
such carving skill.
"Surely this is something
the guards at the wall
of the Inner City should see," they said.
So, taking the old man by the arm,
they guided him
to the great walls of the Inner City.

415

When these guards saw the seeing stick,
they were surprised and delighted.
"Carve our faces, too,"
they begged like children.
So, laughing and touching their faces
as any fond grandfather would,
the old man did as they bid.

In no time at all,
the guards of the Inner City
took the old man by his arm.
They led him to the wall
of the Innermost City
and in through the gate
to the great wooden doors
of the emperor's palace.

They arrived at the throne room
of the palace,
leading the old man by the arm.
The emperor's daughter, Hwei Ming,
was sitting by her father's side,
silent, sightless, and still.
As the guards finished telling
of the wonderful pictures
carved on the golden stick,
the princess clapped her hands.
"Oh, I wish I could see
that wonderful stick,"
she said.

"Just so, just so," said the old man.
"I will show it to you.
It is no ordinary piece of wood,
but a stick that sees."

"What nonsense," said her father
in a voice so low it was almost a growl.

But the princess did not hear him.
She had already bent toward
the sound of the old man's voice.
"A seeing stick?"

The old man did not say anything for a moment.
Then he leaned forward
and touched Hwei Ming's head
and patted her cheek.
She was a princess,
but she was also still a child.

417

Then the old man began to tell again
the story of his long journey to Peking.
He carved the wooden doors,
the emperor's palace,
and the princess,
into the golden wood.

When he finished,
the old man reached out
for the princess's small hands.
He took her tiny fingers in his
and placed them on the stick.
Finger on finger,
he helped her trace the likenesses.

"Feel the long flowing hair of the princess,"
the old man said.
"Grown as she herself has grown,
straight and true."
Hwei Ming touched the carved stick.
"Now feel your own long hair," he said.
And she did.

"Feel the lines in the old man's face,"
he said,
"from years of worry and years of joy."
He placed the stick in her hands again,
and the princess's slim fingers
felt the carved stick.

Then he put her fingers onto his face
and traced the same lines there.
It was the first time
the princess had touched
another person's face
since she was a very small girl.

The princess jumped up from her throne
and held out her hands before her.
"Guards, O guards," she cried out.
"Come here to me."
The guards lifted up their faces
to the Princess Hwei Ming's hands.
Her fingers,
like little breezes,
brushed their eyes and noses and mouths,
and then found each one on the carved stick.

Hwei Ming turned to her father.
She reached out
and her fingers ran eagerly
through his hair
and down his nose and cheek
and rested curiously
on the tear they found there.
That was strange, indeed,
for had not the emperor
given up crying when he came to the throne?

They brought her
through the streets of the city.
Princess Hwei Ming
touched men and women
and children as they passed.
Till at last
she stood before the great walls of Peking
and felt the stones themselves.

Then she turned to the old man.
Her voice was bright
and full of laughter.
"Tell me another tale," she said.

"Tomorrow, if you wish," he replied.

For each tomorrow as long as he lived,
the old man told the princess a story.
Each time
he carved wonderful images
in the stick of golden wood.

As the princess listened,
she grew eyes on the tips of her fingers.
At least that is what
she told the other blind children
whom she taught to see as she saw.
Certainly it was as true
as saying she had a seeing stick.

But the blind Princess Hwei Ming
believed that both things were true.
So did all the blind children
in her city of Peking.
And so did the blind old man.

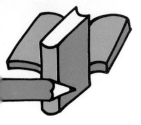

What's the Idea?

When you take notes from an encyclopedia for a report, you write someone else's ideas in your own words. Changing the words in a sentence without changing the meaning of the sentence is called *paraphrasing*.

It is important to learn how to paraphrase for two reasons. First, information in your own words is easier to remember. Second, an author's writing belongs to the author. You must use your own words for your own writing.

Read this sentence from an encyclopedia:

Congress is the law-making branch of government.

There are many ways to paraphrase this sentence. The following are three examples:

1. Congress is the branch of the government that makes our laws.
2. Congress makes our laws.
3. Laws are made by Congress.

Notice that the second and third examples just paraphrase the most important words in the sentence.

Sometimes you may want to paraphrase an entire paragraph. Unimportant words may be omitted, but the meaning of the paragraph should stay the same.

Read the paragraph below and its paraphrase.

Original Paragraph

A pyramid is a large structure. It usually has sides shaped like triangles and a square base. In centuries past, some kings and queens were buried in pyramids.

Paraphrase

Pyramids are large buildings. Most pyramids have square bottoms and sides like triangles. In the past, pyramids were used as places for burying kings and queens.

ACTIVITY A   Write a paraphrase of each sentence on your paper.

1. City officials serve two-year terms.
2. Some animals sting their enemies in order to protect themselves.
3. Dolphins are the brightest of all sea creatures.
4. Some people think dogs make better pets than cats.
5. Scientists use microscopes to study some forms of plant life.

ACTIVITY B   Write a paraphrase of the paragraph below on your paper.

Glaciers are huge bodies of ice. They form high on mountains and in other very cold areas. Some lakes were formed by melting glaciers that slid down mountains.

PAN-AMERICA

The Painting on the Wall

Cars drive up. People stroll by, then stop to stare. Everybody wants to get a good look at the wall. THE WALL? Yes, for on this wall is a painting—a large, outdoor mural. The people enjoy the bold and graceful designs in the painting. They like its bright, tropical colors.

How did this painting happen to be on the wall? A group of young artists in California decided to make a wall painting in their neighborhood. Their neighborhood is the Mission District of San Francisco, where many people of Latin-American descent live. Three of the artists are Mexican-Americans. Their names are Patricia Rodriguez, Irene Perez, and Graciela Carrillo. The fourth is Consuelo Mendez, who is from Venezuela. The four women call themselves *Mujeres Muralistas,* which means "women who paint murals."

The mural they have created is called *Pan-America*. It shows the history and traditions of the people in the Mission District. It also shows everyday life in the neighborhood. One part of the mural shows family life. Another shows familiar figures from Hispanic legends and folktales.

Through the beauty of this mural, the people of the neighborhood feel pride in their heritage. The artists, too, are proud to be able to share their talent and their art with visitors, friends, and neighbors—right in the middle of day-to-day activities on the streets where they live.

CARD HOUSES

Dina Anastasio

The other day, while visiting my family, I came upon an old photograph. It was a picture of me when I was nine years old. In it, I was sitting at a card table. And, on the table, was a tall, skinny house— made entirely of cards.

It's funny, but I can still remember that house. It was all angles and peaks. I remember being afraid to smile too much when my mother took that picture, for fear the house would fall down. Of course, it did fall down as soon as the picture was taken. My card houses almost *always* fell down. That time it was the cat's fault. The flash of the camera frightened him, and he jumped

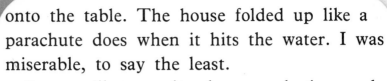

onto the table. The house folded up like a parachute does when it hits the water. I was miserable, to say the least.

I can still remember how much time and patience it took to build a card house. It usually took about two hours, or maybe it just seemed that long. I always started with two cards that I rested carefully against each other at exactly the right angle. Then I put four cards around them for walls and used two more cards for a ceiling. Now I had a first floor. From then on, there was nowhere to go but up. But first I rested a fence against each side of the front door. Of course, no one ever passed through the door, not even two nine-year-old fingers. I was always afraid my houses would fall if I went near them.

In all the houses I ever built, the cards were in perfect order, from the lowest to the highest. I used only twos, threes, fours, and fives for the lower floors. For the middle floors, I used sixes, sevens, eights, and nines. I didn't often reach the upper floors without my house falling. But when I did, I used tens, jacks, queens, and kings for these floors. The aces I saved for last. They became towers and steeples.

The ace of spades was always the last card to be put on a house. I would hold my breath as I picked it up. Carefully I would place the ace on the very top of my house. Then I could sit back in my chair and relax. But, more often than not, at that moment, the whole house would fall together like the pages of a book.

I guess there are many ways to build card houses. But I could never figure out more than two. The first was the kind described above—a tall skinny thing that looked like the Empire State Building.

The second kind was a much more elaborate building that went off in many directions, and looked like a doll house. This was a more exciting house to build, for it had real rooms and openings that looked like little doors.

My houses grew taller and taller as I grew older and older. I remember thinking, each time I began a new house, that if I

could just get to the ace of spades, I wouldn't mind if my house fell down. For the fun, of course, was in the building. Once a card house is built, you see, there really aren't any uses for it. No one can live there, and even if they could, they would be bumping their heads on those narrow ceilings all the time. I know! I lived in an attic once that had a roof that came to a peak. I had a headache the whole time I lived there!

Sometimes, in building my houses, I reached the point where my ace of spades was resting snugly in the clouds. At such times I would sit back in my chair and look at my house for a long time. I hated it when the cat or the wind knocked my house down. But when I did—now that was something else. When I was ready, I would gently touch the two of clubs (always one of the bottom cards), and my house of cards would collapse in a heap. And then I would begin again.

THE HOUSE OF CARDS
Jean-Baptiste-Simeon Chardin
Courtesy of the National Gallery of Art, Andrew W. Mellon Collection, Washington, D.C.

ALL ABOUT GOCARTS

David Newton, age 13

I'll begin by listing the basic things you'll need to make a gocart.

TOOLS

Pencil
Ruler
Saw (carpenter or jig)
Hammer
Drill (electric or hand)
Pliers

MATERIALS

Wood

· A board four or five feet long and one and one-half or two feet wide

2 feet — 5 feet

3 feet

· A two-by-four board (a board two inches thick and four inches wide) about three feet long

Wheels (4, about one foot in diameter)

Axles (2, about two and one-half feet long)

Nails (lots of three-inch nails and some shorter nails)

Bolt (four inches long, with a washer and a nut. A nut is a small metal block with a hole through the center that screws onto a bolt. A washer is a flat piece of metal with a hole in it that makes the nut fit tightly on the bolt.)

Rope (six feet long)

Paint and decals (optional)

WHERE TO GET MATERIALS

Scrap piles, lumber or junkyards, hardware stores, or around your house

(I get my wheels and axles from discarded shopping carts, baby buggies, strollers, or tricycles.)

HOW TO DO IT

The Frame   Start with the frame. Use the board four or five feet long and one and one-half or two feet wide for your frame. If your wood isn't very strong, you may have to use two pieces of the same size, one on top of the other. Or, for extra strength, you could simply nail 3 two-by-fours lengthwise along the board you are using for the frame. Now for the shape of your frame. You could choose one of the shapes shown at the top of the next page.

432

Draw the shape you want your frame to be on your board using a pencil and a ruler. Then cut it out with a saw. The front part should be shorter across than the back, so the front wheels will turn easily without hitting the frame when you steer.

The Axles and Wheels

The size of the wheels is very important. Try to find wheels that are about one foot in diameter. If your wheels are too big or too small, you will have problems.

If your wheels are too small, they will not support the weight of your cart. If they are too big, they will not turn easily. Also, if your cart is too high off the ground, you will tip over easily.

The length of your axles is also very important. Each axle should be about eight inches longer than the width of your frame. The back wheels shouldn't extend more than six inches beyond the frame on either side. If they do, the axle will bend when you sit on your cart.

The back wheels are easy to put on and should be done first. (I save the problem work for last.) Follow these steps:

1. Put back wheels on axle.
2. Tighten nuts to hold wheels in place.

3. Place axle across frame one-half foot from rear of frame.

4. Attach axle with nails by pounding nails halfway into frame.
5. Bend nails around axle to hold it in place.

For added support, you could nail a two-by-four board between the frame and the axle.

I find it easier to attach the front axle to the frame before I put the front wheels on the axle. Cut the two-by-four board so that it is about eight inches shorter than your axle. Lay the axle on your two-by-four so that the axle extends about four inches beyond the two-by-four board on each end. Attach the axle to the two-by-four with nails the same way that you attached the back axle to the frame.

Drill a hole one-half inch in diameter through the *middle* of the two-by-four, bypassing the axle. Now drill a hole in your frame about one foot from the front of the frame to line up with the hole in the two-by-four. Fasten your frame and the two-by-four together carefully with a bolt, washer, and nut. Very good!

Attach the front wheels to their axle the same way you attached the back wheels to their axle.

The Steering   Nail a rope or a piece of wire to each side of the front two-by-four near the wheels. To turn to the left, pull on the left rope. To turn to the right, pull on the right rope.

Alternatives   If you are disappointed because you don't have some of these parts, don't worry. There is always another way. I HAVE A SOLUTION FOR EVERYTHING! For example, if you can't find an axle for the front wheels, get some nails at least four inches long. Hold one wheel up to one end of the two-by-four and hammer the nail through the hole in the wheel and into the two-by-four. Nail the other wheel on the other end of the two-by-four in the same way. No axle is needed.

If you can't get a nut and a bolt, you can use a very long, strong nail to attach the front two-by-four to the frame. Simply hammer the nail through the frame and the two-by-four in the same place that you would have put the bolt. Just be sure to hammer down the end of the nail (if it comes through the bottom of the wood) so you won't hurt yourself on it.

If you want to add extra things, go right ahead. This is your gocart with class. Never give up!

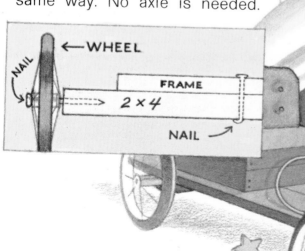

All Stories Are Anansi's

Harold Courlander

In the beginning, all tales and stories belonged to Nyame, the Sky God. But Kwaku Anansi, the spider, wanted to be the owner of all the stories known in the world, and he went to Nyame and offered to buy them.

The Sky God said: "I am willing to sell the stories, but the price is high. Many people have come to me offering to buy, but the price was too high for them. Rich and powerful families have not been able to pay. Do you think you can do it?"

Anansi replied to the Sky God: "I can do it. What is the price?"

"My price is three things," the Sky God said. "I must first have Mmoboro, the hornets. I must then have Onini, the great python. I must then have Osebo, the leopard. For these things I will sell you the right to tell all stories.

Anansi said: "I will bring them."

He went home and made his plans. He first cut a gourd from a vine and made a small hole in it. He took a large calabash and filled it with water. He went to the tree where the hornets lived. He poured some of the water over himself, so that he was dripping. He threw some water over the hornets, so that they too were dripping. Then he put the calabash on his head, as though to protect himself from a storm, and called out to the hornets: "Are you foolish people? Why do you stay in the rain that is falling?"

The hornets answered: "Where shall we go?"

"Go here, in this dry gourd," Anansi told them.

The hornets thanked him and flew into the gourd through the small hole. When the last of them had entered, Anansi plugged the hole with a ball of grass, saying: "Oh, yes, but you are really foolish people!"

He took his gourd full of hornets to Nyame, the Sky God. The Sky God accepted them. He said: "There are two more things."

Anansi returned to the forest and cut a long bamboo pole and some strong vines. Then he walked toward the house of Onini, the python, talking to himself. He said: "My wife is wrong. I say he is longer and stronger. My wife says he is shorter and weaker. I give him more respect. She gives him less respect. Is she right, or am I right? I am right, he is longer. I am right, he is stronger."

When Onini, the python, heard Anansi talking to himself, he said: "Why are you arguing this way with yourself?"

The spider replied: "Ah, I have had a dispute with my wife. She says you are shorter and weaker than this bamboo pole. I say you are longer and stronger."

Onini said: "It's useless and silly to argue. Bring the pole, and we will measure."

So Anansi laid the pole on the ground, and the python came and stretched himself out beside it.

"You seem a little short," Anansi said.

The python stretched further.

"A little more," Anansi said.

"I can stretch no more," Onini said.

"When you stretch at one end, you get shorter at the other end," Anansi said. "Let me tie you at the front so you don't slip."

He tied Onini's head to the pole. Then he went to the other end and tied the tail to the pole. He wrapped the vines all around Onini until the python couldn't move.

"Onini," Anansi said, "it turns out that my wife was right, and I was wrong. You are shorter than the pole and weaker. My opinion wasn't as good as my wife's. But you were even more foolish than I, and you are now my prisoner."

Anansi carried the python to Nyame, the Sky God, who said: "There is one thing more."

Osebo, the leopard, was next. Anansi went into the forest and dug a deep pit where the leopard was accustomed to walk. He covered it with small branches and leaves and put dust on it, so that it was impossible to tell where the pit was. Anansi went away and hid. When Osebo came prowling in the black of night, he stepped into the trap Anansi had prepared and fell to the bottom. Anansi heard the sound of the leopard falling, and he said: "Ah, Osebo, you are half-foolish!"

When morning came, Anansi went to the pit and saw the leopard there.

"Osebo," he asked, "what are you doing in this hole?"

"I have fallen into a trap," Osebo said. "Help me out."

"I would gladly help you," Anansi said. "But I'm sure that if I bring you out, I will have no thanks for it. You will get hungry, and later on you will be wanting to eat me and my children."

"I swear it won't happen!" Osebo said.

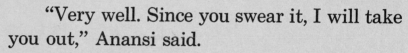

"Very well. Since you swear it, I will take you out," Anansi said.

He bent a tall green tree toward the ground, so that its top was over the pit, and he tied it that way. Then he tied a rope to the top of the tree and dropped the other end of it into the pit.

"Tie this to your tail," he said.

Osebo tied the rope to his tail.

"Is it well tied?"

"Yes, it is well tied," the leopard said.

"In that case," Anansi said, "you are not merely half-foolish, you are all-foolish."

And he took his knife and cut the other rope, the one that held the tree bowed to the ground. The tree straightened up with a snap, pulling Osebo out of the hole. He hung in the air, head downward, twisting and turning. And while he hung this way, Anansi killed him with his weapons.

441

Then he took the body of the leopard and carried it to Nyame, the Sky God, saying: "Here is the third thing. Now I have paid the price."

Nyame said to him: "Kwaku Anansi, great warriors and chiefs have tried, but they have been unable to do it. You have done it. Therefore, I will give you the stories. From this day onward, all stories belong to you. Whenever people tell a story, they must acknowledge that it is Anansi's tale."

In this way Anansi, the spider, became the owner of all stories that are told.

BREAKING THE CODE

Have you ever thought as you were reading that you were really breaking a code? To break a code, you need to know certain things about the code. For example, if you want to break the reading code, you need to know that one letter can stand for more than one sound.

Look at the letter *g* in the words below. What two different sounds does the letter *g* stand for in these words?

game   giant

To break the reading code, you also need to know that sometimes two or more letters spell one sound. What sound is spelled by the underlined letters in these words?

fire   phone

muffin   half   laugh

Now read the words in Column 1 or listen as your teacher reads them. Notice the underlined letters. What sound is the same in all three words? How many ways is this sound spelled? What letter or letters spell this sound?

Column 1	Column 2
leopard	people
pet	be
bread	meat

Next read the words in Column 2. What sound is the same in these words? How many ways is it spelled? What letter or letters spell this sound?

Compare the words in both columns. What do you notice about the underlined letters?

Now do you see why reading is like breaking a code? When you read, you match the sounds of spoken English with the letters in the written words. The more you know about the different ways letters are used to stand for sounds, the better reader you will be. How good are you at breaking the code?

The Pink Slipper

Carol H. Behrman

Anna Pavlova stood in the long hall. She looked about.

There were so many doors! Which was the right one? She had made her way through many halls, all lined with large black doors. Now she was not at all sure that she had come in the right direction.

A footman passed, dressed in bright red. He noticed the confusion of the thin, small, wide-eyed girl.

"Are you lost?"

"I'm looking for the Director's office."

"You must be a new student here, little one." He smiled down at her.

Anna drew herself up to her full height, which still made her look far younger than her fifteen years. "I have been at the Imperial Ballet School almost five years!" she declared, lifting her chin proudly. "I am a senior pupil. I have a message for the Director from the wardrobe mistress."

The footman laughed. "Of course then,

an old-timer like yourself must know that
the office of the Director is at the end
of this hall."

"Of course!" Anna replied. "I just
forgot." She walked gracefully down the hall,
her head high, her step firm. She did not know
where the Director's office was because she had
never been there. No one went to the Director's
office without being called. And that happened
for only the most terrifying reasons. It was very
unusual for Anna to be going there now, but the
Director had not sent the costume list for the
new ballet. The wardrobe mistress needed it and
had sent Anna to get it.

Anna stood still for a minute at the end of

the hall. Then she knocked and entered.

The Director was not alone. Mr. Gerdt, the ballet teacher, was with him. Anna feared Mr. Gerdt almost as much as the Director. He was always bullying her, always asking for more, more. He was never satisfied.

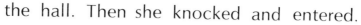

"Ah, the little Pavlova." Mr. Gerdt beckoned Anna to draw near.

As she approached, she noticed a pale pink ballet slipper set all alone on a table between the two men.

Her eyes, with a will of their own, fastened upon the slipper. There was something about that slipper—something that seemed to lift Anna out of this time and place.

"That is Taglioni's slipper," the Director said. "It is for our museum."

Anna gasped. Taglioni! The name caused a thrill to pass through her. Taglioni—the greatest ballerina of all time.

"Alas," the Director continued. "There is no one who could wear that shoe today. Taglioni's feet were tiny—tiny and perfect."

Mr. Gerdt looked at Anna's shining eyes. She was staring at the slipper, hardly aware that anyone else was in the room. He leaned over and whispered in the Director's ear.

The Director smiled. "How would you like to try it on?" he asked Anna.

As in a dream, Anna pulled off one of her black shoes. She was dazed. No student at the Imperial Ballet School ever received even the smallest amount of praise. In all her years of hard work, the nearest thing to praise she had ever heard was a hard-won, "Well, that's a bit better, isn't it?" Anna felt that she was good. The other students praised her. But the teachers—never!

And here she was, putting on Taglioni's slipper! She stood, perfectly balanced on one tiny foot, and pulled on the pink slipper.

"Why, it fits perfectly!" came a surprised woman's voice from the other side of the room. Anna looked up. She hadn't noticed the woman seated in the corner.

The woman leaned forward into the light. It was the prima ballerina of the Imperial Ballet.

Anna's face turned red as she pulled off the slipper. To be in such company!

"Are you Pavlova?" the ballerina asked.

"Yes, Madame."

"I have seen you dance. You are very good. Go on working hard." And the prima ballerina settled back into the shadows.

Still in a dream, Anna received the
list from the Director and brought it back to
the wardrobe mistress. But the voice of the
prima ballerina echoed in her mind.

"You are very good!"

And she had worn Taglioni's slipper!

She, little Anna Pavlova, was going to
be a great dancer. She had known this in her
heart ever since she was a little girl, dancing
as soon as she walked, always dancing. But
now, Anna knew it in her mind as well.

Dancing was Anna's life. One day,
through the perfection of her art, she would
show the beauty and poetry of ballet to
Russia and to all the world.

"I want to dance for everybody in the
world," Anna Pavlova said. And this was the
dream for which she lived her life. After
graduation from the Imperial Ballet School,
Pavlova was accepted into the ballet company.
She soon became one of the leading dancers,
then prima ballerina. But her greatest
contributions to ballet came later, when she
began to dance outside of Russia. Her tours
took her all over the world. Her great dancing
created a love of ballet everywhere she went.

Another Kind of Dance...Tap

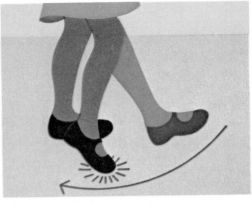

→ Bend knee, swing foot forward in an arc, tap floor with toe as it goes by other foot.

← Swing foot backward in an arc, tap floor with toe as it swings back.

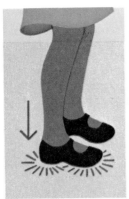

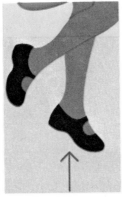

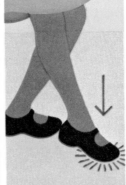

● Step tap

↰ Hop from right foot to left foot

↑ Extend leg forward, point toe, tap floor with toe

⤓ Bend knee, tap floor with toe

Right Foot		Left Foot	
→ Tap forward	↰ Hop to left foot	⇐ Tap forward	⤳ Hop to right foot
← Tap backward	↑ Point tap	⇒ Tap backward	↑ Point tap
● Step tap	⤓ Toe tap	○ Step tap	⤓ Toe tap
			R Rest

I'm Looking Over a Four Leaf Clover

Music by Harry Woods   Words by Mort Dixon   Dance steps by Cle Kinney

PETER AND THE WOLF

Sylvia Chermak

A pantomime is a play in which the actors use only actions, facial expressions, and movements to tell the story. The actors in a pantomime do not speak. If there are narrators, they describe what is happening while the actors act out the story.

CHARACTERS

Peter   **Grandfather**   **Bird**
Duck   **Wolf**   **Hunters**
Cat   **Three Narrators**

SETTING

A Meadow

There is a fence with a gate along the left side of the meadow. A low stone wall runs along the back and the right side of the meadow. Upstage right, a tree stands in front of the wall. Flowers grow in the meadow, and there is a pond near the back of the meadow.

As the curtain rises, Three Narrators *sit on stools, downstage right.* Bird *is asleep, its head resting under one wing.*

Peter *dances onto the stage, looks around, opens the gate, runs into the meadow, skips about, and bends over to pick a flower.*

First Narrator: Early one morning, Peter opened the gate and went into the big, green meadow. On the branch of a big tree sat a little bird who was Peter's friend.

Peter stares at Bird, *who begins to stir, wakens, raises its head, and looks about with quick bird-like movements.* Bird *sees* Peter.

Second Narrator: As Peter continued to dance around in the meadow, he suddenly saw the bird and stopped in front of the tree to look at it.

Peter *continues to stand in front of the tree, looking at* Bird.

Third Narrator: When the bird saw Peter, it chirped at him gaily, "All's quiet here."

Duck *waddles in and stops briefly near the gate. Duck walks to the gate, smiles, waddles through it, stops a moment, then waddles over to the edge of the pond.*

First Narrator: Soon a duck came waddling in. The duck was delighted to see that Peter had not closed the gate and decided to have a nice swim in the cool, deep pond in the meadow.

Bird *flies to* Duck. Duck *dives into the pond and swims around. All this time,* Peter *has been* *watching them with interest from the other side of the meadow.*

Second Narrator: When the little bird saw the duck, it flew down and settled in the grass beside the duck and talked to it. "What kind of bird are you anyway, if you can't even fly?" asked the bird. To this the duck replied, "What kind of bird are *you,* if you can't swim?" Then the duck dived into the pond. They argued and argued—the duck swimming in the pond, and the little bird hopping back and forth along the bank.

Cat *creeps in, sneaks along behind the fence, and comes up behind* Bird *at the edge of the pond.*

Third Narrator: Suddenly, something caught Peter's eye. It was a cat crawling through the grass. The cat said to itself, "Now that the bird is busy arguing with the duck, I'll just grab it!" On its quiet paws, the cat drew closer to the bird.

Cat *lunges at* Bird *and misses. Then* Cat *follows* Bird *over to* *the tree.* Cat *continues to walk about, looking longingly at* Bird *in the tree.*

Second Narrator: "Look out! Look out!" cried Peter—and the bird flew quickly into the tree; while from the middle of the pond, the duck quacked angrily at the cat. The cat walked fiercely round and round the tree and thought, "Is it worth climbing up there to try to catch the bird? By the time I get there, the bird will have flown away."

Grandfather *enters, leaning on his cane, his knees bent. He walks slowly but firmly over to the fence.* Grandfather *shakes his fist angrily at* Peter. Peter *boldly dances away from* Grandfather. Grandfather *takes* Peter *very firmly by the hand, drags him through the gate, locks it, and goes out.* Peter *hangs back but is dragged along, offstage.*

Third Narrator: All at once, Grandfather appeared. He was angry because Peter had gone into the meadow. "The meadow is a dangerous place," he cried to Peter. "What if a wolf should come out of the forest? What would you do then?" But Peter paid no attention to Grandfather. Children like Peter are not afraid of wolves. So Grandfather took Peter by the hand, locked the gate, and led him home.

Wolf *creeps onto stage and looks around fiercely.* Cat *jumps up onto a tree branch.* Duck *begins to quack loudly and flap its wings in fear.*

First Narrator: No sooner had Peter gone than a big wolf *did* come out of the forest. At once, the cat sprang up into the tree. The duck quacked in great excitement. In its excitement, the duck jumped out of the pond. The wolf was getting nearer and nearer and nearer—closer and closer.

Duck *begins to waddle about awkwardly, as* Wolf *first circles* Duck *and then begins to chase around* Duck *in smaller circles.* Duck *runs off to the right.* Wolf *runs off to the right.* Narrators *look off after them.*

Second Narrator: There seemed to be no escape for the duck. It made one last effort to escape the wolf and ran into the forest with the wolf running after. Poor duck never had a chance! The wolf swallowed the duck in one gulp.

Wolf *re-enters, looking very pleased, rubbing its stomach and licking its lips.* Wolf *goes over to the tree and begins to circle the tree slowly.* Peter *enters quietly from the left and stands behind the gate, watching.* Peter *exits.* Peter *re-enters, carrying a rope.* Peter *walks to the side of the tree and stands on the wall. He grabs a branch of the tree, then pulls himself onto the tree.*

Third Narrator: Now this was how things stood. The cat was sitting on one branch up in the tree, the bird on another—not too close to the cat. The wolf was walking round and round the tree, looking at them both with greedy eyes. In the meantime, Peter, without the slightest fear, stood watching all that was going on. Presently, Peter ran out and returned quickly with a piece of strong rope. He went over to the low wall behind the tree, climbed up on it, and from there climbed over into the tree.

Bird *flies down and begins to hop around* Wolf. Wolf *sits under the tree and occasionally lunges at* Bird. Peter *slowly lets down a lasso from his perch in the tree, dangling it near* Wolf's *tail. The lasso drops behind* Wolf, *and, unseen by the audience, wraps around* Wolf's *tail.* Peter *begins to pull on the lasso, and* Wolf *jumps about wildly, trying to get its tail loose.*

Second Narrator: Peter said to the bird, "Fly down and circle around the wolf, but make sure the wolf does not catch you!" The bird got closer and closer to the wolf and almost touched the wolf's head with its wings. The wolf snapped angrily at the bird, but the bird always jumped back just in time. How that bird did bother the wolf! And, oh, how that wolf tried to catch the bird! But the bird was too clever for the wolf, and the wolf simply couldn't do anything about it. Meanwhile, Peter had made a lasso; and, carefully letting it down, he caught the wolf by the tail. Peter pulled with all his might. The wolf, jumped up and tugged and pulled wildly, trying to get its tail out of the lasso.

Hunters' *shots are heard from offstage. Then* Hunters *enter from the forest. They lower their guns and look in surprise at* Wolf *held fast in* Peter's *lasso.*

First Narrator: Just then, a band of hunters came out of the woods, their guns raised as they took aim at the wolf, whose trail they had been following. But Peter, sitting up in the tree, still holding tightly to the rope attached to the wolf's tail, cried out, "Oh, don't shoot! Don't shoot! The bird and I have already caught the wolf. Just help us take the wolf to the zoo!" The hunters were only too willing.

Peter *gets down from the tree, first lowering his end of the rope so that it can be held by one of the hunters.* Grandfather *enters and watches in surprise.* Peter *takes firm hold of the rope again and leads the procession off the stage, pulling* Wolf *behind him.* Hunters *follow* Peter *out. After them go* Grandfather, Cat, *and finally* Bird, *who has been chirping happily about catching* Wolf. Bird *exits at end of procession.*

Third Narrator: And so they went! Imagine the triumphant procession: Peter at the head, leading the wolf; after the wolf, the hunters; and winding up the procession, Grandfather and the cat. Grandfather tossed his head. "This is all very well, but if Peter had not caught the wolf—what then?" Above them flew the little bird, merrily chirping. "Aren't we smart, Peter and I? Just see what we caught!" And if you listened very carefully, you could have heard the duck—quacking away inside the wolf—because in hurrying, the wolf had swallowed the duck alive!

The End

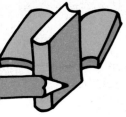

Special Illustrations

There is an old saying which states: "A picture is worth a thousand words." The saying may not always be true. But it is true that a diagram often helps you understand information. Look at these examples of two ways to give the same information.

Paragraph

    The downhill ski is a long, narrow runner. It curves up at the front, or tip. The back of the ski is called the tail. The binding has two parts: the toe binding and the heel binding. The safety strap is attached to the heel binding. Most downhill skis have metal strips along the bottom edge of the runner.

Diagram

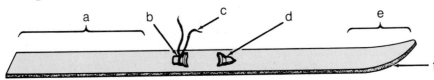

a. tail   **b.** heel binding
c. safety strap   **d.** toe binding
e. tip   **f.** metal strip

The paragraph uses words to describe the downhill ski. The diagram and its key show how the parts of the ski are related to the whole ski. Which is easier to understand, the paragraph or the diagram?

ACTIVITY A Study the diagram below. Then use the diagram to answer the questions. Write the answers on your paper.

Cross Section of a Baseball

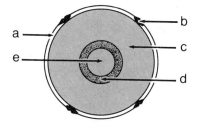

a. cowhide covering
b. red-thread stitching
c. wrapped yarn
d. rubber
e. cork

1. What is the title of this diagram? What important information does it give you?
2. Which letter points out the part of a baseball that is made of rubber?
3. What material is in the center of a baseball?
4. What material is used for the covering?
5. To answer the questions above, you named three of the five materials used in making a baseball. What are the other two?

ACTIVITY B On your paper, write a title for the diagram below. Then write the letters a, b, c, d. Beside each letter, write the correct label for the part of the diagram shown by the letter.

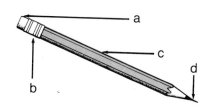

Labels:
metal band
wooden case
lead point
eraser

465

Who Is Leonard Bernstein?

Leonard Bernstein started taking piano lessons when he was eleven years old. He practiced very hard, not because anyone made him, but because he loved music. By the time Leonard went to high school, he knew that he was going to be a musician, even though his father didn't like the idea. After Leonard graduated from college, his father offered him a job in the family business. Leonard turned it down. Instead, he decided to go to a famous music school in Philadelphia. He studied the piano and conducting and composing—all three.

Today Leonard Bernstein is known the world over as a conductor, a pianist, and a composer. He was the first musician born in the United States to become music director of the New York Philharmonic Symphony Orchestra. As director of the Philharmonic, Leonard began giving concerts and lectures on television. He enjoyed sharing his love and understanding of fine music with children. His nationally televised Young People's Concerts were very popular. The essay you are going to read is from one of these concerts. In 1969, he retired as director of the Philharmonic to have more time for composing.

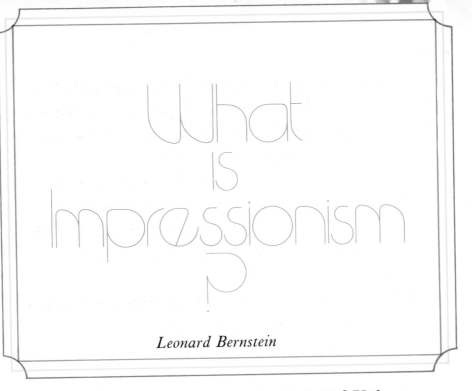

What is Impressionism?

Leonard Bernstein

You may have heard him called **DAY-bussy** or even **De-BYOU-sy.** But however you say his name, Claude **DE-bus-sy** wrote *La Mer* (which means "The Sea"). It is the most famous piece of music ever written about the sea.

When I was a child in Boston, it was hard for me to believe that there were people who had never seen the ocean. There were people in Winnipeg, for instance, smack in the middle of Canada, who had never been *near* the ocean. Now, if I wanted to tell someone in Winnipeg what the sea is like, I could do it with facts and figures. Or I could send him a picture postcard from Coney Island. But that wouldn't give him the real *quality* of the sea. It wouldn't show him what it feels like to look at it or to smell it or to hear it. What our friend in Winnipeg would need is an *impression* of the sea, not just facts and figures. And that brings us to the subject at hand—*impressionism*.

This sea piece by Debussy is what is called an *impressionistic* piece of music. It tells you no facts at all. It does not describe the sea in real terms. Instead it is all color and movement and *suggestion*.

That was the idea that all impressionist artists had in mind, whether they were poets or painters or composers. By the way, they're almost all French.

Now, of course, the real job of music is not to describe anything at all. Its job is just to be music and to give pleasure. But some music has been written *about* things, about nature or stories or thoughts. This music is called program music. Impressionistic music is almost *always* program music. It's *about* something—scenery or a poem or a picture. The whole idea of impressionism began with painters—French painters like Manet, Monet, and Renoir.

Have you ever looked at an impressionistic French painting? I'm sure you have, but maybe you didn't know it. You just saw a picture that seemed to you blurry or hazy. It didn't have a "real" sort of look. On the next page, we have an example of this type of painting.

"Rouen, Cathedral: Sunset"—Claude Monet

Courtesy of the Museum of Fine Arts, Boston. Juliana Cheney Edwards Collection.
Bequest of Hannah Marcy Edwards in memory of her mother.

470

This is a painting of the front of a church in Rouen, France. It was painted by the great impressionist Claude Monet. You see how misty it is? You almost cannot tell *what* it is at first sight. Now take a look at the photograph of that same church next to the painting. See the difference?

The photograph shows the clean outlines and edges and shapes. A realistic painter would want to make the church as real as he could. He would make the light and shapes exact, like the photograph. But not Monet. He doesn't want you to see only a church. He wants you to see light itself, and colors, as they look to him reflecting *on* a church. This is almost like a *dream* of a church. It is an impression of it at a certain time of day when the light was a certain way. Here the church is painted in a sunset. The setting sun has turned the stone into a dazzling, blurry dance of blues and oranges and purples. That is one *impression* of this church at Rouen.

Of course, music is much different from
painting. Music can't *ever* really be realistic.
Notes can't ever give you the exact size of a
church or the exact shape of somebody's nose.
But music can be more or less realistic in its own
way. It can have a straightforward, clear idea,
like this music by Beethoven:

The message is clear, direct—like your father saying,
"Go to bed!" Or music can *suggest* with fuzzy little
wisps of melody as Debussy does:

This is like hinting at happy dreams.
Suggestion, you see? That's impressionism.

La Mer is made up of three parts, called
movements. The first movement is called "From
Dawn to Noon on the Sea." In it you get all
kinds of impressions or suggestions. There is the
complete stillness of the ocean just before dawn.
This comes right at the beginning. Then there
are the first spooky rays of light coming up. Next
the first faint cries of sea birds can be heard.
And the waters begin to stir and rock as the first
breeze comes up. Then, as the movement goes on,

472

there is a bright new sound from the cellos and horns as the sun appears in the sky. From there on, the music grows in power and color and movement. At the very end, the sun has climbed to the height of noon. It hangs there, blazing in space. This is a great moment of musical painting.

"The Cliff at Etretat"—Claude Monet

Courtesy of the Metropolitan Museum of Art, New York
Bequest of William Church Osborn

You can almost see the sun shining there like a big ball, blazing at noontime. It is a wonderful piece of tone-painting—for that's just what it is: painting for the ear instead of the eye.

And that is what impressionism is all about.

IMPRESSIONS

Painters and composers convey their impressions through colors and music. Writers use words. Words can tell how something looks or how it feels when you touch it. Words can also describe tastes, smells, and sounds.

One way a writer uses words to convey an impression of something is to compare it to something else. Look at these two sentences:

> The sun floats across the sky like a giant
> yellow balloon.
> The sun is a giant yellow balloon.

Both sentences describe something—the sun—by comparing it to something else—a giant yellow balloon.

The first sentence describes the sun by saying it is *like* a balloon. When the word *like* or *as* is used to compare two things, the writer is using a **simile**.

The second sentence says that the sun *is* a balloon. When a sentence describes something by saying that it *is* something else, the writer is using a **metaphor**.

Similes and metaphors are kinds of figurative language. The sentences below are examples of the use of figurative language. Which sentences are similes? Which ones are metaphors?

1. The cat looked like a wet, stringy mop.
2. My desk is a mountain of books and papers.
3. Those rocks are as big as doghouses.
4. Stars are like pinholes in a black blanket.
5. The seashore is a storehouse for shells.

How would you use a simile or a metaphor to describe clouds? Raindrops? Thunder?

What Spider Woman Taught

Marion E. Gridley

"It was Spider Woman who taught us to weave," the Navaho say.

Many hundreds of years ago, a woman looked down into a small hole. There she saw Spider Woman at work weaving a web. Spider Woman taught her how to weave four different blankets, and she said that a spider hole must be made in all weavings.

At first the blankets were used for robes and dresses. Today they are rugs. Early weavers used the natural colors of the wool— white, black, brown, and a gray that was a mixture of black and white wool. Soon they started to use other colors also. They made lovely, soft colors from vegetable dyes.

In all of the early blankets, the spider hole was there. The weavers created hundreds of patterns, but no two were alike. A design was never duplicated, for this would bring bad luck. A small "mistake" was made in every blanket to let the weaver's mind escape. For in creating her design, the weaver became a part of it. If her mind had no way to escape, it would be caught in the design forever.

ANNIE AND THE OLD ONE

Miska Miles

Annie's Navaho world was good—a world of rippling sand, of high copper-red bluffs in the distance, of the low mesa near her own snug hogan. The pumpkins were yellow in the cornfield, and the tassels on the corn were turning brown.

Each morning, the gate to the night pen near the hogan was opened wide, and the sheep were herded to pasture on the desert.

Annie watched the sheep. She carried pails of water to the cornfield. And every weekday, she walked to the bus stop and waited for the yellow bus that took her to school and brought her home again.

Best of all were the evenings when she sat at her grandmother's feet and listened to stories of times long ago.

Sometimes it seemed to Annie that her grandmother was her age—a girl who had seen no more than nine or ten harvestings.

If a mouse skittered and jerked across the hard dirt floor of their hogan, Annie and her grandmother laughed together.

And when they prepared the fried bread for the evening meal, if it burned a bit black at the edges, they laughed and said it was good.

There were other times when her grandmother sat small and still, and Annie knew that she was very old. Then Annie would cover the thin knees of the Old One with a warm blanket.

It was at such a time that her grandmother said, "It is time you learn to weave, my granddaughter."

Annie touched the web of wrinkles that crisscrossed her grandmother's face and slowly went outside the hogan.

Beside the door, her father sat cross-legged, working with silver and fire, making a handsome, heavy necklace. Annie passed him and went to the big loom where her mother sat weaving.

Annie sat beside the loom, watching, while her mother slid the weaving stick in place among the strings of the warp. With red wool, her mother added a row to a slanting arrow of red, bright against the dull background.

Annie's thoughts wandered. She thought about the stories her grandmother had told— stories of hardship when rains flooded the desert—of dry weather when rains did not fall and the pumpkins and corn were dry in the field.

Annie looked out across the sand where the cactus bore its red fruit and thought about the coyote—God's Dog—guarding the hogans of the Navahos.

Annie watched while her mother worked. She made herself sit very still.

After a time, her mother looked at her and smiled. "Are you ready to weave, my daughter?"

Annie shook her head.

She continued to watch while her mother twisted the weaving stick in the warp, making a shed for the strands of gray and red wool.

At last her mother said softly, "You may go," almost as though she knew what Annie wanted.

Annie ran off to find her grandmother, and together they gathered twigs and brush to feed the small fire in the middle of the hogan.

When the evening meal was done, the old grandmother called her family together.

Annie and her mother and father stood quietly, waiting for the grandmother to speak.

A coyote called shrilly from the mesa.

There was no sound in the hogan. There was no sound at all, except a small snap of the dying fire.

Then the grandmother spoke softly.

"My children, when the new rug is taken from the loom, I will go to Mother Earth."

Annie shivered and looked at her mother.

Her mother's eyes were shining bright with tears that did not fall, and Annie knew what her grandmother meant. Her heart stood still, and she made no sound.

The Old One spoke again.

"You will each choose the gift that you wish to have."

Annie looked at the hard earth.

"What will you have, my granddaughter?"

Annie looked at a weaving stick propped against the wall of the hogan. This was the grandmother's own weaving stick, polished and beautiful with age. Annie looked directly at the stick.

As though Annie had spoken, her grandmother nodded.

"My granddaughter shall have my weaving stick."

On the floor of the hogan lay a rug that the Old One had woven long, long ago. Its colors were mellowed, and its warp and weft were strong.

Annie's mother chose the rug.

Annie's father chose the silver belt studded with turquoise that was now loose around the waist of the Old One.

Annie folded her arms tightly across her stomach and went outside, and her mother followed.

"How can my grandmother know she will go to Mother Earth when the rug is taken from the loom?" Annie asked.

"Many of the Old Ones know," her mother said.

"How do they know?"

"Your grandmother is one of those who lives in harmony with all nature—with earth, coyote, birds in the sky. They know more than many will ever learn. Those Old Ones know." Her mother sighed deeply. "We will speak of other things."

In the days that followed, the grandmother went about her work much as she had always done.

She ground corn to make meal for bread.

She gathered dry twigs and brush to make fire.

And when there was no school, she and Annie watched the sheep and listened to the sweet, clear music of the bell on the collar of the lead goat.

The weaving of the rug was high on the loom. It was almost as high as Annie's waist.

"My mother," Annie said, "why do you weave?"

"I weave so we may sell the rug and buy the things we must have from the trading post. Silver for silvermaking. Deer hide for boots—"

"But you know what my grandmother said—"

Annie's mother did not speak. She slid her weaving stick through the warp and picked up a strand of rose-red wool.

Annie turned and ran. She ran across the sand and huddled in the shallow shade of the small mesa. Her grandmother would go back to the earth when the rug was taken from the loom. The rug must not be finished. Her mother must not weave.

The next morning, where her grandmother went, Annie followed.

When it was time to go to the bus stop to meet the school bus, she dawdled, walking slowly and watching her feet. Perhaps she would miss the bus.

And then, quite suddenly, she did not want to miss it. She knew what she must do.

She ran hard, as fast as she could—breathing deeply—and the yellow bus was waiting for her at the stop.

She climbed aboard. The bus moved on, stopping now and then at hogans along the way. Annie sat there alone and made her plan.

In school she would be bad, so bad that the teacher would send for her mother. and father.

And if her mother and father came to school to talk to the teacher, that would be one day when her mother could not weave. One day.

On the playground, Annie's teacher was in charge of the girls' gym class.

"Who will lead the exercises today?" the teacher asked.

No one answered.

The teacher laughed. "Very well. Then I shall be leader." The teacher was young, with yellow hair. Her blue skirt was wide, and the heels on her brown shoes were high. The teacher kicked off her shoes, and the girls laughed.

Annie followed the teacher's lead—bending, jumping, and she waited for the time when the teacher would lead them in jogging around the playground.

As Annie jogged past the spot where the teacher's shoes lay on the ground, she picked up a shoe and hid it in the folds of her dress.

And when Annie jogged past a trash can, she dropped the shoe inside.

Some of the girls saw her and laughed, but some frowned and were solemn.

When the line jogged near the schoolhouse door, Annie slipped from the line and went inside to her room and her own desk.

Clearly she heard the teacher as she spoke to the girls outside.

"The other shoe, please." Her voice was pleasant. There was silence.

Limping, one shoe on and one shoe gone, the teacher came into the room.

The girls followed, giggling and holding their hands across their mouths.

"I know it's funny," the teacher said, "but now I need the shoe."

Annie looked at the boards of the floor. A shiny black beetle crawled between the cracks.

The door opened, and a man teacher came inside with a shoe in his hand. As he passed Annie's desk, he touched her shoulder and smiled down at her.

"I saw someone playing tricks," he said.

The teacher looked at Annie, and the room was very still.

When school was over for the day, Annie waited.

Timidly, with hammering heart, she went to the teacher's desk.

"Do you want my mother and father to come to the school tomorrow?" she asked.

"No, Annie," the teacher said. "I have the shoe. Everything is all right."

Annie's face was hot, and her hands were cold. She turned and ran. She was the last to climb on the bus.

Finally there was her own bus stop. She hopped down and slowly trudged the long way home. She stopped beside the loom.

The rug was now much higher than her waist.

That night she curled up in her blanket. She slept lightly and awakened before dawn.

There was no sound from her mother's sheepskin. Her grandmother was a quiet hump in her blanket. Annie heard only her father's loud, sleeping breathing. There was no other sound on the whole earth, except the howling of a coyote from far across the desert.

In the dim light of early morning, Annie crept outside to the night pen where the sheep were sleeping.

She tugged at the sleeping sheep until one stood quietly. Then the others stood also, uncertain—shoving together. The lead goat turned toward the open gate, and Annie slipped her fingers through his belled collar. She curled her fingertips across the bell, muffling its sound, and led the goat through the gate. The sheep followed.

She led them across the sand and around the small mesa where she released the goat.

"Go," she said.

She ran back to the hogan and slid under her blanket and lay shivering. Now her family would hunt the sheep all day. This would be a day when her mother would not weave.

When the fullness of morning came and it was light, Annie watched her grandmother rise and go outside.

Annie heard her call.

"The sheep are gone."

Annie's mother and father hurried outside, and Annie followed.

Her mother moaned softly, "The sheep— the sheep—"

"I see them," the grandmother said.

Annie went with her grandmother, and when they reached the sheep, Annie's fingers slipped under the goat's collar, and the bell tinkled sharply as the sheep followed back to the pen.

In school that day, Annie sat quietly and wondered what more she could do. When the teacher asked questions, Annie looked at the floor. She did not even hear.

When night came, she curled up in her blanket, but not to sleep.

When everything was still, she slipped from her blanket and crept outside.

The sky was dark and secret. The wind was soft against her face. For a moment she stood waiting until she could see in the night. She went to the loom.

She felt for the weaving stick there in its place among the warp strings. She separated the warp and felt for the wool.

Slowly she pulled out the strands of yarn.

One by one, she laid them across her knees.

And when the row was removed, she separated the strings of the warp again and reached for the second row.

When the woven rug was only as high as her waist, she crept back to her blanket, taking the strands of wool with her.

Under her blanket, she smoothed the strands and made them into a ball. And then she slept.

The next night, Annie removed another day's weaving.

In the morning when her mother went to the loom, she looked at the weaving—puzzled—

For a moment, she pressed her fingers against her eyes.

The Old One looked at Annie oddly. Annie held her breath.

The third night, Annie crept to the loom.

A gentle hand touched her shoulder.

"Go to sleep, my granddaughter," the Old One said.

Annie wanted to throw her arms around her grandmother's waist and tell her why she had been bad. But she could only stumble to her blanket and huddle under it and let the tears roll into the edge of her hair.

When morning came, Annie unrolled herself from the blanket and helped prepare the morning meal.

Afterward she followed her grandmother through the cornfield. Her grandmother walked slowly, and Annie fitted her steps to the slow steps of the Old One.

When they reached the small mesa, the Old One sat, crossing her knees.

Annie knelt beside her.

The Old One looked far off toward the rim of the desert where sky met sand.

"My granddaughter," she said, "you have tried to hold back time. This cannot be done." The desert stretched yellow and brown away to the edge of the morning sky. "The sun comes up from the edge of the earth in the morning. It returns to the edge of the earth in the evening. Earth, from which good things come for the living creatures on it. Earth, to which all creatures finally go."

Annie picked up a handful of brown sand and pressed it against the palm of her hand. Slowly she let it fall to earth. She understood many things.

The sun rose, but it also set.

The cactus did not bloom forever. Petals dried and fell to earth.

She knew that she was a part of the earth and the things on it. She would always be a part of the earth, just as her grandmother had always been, just as her grandmother would always be, always and forever.

And Annie was breathless with the wonder of it.

They walked back to the hogan together, Annie and the Old One.

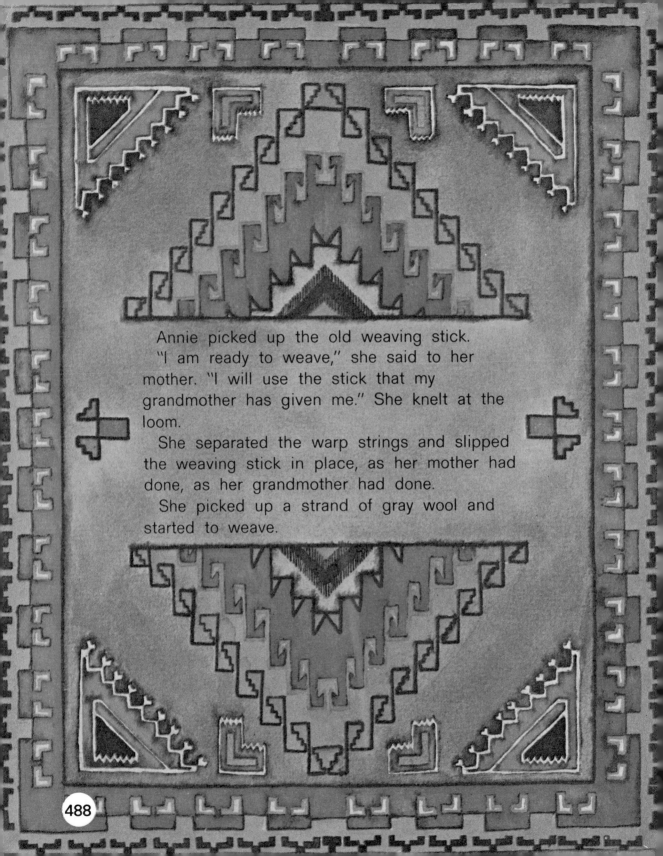

Annie picked up the old weaving stick. "I am ready to weave," she said to her mother. "I will use the stick that my grandmother has given me." She knelt at the loom.

She separated the warp strings and slipped the weaving stick in place, as her mother had done, as her grandmother had done.

She picked up a strand of gray wool and started to weave.

Photo courtesy of The New York Historical Society, New York

SCRIMSHAW: The Art Done by Sailors on Whaling Ships

Jean and Cle Kinney

The word *scrimshank* is an old British word that means "avoiding regular work" or "fooling around." It may be the basis of the word *scrimshaw*, which is the name given to the art work done by sailors on American whaling ships. Certainly carving on ivory was not the "regular work" of sailors, and engraving pictures on whales' teeth was probably thought of as "fooling around."

New England boys knew when they signed up for a whaling trip that they would not be home until every barrel on the ship was filled with whale oil. With a lucky captain, a ship could be full in a year and a half, but most ships stayed out three years. When there were no whales in sight, there was little for the sailors to do. A number of them spent their spare time making beautiful engravings, which are now in museums.

To make a piece of scrimshaw of your own, you will need the following:

- An empty, white, plastic bottle (for example, one that held liquid soap or bleach)

- A large needle or sharpened nail

- Carbon (formed by holding a lighted candle under a white saucer)

- Pencil and paper

Here's all you do:

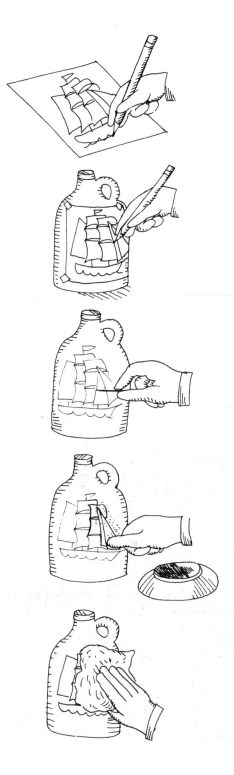

1. Draw on paper the picture you want on your bottle.

2. Lightly draw or trace this picture on your white plastic bottle.

3. Scratch the bottle with your needle or nail along the lines of your drawing.

4. Fill in the cut marks with black carbon by rubbing your thumb on the bottom of the blackened saucer and then rubbing the carbon into the engraving.

5. Clean off the excess carbon by wiping the bottle lightly with a paper towel dampened with a drop or two of liquid detergent.

When finished, your design will stand out like the ones on the opposite page.

Daybreak in Alabama

When I get to be a composer
I'm gonna write me some music about
Daybreak in Alabama
And I'm gonna put the purtiest songs in it
Rising out of the ground like a swamp mist
And falling out of heaven like soft dew.
I'm gonna put some tall trees in it
And the scent of pine needles
And the smell of red clay after rain
And long red necks
And poppy colored faces
And big brown arms
And the field daisy eyes
Of black and white black white black people
And I'm gonna put white hands
And black hands and brown and yellow hands
And red clay earth hands in it
Touching everybody with kind fingers
And touching each other natural as dew
In that dawn of music when I
Get to be a composer
And write about daybreak
In Alabama.

—*Langston Hughes*

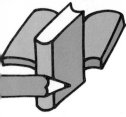

Look It Up!

A dictionary contains information about words. The words are listed in alphabetical order. Look at the dictionary entry for the word *talent*. This word also appears in the glossary of this book.

> **tal·ent** (tal′ent) *n.* **1.** a special natural ability or aptitude: *He has musical talent.* **2.** a person or persons having talent: *The movie producer was always looking for new acting talent.*

1. An *entry word* is a word that is defined in a dictionary. The entry word is printed in heavy, dark type.

2. The dictionary shows the number of *syllables* in an entry word. The syllables are separated by a dot. How many syllables are in *talent*?

3. The pronunciation of an entry word appears in parentheses. The letters in parentheses are symbols. The *pronunciation key* at the beginning of a dictionary shows what the symbols mean and how to use them to pronounce a word.

4. If a word has more than one syllable, a *stress mark* appears with the pronunciation symbols in parentheses. This mark shows which syllable is stressed when you say the word. Which syllable is stressed in *talent*?

5. The *letter* after the pronunciation symbols tells you whether the entry word is a noun, a

verb, an adjective, or an adverb. How can you tell that *talent* is a noun?

6. Many words have more than one meaning. These meanings are numbered in a dictionary. How many meanings are given for the word *talent*?

7. Sometimes a sample sentence or phrase using the word follows the definition. Read the sample sentence after each definition of *talent*.

ACTIVITY A   Read the dictionary entry below. Write the answers to the questions on your paper.

> **de · scent** (di sent′) *n.* **1.** movement from a higher place to a lower one: *the descent of an elevator.* **2.** downward slope or inclination: *a hill with a steep descent.* **3.** ancestry or birth: *Our family is of English descent.*

1. What is the entry word shown above?
2. How many syllables are there in the entry word?
3. Which syllable is stressed?
4. Is the entry word a noun or a verb?
5. How many meanings are given for the entry word?

ACTIVITY B   Read each sentence. Use the dictionary entries on these pages to decide the meaning of each underlined word. Write the word and its meaning on your paper.

1. The <u>descent</u> from the mountain took two hours.
2. She has artistic <u>talent</u>.
3. Her mother is of Irish <u>descent</u>.
4. He is a new <u>talent</u> in the dance troupe.
5. The slide at the park has a gradual <u>descent</u>.

IMPRESSIONS

In "Impressions," you read about many ways to convey impressions such as carving, weaving, painting, dancing, and music. You learned that each person sees and does things just a little differently. Some of the selections you read were about real people. Some were about fictional characters. But in each selection, you saw how things that we make and do leave impressions that make life richer and more enjoyable.

Thinking About "Impressions"

1. "The Seeing Stick" and "Annie and the Old One" are fictional selections. How does a young character in each learn from an older one?
2. "Card Houses" and "All About Gocarts" are nonfictional selections that tell about making something. How are they alike? How are they different?
3. What did you learn about Leonard Bernstein from the short selection about his life?
4. "Peter and the Wolf" is a play. How does it differ from some of the other selections?
5. What special talents would you like to share?
6. Think about your favorite painting or piece of music. Write a paragraph describing your impressions.

HAPPENINGS

How do we learn? How do our experiences help us grow? In "Happenings," special things happen to both animals and people. What happens to these characters helps them learn something about themselves and their lives. Some characters grow because of what they learn from others. Some grow because of what happens to them. But all the characters finally realize that the most important thing is to be themselves.

One of the characters you will meet is Wilbur, the pig, who discovers that he cannot be like someone else, but people like him the way he is. You will meet a baby bat and share her adventures. You will meet a boy who has always wanted to fly. You will also meet a boy who tries to protect a special friend.

As you read, think about how the characters in the stories grow. Think about how they change and learn to be themselves. How have your experiences changed you and helped you grow?

Familiar Friends

The horses, the pigs,
And the chickens,
The turkeys, the ducks,
And the sheep!
I can see all my friends
From my window
As soon as I waken
From sleep.

The cat on the fence
Is out walking.
The geese have gone down
For a swim.
The pony comes trotting
Right up to the gate;
He knows I have candy
For him.

The cows in the pasture
Are switching
Their tails to keep off
The flies.
And the old mother dog
Has come out in the yard
With five pups to give me
A surprise.

—*James S. Tippett*

Wilbur's Boast

FROM THE NOVEL,

Charlotte's Web,

BY E. B. WHITE

Charlotte's Web *is the story of a pig named Wilbur and his very special friend, the spider Charlotte A. Cavatica.*

Wilbur and Charlotte lived with other animals on a farm owned by the Zuckermans. At first, Wilbur didn't like the farm. Lurvy, the farmhand, fed him three times a day. Fern, the young girl who cared for him when he was a weak, little piglet, came to visit every day—if it didn't rain. Still, Wilbur was lonely—until he met Charlotte and found a new friend.

Then an old sheep told Wilbur that one day, when he grew fat, he would be turned into bacon and ham. The news frightened Wilbur. But his friend Charlotte promised to think of a way to save him.

Charlotte did her thinking as she hung from her web, and she weaved on her web every day. One day, however, her work was interrupted by Wilbur's boasting. After that, Charlotte, Fern, and the rat, Templeton, watched a most unusual event.

A spider's web is stronger than it looks. Although it is made of thin, delicate strands, the web is not easily broken. However, a web gets torn every day by the insects that kick around in it, and a spider must rebuild it when it gets full of holes. Charlotte liked to do her weaving during the late afternoon, and Fern liked to sit nearby and watch. One afternoon, she heard a most interesting conversation and witnessed a strange event.

"You have awfully hairy legs, Charlotte," said Wilbur, as the spider busily worked at her task.

"My legs are hairy for a good reason," replied Charlotte. "Furthermore, each leg of mine has seven sections—the coxa, the trochanter, the femur, the patella, the tibia, the metatarsus, and the tarsus."

Wilbur sat bolt upright. "You're kidding," he said.

"No, I'm not either."

"Say those names again. I didn't catch them the first time."

"Coxa, trochanter, femur, patella, tibia, metatarsus, and tarsus."

"Goodness!" said Wilbur, looking down at his own chubby legs. "I don't think *my* legs have seven sections."

"Well," said Charlotte, "you and I lead different lives. You don't have to spin a web. That takes real leg work."

"I could spin a web if I tried," said Wilbur, boasting. "I've just never tried."

"Let's see you do it," said Charlotte. Fern chuckled softly, and her eyes grew wide with love for the pig.

"O.K.," replied Wilbur. "You coach me and I'll spin one. It must be a lot of fun to spin a web. How do I start?"

"Take a deep breath!" said Charlotte, smiling. Wilbur breathed deeply. "Now climb to the highest place you can get to, like this." Charlotte raced up to the top of the doorway. Wilbur scrambled to the top of the manure pile.

"Very good!" said Charlotte. "Now make an attachment with your spinnerets, hurl yourself into space, and let out a dragline as you go down!"

Wilbur hesitated a moment, then jumped out into the air. He glanced hastily behind to see if a piece of rope was following him to check his fall. But nothing seemed to be happening in his rear, and the next thing he knew he landed with a thump. "Ooomp!" he grunted.

Charlotte laughed so hard her web began to sway.

"What did I do wrong?" asked the pig, when he recovered from his bump.

"Nothing," said Charlotte. "It was a nice try."

"I think I'll try again," said Wilbur, cheerfully. "I believe what I need is a little piece of string to hold me."

The pig walked out to his yard. "You there, Templeton?" he called. The rat poked his head out from under the trough.

"Got a little piece of string I could borrow?" asked Wilbur. "I need it to spin a web."

"Yes, indeed," replied Templeton, who saved string. "No trouble at all. Anything to oblige." He crept down into his hole, pushed the goose egg out of the way, and

returned with an old piece of dirty, white string. Wilbur examined it.

"That's just the thing," he said. "Tie one end to my tail, will you, Templeton?"

Wilbur crouched low, with his thin, curly tail toward the rat. Templeton seized the string, passed it around the end of the pig's tail, and tied two half hitches. Charlotte watched in delight. Like Fern, she was truly fond of Wilbur, whose smelly pen and stale food attracted the flies she needed, and she was proud to see that he was not a quitter and was willing to try again to spin a web.

While the rat and the spider and the little girl watched, Wilbur climbed again to the top of the manure pile, full of energy and hope.

"Everybody watch!" he cried. Then summoning all his strength, he threw himself into the air, head-first. The string trailed behind him. But as he had neglected to fasten the other end to anything, it didn't do any good, and Wilbur landed with a thud, crushed and hurt. Tears came to his eyes. Templeton grinned. Charlotte just sat quietly. After a bit, she spoke.

"You can't spin a web, Wilbur, and I advise you to put the idea out of your mind. You lack two things needed for spinning a web."

"What are they?" asked Wilbur, sadly.

"You lack a set of spinnerets, and you lack know-how. But cheer up, you don't need a web. Zuckerman supplies you with three big meals a day. Why should you worry about trapping food?"

Wilbur sighed. "You're ever so much cleverer and brighter than I am, Charlotte. I guess I was just trying to show off. Serves me right."

Templeton untied his string and took it back to his home. Charlotte returned to her weaving.

"You needn't feel too badly, Wilbur," she said. "Not many creatures can spin webs. Even men aren't as good at it as spiders, although they *think* they're pretty good, and they'll *try* anything. Did you ever hear of the Queensborough Bridge?"

Wilbur shook his head. "Is it a web?"

"Sort of," replied Charlotte. "But do you know how long it took men to build it? Eight whole years. My goodness, I would have starved to death waiting that long. I can make a web in a single evening."

"What do people catch in the Queensborough Bridge —bugs?" asked Wilbur.

"No," said Charlotte. "They don't catch anything. They just keep trotting back and forth across the bridge thinking there is something better on the other side. If they'd hang head-down at the top of the thing and wait quietly, maybe something good would come along. But no —with men, it's rush, rush, rush, every minute. I'm glad I'm a sedentary spider."

"What does sedentary mean?" asked Wilbur.

"Means I sit still a good part of the time and don't go wandering all over creation. I know a good thing when I see it, and my web is a good thing. I stay put and wait for what comes. Gives me a chance to think."

"Well, I'm sort of sedentary myself, I guess," said the pig. "I have to hang around here whether I want to or not. You know where I'd really like to be this evening?"

"Where?"

"In a forest looking for beechnuts and truffles and delectable roots, pushing leaves aside with my wonderful strong nose, searching and sniffing along the ground, smelling, smelling, smelling . . ."

"You smell just the way you are," remarked a lamb who had just walked in. "I can smell you from here. You're the smelliest creature in the place."

Wilbur hung his head. His eyes grew wet with tears. Charlotte noticed his embarrassment, and she spoke sharply to the lamb.

"Let Wilbur alone!" she said. "He has a perfect right to smell, considering his surroundings. You're no bundle of sweet peas yourself. Furthermore, you are interrupting a very pleasant conversation. What were we talking about, Wilbur, when we were so rudely interrupted?"

"Oh, I don't remember," said Wilbur. "It doesn't make any difference. Let's not talk any more for a while,

Charlotte. I'm getting sleepy. You go ahead and finish fixing your web, and I'll just lie here and watch you. It's a lovely evening." Wilbur stretched out on his side.

Twilight settled over Zuckerman's barn, and a feeling of peace. Fern knew it was almost suppertime, but she couldn't bear to leave. Swallows passed on silent wings, in and out of the doorways, bringing food to their young ones. From across the road, a bird sang, "Whippoorwill, whippoorwill!" Lurvy sat down under an apple tree and lit his pipe; the animals sniffed the familiar smell of strong tobacco. Wilbur heard the trill of the tree toad and the occasional slamming of the kitchen door. All these sounds made him feel comfortable and happy, for he loved life and loved to be a part of the world on a summer evening. But as he lay there, he remembered what the old sheep had told him. The thought of death came to him, and he began to tremble with fear.

"Charlotte?" he said, softly.

"Yes, Wilbur?"

"I don't want to die."

"Of course you don't," said Charlotte, in a comforting voice.

"I just love it here in the barn," said Wilbur. "I love everything about this place."

"Of course you do," said Charlotte. "We all do."

The goose appeared, followed by her seven goslings. They thrust their little necks out and kept up a musical whistling, like a tiny troupe of pipers. Wilbur listened to the sound with love in his heart.

"Charlotte?" he said.

"Yes?" said the spider.

"Were you serious when you promised you would keep them from killing me?"

"I was never more serious in my life. I am not going to let you die, Wilbur."

"How are you going to save me?" asked Wilbur, whose curiosity was very strong on this point.

"Well," said Charlotte, vaguely, "I don't really know. But I'm working on a plan."

"That's wonderful," said Wilbur. "How is the plan coming, Charlotte? Have you got very far with it? Is it coming along pretty well?" Wilbur was trembling again, but Charlotte was cool and collected.

"Oh, it's coming all right," she said, lightly. "The plan is still in its early stages and hasn't completely shaped up yet, but I'm working on it."

"When do you work on it?" begged Wilbur.

"When I'm hanging head-down at the top of my web. That's when I do my thinking, because then all the blood is in my head."

"I'd be only too glad to help in any way I can."

"Oh, I'll work it out alone," said Charlotte. "I can think better if I think alone."

"All right," said Wilbur. "But don't fail to let me know if there's anything I can do to help, no matter how slight."

"Well," replied Charlotte, "you must try to build yourself up. I want you to get plenty of sleep, and stop worrying. Never hurry and never worry! Chew your food thoroughly and eat every bit of it, except you must leave just enough for Templeton. Gain weight and stay well — that's the way you can help. Keep fit, and don't lose your nerve. Do you think you understand?"

"Yes, I understand," said Wilbur.

"Go along to bed, then," said Charlotte. "Sleep is important."

Wilbur trotted over to the darkest corner of his pen and threw himself down. He closed his eyes. In another minute, he spoke.

"Charlotte?" he said.

"Yes, Wilbur?"

"May I go out to my trough and see if I left any of my supper? I think I left just a tiny bit of mashed potato."

"Very well," said Charlotte. "But I want you in bed again without delay."

Wilbur started to race out to his yard.

"Slowly, slowly!" said Charlotte. "Never hurry and never worry!"

Wilbur checked himself and crept slowly to his trough. He found a bit of potato, chewed it carefully, swallowed it, and walked back to bed. He closed his eyes and was silent for a while.

"Charlotte?" he said in a whisper.

"Yes?"

"May I get a drink of milk? I think there are a few drops of milk left in my trough."

"No, the trough is dry, and I want you to go to sleep. No more talking! Close your eyes and go to sleep!"

Wilbur shut his eyes. Fern got up from her stool and started for home, her mind full of everything she had seen and heard.

"Good night, Charlotte!" said Wilbur.

"Good night, Wilbur!"

There was a pause.

"Good night, Charlotte!"

"Good night, Wilbur!"

"Good night!"

"Good night!"

In the days and weeks that followed, Charlotte's plan to save Wilbur gradually took shape. She was growing old, but she was determined to keep her promise to Wilbur. She even persuaded Templeton, the rat, to help her.

Would you like to know Charlotte's plan? Do you think it worked? Why don't you read the novel, Charlotte's Web, *to find out?*

Feather or Fur

When you watch for
Feather or fur
Feather or fur
Do not stir
Do not stir.

Feather or fur
Come crawling
Creeping
Some come peeping
Some by night
And some by day.
Most come gently
All come softly
Do not scare
A friend away.

When you watch for
Feather or fur
Feather or fur
Do not stir
Do not stir.

—John Becker

513

Wufu

Berniece Freschet

Part One

Spring

It was a warm rainy night. High in the rafters of an old deserted barn, Wufu, a little brown bat, was born.

The mother bat caught her new baby in her wide wings. She wrapped her wings close about the baby. The tiny, naked, newborn bat snuggled against her mother's warm body and began to nurse.

Wufu's mother hung under the roof in a far corner of the barn, away from a large family of bats. There were sixty-seven members in the bat family. Counting Wufu, now there were sixty-eight. There were uncles, aunts, brothers, sisters, and many, many cousins—all hanging together—upside down—high in the rafters of the old barn.

After a while, the mother bat moved over beside her family. It was cozy here in the darkness. The musty smell of hay drifted up from the hayloft. The little bats all pressed close together for warmth and comfort.

The falling rain made a soft whispering sound against the roof. Soon, when Wufu's stomach was full of milk, she burrowed into her mother's soft fur and slept.

Because of the spring rain, the bats did not leave the barn this night. But the next day, the rain stopped. That evening the bats started out on their usual hunt for food and water.

With a fluttering and flapping of their wide wings, the bats flew out the open door of the hayloft. Three times they circled around the barn. Then, flying high above the treetops, the bats sailed over a wooded hill and swooped down to a small lake.

The darkening air was filled with the sounds of a May twilight. At the edge of the lake, hidden in the reeds, a chorus of toads and frogs croaked a spring concert. From a tree branch above the still water, a hermit thrush answered with its clear, sweet song.

Under a dogwood bush, a marsh hen fluffed out her feathers and settled herself more comfortably over her nest of eggs.

A turtle plunged off a rock and splashed into the lake.

Here and there, a fish leaped up to catch a mosquito, making wide circles of ripples on the water.

Wufu clung tightly to her mother's fur. The mother skimmed low over the lake. She dipped so low that her wing tips almost brushed the surface. She dipped her head down and scooped up a small mouthful of water. She did this several times, flying back and forth, back and forth — each time lapping up a tiny sip of water until her thirst was satisfied.

Suddenly, right in front of her, a fat trout jumped out of the water. His big mouth opened wide. There was no time to move out of his way. Quickly the mother bat dived under the trout. Then, with great energy, she swooped high into the air. She and Wufu had barely missed making a supper for the hungry fish.

The bat family climbed up into the sky and off toward a marshy bog about a mile away. At the bog, the bat family hunted insects to eat. They caught hundreds and hundreds of moths, mosquitoes, and gnats—almost any insect in the air.

The farmer, who lived over the hill, was glad that the bat family had come to live in the old barn. They would catch many of the harmful insects that otherwise would ruin his apple orchard and the new tender plants in his vegetable garden. The bats did the

farmer a great service. He hoped they would stay a long time in the old barn.

As the bats dipped low over the marshy bog, they made a series of high piercing cries. These sounds guided the bats and told them what was ahead of them.

The sounds bounced off any object in their path. With their sensitive ears, the bats could tell from the echo how big the object was and how far away it was. If the object was moving, the echo told them which way it was going. They could even tell the texture of the object. The echoes were different when they came from a stone, a moth, or just a leaf blowing in the wind.

The bats could see in the daytime, but their eyes were small. So at night, they used their ears to "see".

At dawn, the bats flew back to the lake for a last drink of water. Then they headed for their home in the barn.

The sun pushed up over the hill. Its first warm rays inched across the barnyard. They touched the bent and rusty hayfork — then, the smooth round stones in the wall. The rays moved past the old, twisted apple tree and then slowly slanted up the gray, weathered side of the barn—bathing everything in warm, yellow light.

The bat family circled once around the barn and then quickly darted inside the hayloft door. With a great fluttering and flapping of wings, they perched on the rafters. Then, clinging with their long, curved hind toes to the rafters, they swung themselves up-side down and huddled together. The mother bat wrapped her wide wings around Wufu.

Here, hanging from the rafters and folded inside their wings, the little brown bats went to sleep in the air.

Every evening, for almost two weeks, the mother bat took her baby with her. But soon Wufu was too heavy to carry. One evening, before the mother bat flew off to hunt for food, she carefully hung Wufu up on a limb of the old apple tree that stood at the side of the barn. All night long, while the bat family looked for insects to eat, Wufu would stay there. She was well-hidden among the leaves and the sweet-smelling apple blossoms in the tree.

The moon came up. A dark shadow skimmed overhead. Silently, the shadow swooped through the hayloft door. It was a barn owl — a dangerous enemy. He was looking for something to eat — a small bat would be a tempting morsel for his supper. Finding nothing in the barn, the owl flew outside and perch-ed at the top of the apple tree.

He flapped his wings and snapped his sharp beak.

His head turned slowly from side to side.

His round yellow eyes looked out. His sight was very sharp. He could see the black beetle that stirred the grasses below.

The hungry owl watched and waited.

Wufu hung silently on the limb. Her small, dark body blended into the shadow of leaves. The little bat slept soundly. She did not know that an enemy was near. A soft wind ruffled the leaves. It gently rocked Wufu back and forth on her limb. In the darkness, she looked like just another leaf swaying in the breeze.

Below, beside the stone wall, a meadow mouse poked her head out of a hole.

The owl blinked. His eyes stared down into the darkness.

The mouse pushed outside and sat up on her hind legs. She looked around — sniffing the air for signs of danger. Then, quickly, she scurried up the wall and ran over the top of the smooth stones.

The owl leaped far out. The quiet hunter dived low. His sharp claws spread wide.

The owl's shadow passed over the mouse. Squeaking with fright, the mouse jumped — flattening herself into a crack between the stones.

Tonight the mouse and the little brown bat were lucky. They had escaped the quiet hunter.

The barn owl pulled in his claws, dipped his wings, and swooped upward. From out of the darkness came his cry as he silently glided away: "Whoo — whoo — whoo — "

During the day, when the other bats were sleeping, sometimes Wufu would awake. Gradually, she became aware that there were other creatures who lived below her in the barn.

Inside an old, worn horse collar that hung from a peg on the barn wall, lived a family of field mice. The mouse babies were still too young to leave the nest. Sometimes, when their mother was away looking for food, the young mice poked their heads out of a hole in the collar. Five pairs of black, shiny eyes looked out. Five tiny noses twitched. What a big world waited outside their home!

One day, a black snake crawled into the barn. Slowly, she slithered forward. Her scales made a soft rustling sound against the dry dirt floor.

The young mice watched the black snake wriggling nearer. The snake's tongue flicked in and out, in and out, testing the air for scent of prey. The snake smelled mouse. She raised her body high.

But the wise mother mouse had chosen a good place to have her family. The black snake could not reach the baby mice in the horse collar on the wall.

Finally, the snake turned and slowly crawled out of the barn. But she would be back.

High above, Wufu clung tightly to her mother's fur. If she were to fall, the black snake would enjoy a breakfast of bat almost as much as one of mouse.

On the other side of the barn, underneath the corncrib, lived a skunk. Most of the time, she slept during the day and, like the bat family, hunted for her food at night. But sometimes, she came out in the daytime and shuffled about the barn, sniffing into the dark corners looking for insects to eat.

One morning, three baby skunks followed her out of the corncrib. From above, Wufu watched the skunk family.

At first, the babies stayed close to the crib. When they walked, they staggered about and bumped into each other. But gradually, their legs grew strong. Soon they were playing together. They began to stray farther and farther from the safety of their home.

But whenever a baby skunk wandered too far, the mother skunk went after it. Holding it in her mouth by the scruff of its neck, she carried it back to the safety of the corncrib.

One evening, as the bats fluttered out of the hayloft, the mother skunk was leading her babies out the door. It was time for the youngsters to learn how to find their own food.

While the bats hunted in the sky, the mother skunk was teaching her young to hunt on the ground. They learned to poke under logs and rocks for grubs and beetles. They found the place where the snapping turtle had laid her eggs on the shore of the lake. They learned how to use their quick paws to bat minnows out of the water.

At dawn, the bat family came swooping back into the hayloft.

At the same time, the mother skunk was leading her weary youngsters into the barn, back to the corncrib for a long, well-earned day's rest.

It had been a busy night for the little skunks. They were very tired. They curled up into furry balls and were soon asleep.

Hanging from their rafters above, the sleepy cluster of bats snuggled together. The old barn grew quiet.

Part Two

Summer, **Autumn,** Winter

Small green knobs began to form on the branches of the apple tree.

Wufu was growing. She was three and a half weeks old now and almost four inches long. For several nights, she had taken short practice flights out from her limb on the apple tree. She was beginning to get the feel of flying through the air. She was learning how to use her remarkable wings.

Wufu's wings were leathery membranes. They stretched between the long bones of her four fingers like a web. The wings stretched from her shoulders to her hind feet and back to her tail. A membrane was attached to all four legs and to her tail. It made a kind of parachute above her body as she flew. These wings made the little brown bat one of the most skillful fliers in the sky. But on the ground, Wufu was almost totally helpless.

Her hind legs were smaller than her forearms. Because her knee joints bent backward, it was difficult for her to walk. She moved by pushing her wings against the ground, awkwardly hitching herself forward.

If an enemy were to catch Wufu on the ground, it would be very dangerous for the little bat.

Moonlight shone through the open spaces of the apple tree. It made lacy leaf shadows on the ground. Wufu fluttered out from her branch. She circled the tree and then darted back to her favorite limb.

Above, the owl sat at the top of the tree. His round yellow eyes watched the bat's every move. On her next practice flight from the tree, just as Wufu was fluttering back to her branch — the barn owl sprung outward.

He dived at the little bat!

Wufu did not see the owl, but her sensitive ears heard the vibrations of even this great soft flier. The bat swooped upward.

Quickly, the barn owl followed. But the bat's leathery wings had grown strong. The owl was no match in the sky for the speed of the little brown bat.

Away Wufu sailed — over the treetops — over the hill — skimming across the lake, and then darting down to join her family at the bog.

Soon she, too, was catching the moths and gnats that flitted through the darkness.

No one had to teach her to catch insects. She knew by instinct. She curled her tail forward, making a net that scooped the insects out of the air.

Bending her head forward, she grasped the insects in her mouth. Wufu caught and ate hundreds and hundreds of gnats and moths. She ate almost a fourth of her own weight during just this one night's hunt.

Wufu would have to do this every night of her life. Now she was on her own. She was a hunter. She swooped through the air — a true member of the bat family.

High above, the stars made silver pinpoints of light in a black velvet sky. The moon shone down on the bog. The warm summer night was filled with the soft sounds and quiet movements of the night creatures.

Below, two raccoons sat dipping their paws into the water looking for snails and crayfish to eat. A mother possum, her babies clinging to her back, slowly felt her way down the river's bank. The possums pushed through clumps of rose-colored wild geraniums. The possums had come to the bog for their evening drink and to look for root bulbs to eat.

Under lacy ferns, crickets chirruped. At the swampy edge of the bog, among tall stalks of cattails, frogs sang. The sounds of night were all about.

A curlew and a plover probed in the mud with their long beaks. The two birds hunted for worms and chatted together softly.

A porcupine shuffled over the ground, rustling through the wild grasses.

High above, the little brown bats flitted through the air hunting for insects. In the light of the bright moon, the black shadow of their wings could be seen. The bats flew in graceful, gliding waves under the starry sky.

All night long, on wide, silent wings, they swooped and soared. They looped and whirled — up and down — around and around. The little bats danced through the air, performing a beautiful ballet across the sky.

In the east, the horizon grew light. The moon slid behind the hill. One by one, the bright stars grew dim. It was time for the bats to return to their home in the barn. Back they flew.

Clinging to her rafter in the barn, Wufu began to wash herself. The little brown bat liked to keep clean, and sometimes she spent an hour grooming herself. Like a cat, Wufu licked the glossy brown fur on her back and then the lighter fur across her stomach. She moistened the tip of one wing and rubbed it hard across her head, against the fur.

Then, very carefully, Wufu cleaned her ears. Her ears were a matter of life and death to the little bat. So she gave them special care. Licking her thumb, she twisted it around and around in her ear until she was satisfied that it was washed thoroughly clean. Then she scratched behind it.

She also paid particular attention to her wings. She sponged every inch with her long red tongue. Working on the inside, she pulled the wing down over her head. The elastic membrane stretched into odd-looking shapes. The little bat looked as though she were wearing a rubber mask. Finally, she was satisfied with herself.

Wufu's face wrinkled into a wide yawn. She stretched. She was tired from her first long, all-night flight. Soon she dozed. Later she half awoke and snuggled over closer beside her mother. Suddenly — a piece of rotting wood gave way. Wufu lost her grip on the rafter. She plunged downward!

She had barely enough time to half spread her wings and break the fall before she hit the ground.

The fall stunned her. She closed her eyes and huddled against the floor. She was afraid and didn't know what to do.

She heard a soft rustling sound moving near. A blurred shadow crawled through the barn doorway and slowly moved toward the bat on the ground.

The big black snake raised her head. Her flicking tongue caught the bat's scent. She weaved forward.

Wufu struggled to her feet. She knew she was in serious danger. It was hard for her to move across the floor. But the confused little bat tried hard to get away from the enemy.

Slowly, softly the snake slithered nearer. She raised her head and pulled it back, ready to strike —

Wufu spread her wings. With her last bit of strength, she lifted herself upward. Then she was in the air — flying! But she did not have enough strength to reach the rafters high above. Suddenly, her wings folded and hung limp. Wufu was falling again.

She flung out her feet behind her. Her long toenails dug into the horse-collar peg. She clung there. For a moment, she was safe.

A mouse peeked out of her hole in the horse-collar. With angry squeaks, she scolded the bat for disturbing her sleep.

Wufu rested. She waited for her strength to return. She paid little attention to the angry mouse.

The bat and the mouse looked as though they might be cousins. With her pug nose and her small black eyes almost hidden in the folds of her wrinkled skin, Wufu looked very much like a furry mouse with wings.

The hungry snake grew tired of waiting for the bat to fall. She crawled away, out the barn door.

The apples on the old twisted tree grew round and red.

All summer long, the bats hunted at the bog. They returned early each morning to sleep away the hot summer days under the roof of the cool, dark barn.

For weeks they had been eating and eating, and they had grown fat. Each day, the bats moved a little slower and slept longer. Now it was almost time for the bat family to go into hibernation, to move into their cave up in the hills. There they would sleep through the long winter.

The autumn nights grew crisp and cold.

Ripe apples fell from the apple tree.

A hungry family of deer came and ate the fruit.

The pumpkins in the farmer's garden grew round and golden.

One twilight evening the bats swooped away — over the treetops — over the hills. Their wide scalloped wings made a beautiful black pattern against the red sunset. This time, they would not return to the barn at dawn.

The farmer watched them go. His harvest had been good. He was grateful for the little brown bats' help. He would be glad when they returned in the spring.

Snows drifted deep against the stone wall and the gray weathered sides of the barn. Cold winds whistled through the bare branches of the apple tree.

In the hills, deep underground in their warm cave, the bats slept — snuggled close. All through the long winter, the bats would sleep their deep sleep.

When the warm breezes of spring come and melt the snow, and the sap once again rises in the apple tree and tiny green buds push out, the brown bats will return.

Then Wufu and the bat family will stay, high in the rafters under the roof of the old, deserted barn — their home.

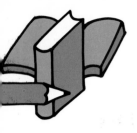

Getting to Know You

Reading a story is like moving to a new town. When you read, you have a chance to explore a new place and meet new friends. The people you meet in a story are the *characters*. You learn about them from the things they think, do, and say. You also learn about them from the way they behave toward other characters.

You learned many things about Charlotte, the spider, in "Wilbur's Boast." For example, Charlotte liked Wilbur, the pig, and was a good friend to him. You learned how she felt about Wilbur from the way she acted and spoke. She enjoyed talking to Wilbur. When he wanted to spin a web, she showed him how and encouraged him. When he realized he couldn't, she consoled him. She explained things to Wilbur that he didn't understand. She came to Wilbur's defense and spoke sharply to the lamb who insulted him. Charlotte also comforted Wilbur by telling him she was working on a plan to save him.

You learned about Wilbur, too, from the things he said, thought, and did. You learned that he could be very determined and wouldn't give up when he made up his mind. For example, he tried twice to spin a web. Then, when he told Charlotte how smart she was, you learned that he looked up to her.

Read the story below. As you read, pay close attention to the character named Tommy.

Tommy was a lazy young man. He never did his work until the last minute. His friends often teased him. "Some day you'll be sorry," they warned. But Tommy just laughed at their warnings.

In school, the teacher gave the students three weeks in which to prepare a report. The other students went to the library immediately. But Tommy didn't go.

"I'll do my work on the last day," he thought. But on the last day, it snowed heavily. Tommy couldn't get to the library. The next day, he told his teacher what had happened. Some children laughed to themselves. Others laughed aloud.

Tommy thought, "I'm really ashamed of myself." Then he said aloud, "I've learned my lesson."

Tommy was never late again.

Now write a sentence from the story that proves each statement below:

1. Tommy's own thoughts showed that he was lazy.
2. Tommy's own actions showed that he was lazy.
3. Other people's actions showed that Tommy was not respected.
4. Tommy's own thoughts showed that he was sorry.
5. Tommy's own words told you he was sorry.
6. Tommy's own actions showed that he was truly sorry.

HAWK,
I'm Your Brother

Byrd Baylor

Rudy Soto
dreams
of flying . . .

wants
to float
on the wind,
wants
to soar
over canyons.

He doesn't see himself
some little
light-winged bird
that flaps
and flutters
when it flies.
No cactus wren.
No sparrow.

He'd be
more like
a HAWK

gliding

smoother
than anything else
in the world.

He sees himself
a hawk
wrapped up in wind

lifting

facing the sun.

That's how
he wants
to fly.

That's all
he wants—
the only wish
he's ever had.

No matter what happens
he won't give it up.
He won't trade it
for easier wishes.

There,
playing alone
on the mountainside,
a dark skinny boy
calling out
to a hawk . . .

That's Rudy Soto.

People here say
that the day he was born
he looked at the sky
and lifted his hands
toward birds
and seemed to smile
at Santos Mountain.

The first words
he ever learned
were the words for
FLYING
and for
BIRD
and for
UP THERE . . . UP THERE.

And later on
they say that
every day
he asked his father,
"When do I learn to fly?"

(He was too young then
to know
he'd never get his wish.)

His father said,
"You run.
You climb over rocks.
You jump around like a crazy
whirlwind.
Why do you need to fly?"

"I just do.
I need to fly."

In those days
he thought that
somebody
would give him
the answer.
He asked
everybody . . .

everybody.

539

And they always said,
"People don't fly."

"Never?"

"Never."

But Rudy Soto
told them this:
"*Some* people do.
Maybe we just don't know
those people.
Maybe they live
far away from here."

And when he met new people
he would
look at them
carefully.

"Can you fly?"

They'd only laugh
and shake their heads.

Finally he learned
to stop
asking.

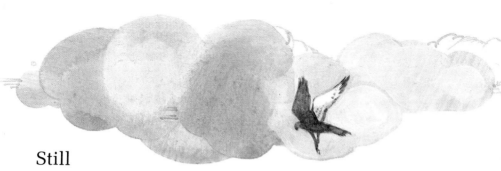

Still
he thought
that maybe
flying
is the secret
old people
keep
to themselves.
Maybe they go sailing
quietly
through the sky
when children
are asleep.

Or maybe
flying
is for
magic people.

And he even thought
that if no one else
in the world
could fly
he'd be the one
who would learn it.

"Somebody ought to,"
he said.
"Somebody.
Me!
Rudy Soto."

There,
barefoot
on the mountainside,
he'd
almost
fly.

He'd dream
he knew
the power
of great wings
and sing
up to the sun.

In his mind
he always seemed
to be a hawk,
the way he flew.

Of course
a boy like that
would know
every nest
this side of the mountain.
He'd know the time
in summer
when the young hawks
learn to fly.
And he'd think
a thousand times,
"Hawk, I'm your
brother.
Why am I stuck
down here?"

You have to know all this
to forgive the boy
for what he did.

And even then
you may not think
that he was right
to steal the bird.
It may seem
cruel
and selfish
and mean—
not worthy of one
who says
he's brother
to all birds.

But anyway
that's what he did.

He stole
a hawk—
a redtail hawk—
out of its nest
before the bird
could fly.

It was a nest
that Rudy Soto
must have seen
all his life,
high on the ledge
of a steep rough
canyon wall.

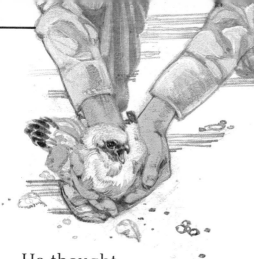

He thought
that nest
might be
the best home
in the world,
up there
on Santos Mountain.

And he even thought
that there might be
some special
magic
in a bird
that came from
Santos Mountain.

Somehow
he thought
he'd share
that
magic

and he'd *fly*.

They say
it used to
be
that way
when
we
knew how
to
talk
to birds

and how
to call
a bird's
wild spirit
down
into our own.

He'd heard
all those
old stories

and he'd seen
hawks
go flying
over mountains
and felt
their power
fill the sky.

It seemed to him
he'd FLY —

if
a hawk
became
his
brother.

That's why
he climbed
the cliff
at dawn
singing . . .

to make
the magic
stronger.

And
that's why
he left
an offering
of food . . .

to show
he was
that
brother.

But
the young hawk
struggled
and screamed,
called
to the birds
circling
overhead,
called
to its nest
on Santos Mountain.

"Listen, bird.
Don't be afraid.
Don't be
afraid
of *me*."

Climbing down,
he held
that bird
so close
he felt
its heartbeat
and
the bird
felt his.

"You'll be
all right.
You'll see."

But even a hawk
too young to fly
knows
he's meant
to fly.
He knows
he isn't meant
to have
a string
tied
to his leg.

He knows
he isn't meant
to live
in a cage.

Every day
he screams.
He pulls
against the string.
He beats
his wings
against the cage.

"You'll be happy
with me, bird.
You will."

But the bird
looks out
with fierce
free
eyes
and calls
to its brothers
in the canyon.

Every day
it is the same.

They see
those
other birds
learning
to fly,
learning
the touch
and roll
and lift
of air,
learning
to
dip
and dive.
They turn
when
the wind
turns.

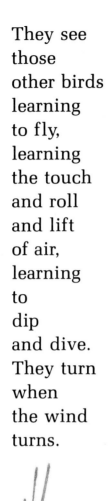

But
down below
with his feet
touching
sand
Rudy Soto's hawk
can only
flap
his wings
and rise
as high
as a string
will let him go.

Not high
enough.

Not far
enough.

Rudy Soto
tells his hawk:
"Someday
we'll fly
together."

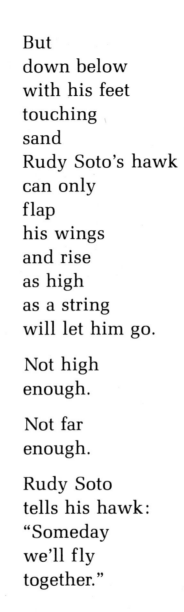

He wants
to please
that hawk.
He's sure
he will.
He's sure
it's going to be
his
brother.

Each day
when the melons
are picked
and the wood
is chopped
and the corn
is hoed
Rudy Soto gives
a long soft call
and he comes
running.

He always says:
"I'm here now,
bird.
What do you want
to do?"

He takes the bird
out of the cage
and ties the string
around its foot
and the bird sits
on his shoulder
as they walk
the desert hills.

They go down
sandy washes
and
follow
deer tracks
into canyons.

Sometimes
they sit
looking off
to
Santos Mountain.

And sometimes
they even go
on the other side
of Santos Mountain
to a place
where
water
trickles
over
flat
smooth
rocks.

The bird
plays
in that
cold water . . .
dips
his wings
into the stream
and jumps
and flaps

and the boy says,
"See.
You're happy
here with me."

But
even
when he says it
he knows
it isn't true
because
the bird
is tugging
at the string

and
you see
sky
reflected in his eyes

and his eyes
flash

and his wings
move
with the
wind.

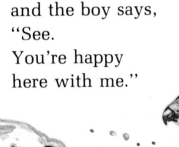

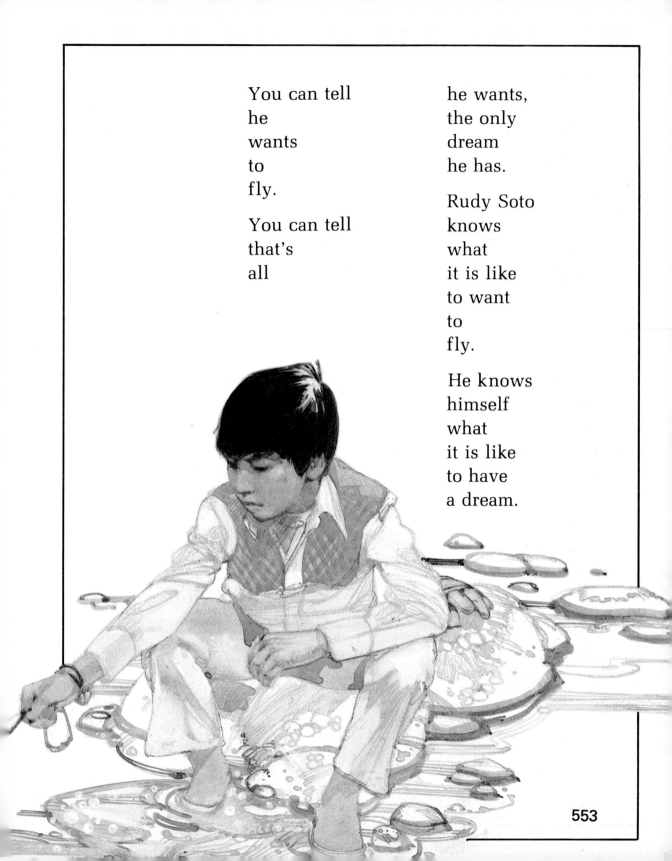

You can tell
he
wants
to
fly.

You can tell
that's
all
he wants,
the only
dream
he has.

Rudy Soto
knows
what
it is like
to want
to
fly.

He knows
himself
what
it is like
to have
a dream.

But even so
he waits
until
the end of summer,
hoping
that
the bird
will be
content.

Every day
it is the same.

The bird
still
tugs
and pulls
and yearns
against the string.

Rudy Soto
knows
that the hawk
will not
give up.

What else
can
a boy
like Rudy Soto
do?

He has to say:
"I don't want
to see you
so unhappy,
bird."

And he has to say:
"One of us
might as well
fly!"

What else
can he
do
if he
really
loves
that bird?

He has to
take him
back
to Santos Mountain
to the place
where *he*
would like
to fly.

That's where
they go —

up
to those
high
red rocks.

There is
a wind
and
clouds move
across
the sky
and
from far away
you can smell
rain.

Now he
unties
the string
that has held
his hawk
so
long.

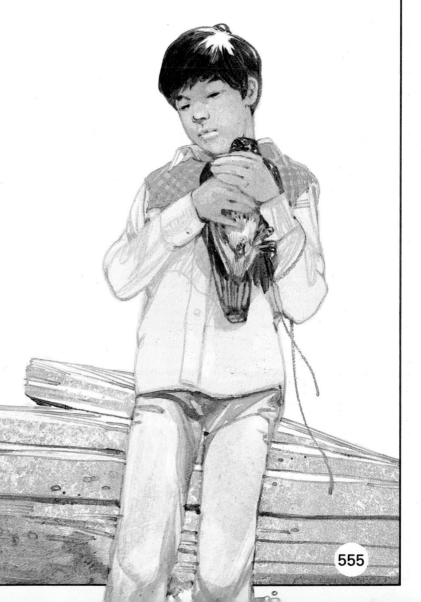

The hawk
is on his
shoulder.

"Fly now,
bird.
Go on."

The hawk
turns.
He moves
his wings.

"Bird,
you can
fly."

The hawk
takes
his
time.

There
on the rocks
he jumps
and
flaps,

rises

and
sinks.

He
has
to learn
the force
of air
and the pull
of wind
and the feel
of
freedom.

Maybe
he jumps
a hundred times
before
he seems
to catch
the wind,
before
he lifts
himself
into
that
summer sky.

At last
he
soars.

His wings
shine
in the sun

and
the way
he
flies
is the way
Rudy Soto
always
dreamed
he'd fly.

The bird
looks
down.

Then
he calls
a long
hawk cry,
the kind of cry
he used to call
to his
brothers.

Brother
to
brother
they call

all through
the afternoon.

High
on the side
of Santos Mountain
Rudy Soto
lifts
his arms.

His hair
blows
in the wind
and
in his mind

he's
FLYING
too.

Only
this time
he calls
to
Rudy Soto

and the sound
floats
on the wind.

Rudy Soto
answers
with
the same
hawk
sound.

Back and forth
they call.

It doesn't
even matter
that
his feet
are on the
ground.

It seems to him
he has
the whole sky
to fly in
when
he hears
that
call.

He knows
he'll keep it
in his mind
forever.

Rudy Soto
doesn't tell
anybody.

He doesn't say:
"Lucky me.
I know
about
flying.
I know
about
wind."

He never says,
"There is a hawk
that is
my brother
so I have
a special
power."

But
people here
can tell
such things.

They notice
that a hawk
calls to him
from
Santos Mountain

and they hear
the way
he answers.

They see
that Rudy Soto
has a
different look
about him.

His eyes
flash
like
a young
hawk's

re is

in those eyes
and it's
the sky
high
over
Santos Mountain.

People here
are not
surprised.

They're
wise enough
to
understand
such things.

Hurt No Living Thing

Hurt no living thing;
Ladybird, nor butterfly,
Nor moth with dusty wing.
Nor cricket chirping cheerily,
Nor grasshopper so light of leap,
Nor dancing gnat, nor beetle fat,
Nor harmless worms that creep.

—Christina Rossetti

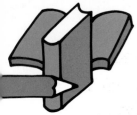

Categories and Labels

Ruth runs a department store. She sells furniture, books, and toys. All the books are on the first floor. All the furniture is on the second floor. The third floor has all the toys.

Bill runs a department store, too. He also sells furniture, books, and toys. However, these items are scattered throughout the store. Some books are on the first floor. Others are on the second and third floors. The same is true of the furniture and the toys.

Suppose you wanted to buy a dictionary. Would you rather shop at Ruth's store or Bill's store? You would save time at Ruth's store. She has grouped all her books together. Bill's dictionaries might be on any one of three floors.

Putting things into groups is called *classifying*. You put things that are alike in the same group. For example, one group of things in a store might be books. The items in that group may be a dictionary, a cookbook, a biography, and an almanac. Here are other groups and some items that might be in these groups.

	Items
562 ure:	chair, table, bed, lamp
	yo-yo, rubber ball, top, blocks

ACTIVITY A Read each set of items. Then read the group names. Choose the correct group name for each set of items. Write the group name on your paper.

1. **Items:** mouse, horse, dog, monkey, squirrel
   Group: colors, animals, shoes
2. **Items:** bread, eggs, cheese, meat, tomatoes
   Group: foods, jobs, countries
3. **Items:** three, six, twelve, nine, twenty
   Group: names of rivers, names of towns, names of numbers

ACTIVITY B Read each set of words. One word in each set names the group. On your paper, write the word that names the group.

1. milk, juice, cream, liquids, water, soda
2. big, small, medium, large, sizes, tiny
3. snow, weather, rain, sunshine, fog, sleet
4. glass, steel, rubber, cotton, wool, materials
5. golf, tennis, sports, baseball, soccer, basketball

ACTIVITY C Read each set of words. Think of a group name for each set. Write the group name on your paper.

1. January, April, July, November, December
2. shirt, pants, socks, sweater, skirt
3. yellow, white, blue, pink, green
4. river, lake, stream, pond, creek
5. Tuesday, Friday, Thursday, Sunday, Wednesday

MY
CARUSO

Earl G. Robbins

PART ONE
I MEET CARUSO

The train slowed, tooted its whistle three times, and came to a full stop in front of the little depot. The kindly conductor, who had looked after me since leaving the city one hundred miles away, collected my ticket and helped me onto the platform. I spied Grandpa on his wagon, holding the mules and making ready to drive us to the farm. "Here I am, Grandpa. Here I am!" I cried, running and climbing on the high seat beside him. "This summer is mine, Grandpa. This summer is mine!" And that summer was mine. No other grandchildren lived within miles, and the nearest neighbors were an hour's wagon ride away.

The very first afternoon, Grandpa and I walked down a hill to a cool pool of water under the railroad trestle. First we swam. I played and paddled in shallow water near the bank. Grandpa swam like a frog. His arms and legs worked sidewise from his body, rather than forward and back, as most people swim. He dove and ducked me playfully. Later we fished. We caught small fish, but threw them back into the stream to grow.

Grandpa joked like a young man, not like one who was seventy years old. He mimicked birds, croaked like frogs, and sang funny songs about varmints we saw in the fields and woods. His clear voice rang from hill to hill when he bellowed:

"'Coon has got a ringey tail,

Possum tail go bare.

Rabbit got no tail at all.

Just a little white bunch of hair."

After Sunday dinner, Grandpa and Uncle George sat in the yard and talked about the weather and their crops. I played with Old Jack, Grandpa's furry dog. I chased him and threw him to the ground. Grandpa laughed and joked with me.

Uncle George talked sadly and looked glum. "The weeds are ruining my corn, Pa. I have no one to help me, now that Fanny's gone," he said sadly.

Late in the afternoon as he was preparing to leave, he called me over to where he sat. "Boy," he said, looking me over sharply. "I might use you a few days if you could drive a team of mules." He moved out of his chair as if to leave. "I doubt if you could handle the job," he said, not quite believing his own judgment.

I threw back my shoulders and stood before him. "Uncle George, I can drive your mules. I'm nine years old, going on ten!" I looked up into his weak gray eyes. Then I turned to Grandpa. "Can't I drive the team, Grandpa?"

"The boy's a good hand with my team, George. We plowed weeds out of the watermelons."

"I'll pay you a quarter a day, son, if you can drive Beck and Julie." Uncle George reached into his pocket and pulled out two shiny quarters.

My eyes grew large. "I'm ready, Uncle George. Let's get started."

"Can we have him back by Wednesday, George? I need him to help me drive the mules to town," said Grandpa.

I bubbled with this attention.

"It depends on how good he is with the team, Pa. I usually plow both fields in two and a half days." Uncle George looked at me questioningly. "It might take three days with him."

I was angry. "I'll show you, Uncle George! Heck, I make Grandpa's big mules gallop. I can drive little Beck and Julie!"

A pale moon lit the sky dimly as Uncle George and I walked slowly along a narrow path through the woods leading to his home. The night was dark and quiet when we reached Uncle George's cabin. "We'll be out early, son," he said, striking a match and lighting the lamp. "I want to be in the field by sunup."

As we ate, we talked. "Will we do anything besides plow corn?" I asked. I was thinking of fishing and swimming as I did with Grandpa.

"That's all, except feed the chickens and milk the cow." Uncle George backed his chair away from the table. "Let's go outside and look at the moon before we go to bed." He moved toward the door. I followed close behind.

Fluffy gray clouds floated slowly across the silent sky. Silhouettes from the pale moon slithered through a dying, half-naked tree beside the cabin. Uncle George's thin frame cast a giant shadow away from his body. A barn owl called softly, "Who, who, who, who are you?" I felt it was talking to me. It gave me an eerie feeling. I shivered and wondered if I had done the right thing in accepting Uncle George's invitation. A strange loneliness in him made me homesick. I wished for Old Jack. He would bark and scare bad things away.

"Let's go to bed so we can be out early," Uncle George finally said. I crawled into bed and slid to the backside near the wall. I pulled the cover high over my head and shut my eyes tightly.

It was yet dark when I was awakened by a voice saying, "Get up, boy, it's time to feed and milk." I jumped out of bed and pulled on my overalls. We had slept soundly, or at least I had, all night long.

Uncle George grinned and pulled on his heavy shoes. "We'll feed the chickens on the way to the barn. Take this basket and get some corn from the bin. I'll start the fire and put my coffee on before we leave."

I scooped corn into the basket and handed him a few sticks of wood to put into the stove. He picked up the milk pail from a bench beside the

door. I walked closely beside him toward the barn. Moist morning air made me feel fresh and clean. Chickens gathered around Uncle George's feet as he stepped through the gate. They clucked, begged, and pecked for favored feeding positions. One rooster, however, did not come close and did not show interest in the plump, yellow grains we scattered over the hungry mob. He stood off and watched like a guard.

Even in the early light, I saw that this rooster was different from the others. His bright feathers and the way he walked gave him a look of royalty. I hoped to see him in full light when we returned.

I did! As we came toward the cabin, he strutted out before us. He threw his head high and gave a clear shrill, "Cock-a-doodle-doo-o." I watched him flap his colorful wings and fly to the top of a post. He arched his shining neck, looked at me, and repeated his "Cock-a-doodle-doo-o." He flew down from his perch and was surrounded by the hens. Other roosters watched with jealousy. He talked, cooed, and moved masterfully among the hens. He strutted, looked toward the less-attractive roosters, and gave another "Cock-a-doodle-doo-o."

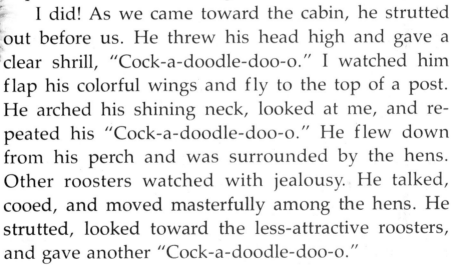

A full-grown pullet with a bright red comb moved coyly near the handsome rooster. She fluffed her pretty feathers and clucked softly. He yanked and tore at a clump of heavy sod; uncovered a plump, white grub; and cooed gently to the pretty pullet, calling her to come see what he had. He fanned dirt from around the grub, picked it up graciously, and laid it at the feet of the enchanted young hen.

I watched excitedly as he continued his courtship and wooing. He carried himself with the air of a king. Like the pullet, I too fell in love with him. He strutted and pranced, displaying his bright colors in the early morning light. He was red, green, gold, and deep violet — a rainbow of colors! His full red comb sat above his shapely head like a king's hunting cap. Beneath his strong, curved beak, silver-white wattles swung and flapped like beads of precious pearls decorating his broad breast. His razor-sharp spurs and long claws gave him a fierce bearing. He acted and looked like a conqueror. I knew I must own him.

At breakfast, I asked Uncle George how much he would take for the handsome rooster. He gulped, held his fork in mid-air, stared at me as if unsure of my question, laid his fork on the table, saucered his coffee, and looked at the bed where Aunt Fanny had lain. Finally, he said in a sad voice, "We never thought of selling *that* rooster, son. Fanny named him just before she died. 'My Caruso' she called him, after that big singer that she once heard on a gramophone machine. He crowed and sang at her window every morning at break of day. She said that rooster's 'Cock-a-doodle-doo-o' was like sweet music to her ears." He drank slowly and seemed to forget that I was in the cabin.

I sensed Uncle George might not part with the rooster, but he seemed to be thinking as he buttered a biscuit and covered it with honey. After a long silence, he stared at me and said, "Son, I've been thinking about what Fanny would want me to do." He looked again at her bed. "If you work real hard and we plow both fields by tomorrow night, I might sell Caruso to you for fifty cents." He cleared his throat with a sip of coffee. "I think Fanny would like for a boy like you to own her Caruso."

"I'm ready to work right now, Uncle George! Let's get started. I'll work hard for you." I squirmed and fretted at Uncle George's tardiness. I gobbled down my breakfast. "Let's get started, Uncle George," I said again. "The mules have eaten their corn by this time. Let's go!" With that, I ran to the barn, and Uncle George followed me.

"You don't have to worry about Caruso's feed, boy. He eats worms, bugs, seeds, and wild berries." Uncle George finished hitching Julie to her whiffletree. "We'll plow the rough hillside field first while you and the mules are fresh." He handed me the lines and called out gently, "Get up, Beck. Come on, Julie. Get up Beck. Come on, Julie."

Soon we were in the tall corn. My job was to guide the mules, keeping them at the proper pace and making sure they didn't tramp on the growing corn. I sat on a sack of straw directly behind the mules. Uncle George walked behind, controlling the plow shovels as they scratched and dug out weeds. He talked kindly to the mules, never raising his voice except when the plow snagged into a wild root or a rock. Then, he hollered, "Whoa! Back, Beck. Back up, Julie! Whoa! Whoa, girl!" He shook the plow handles fiercely. Up and down, up and down, he thrashed at weeds and trash until the plow was free and clean.

I clucked and called loudly to the mules. I shook their lines and encouraged them to walk fast. They walked briskly in the morning coolness, wiggling their long ears and switching their stubby tails. The sharp shovels cut and threw dirt high. I hollered, "Get up Julie!" I tapped her sharply with the line. She jumped and broke into a hopping canter, up and down, up and down. Beck stomped, knocked down corn, and kicked against the plow. Sparks flew into my face. I pulled and yanked hard on the lines. Beck and Julie ran zigzagging between the corn rows.

Uncle George socked the plow shovels deep into the ground. "Hold 'em, boy! Hold 'em! Pull 'em back! Hold 'em down! They're running away!" he hollered. He braced his feet and tried to stop the plow.

I seesawed on the lines. I yanked and pulled. "Whoa, Beck! Whoa, Julie! Whoa! Whoa! Whoa,

girls!" I pleaded. Over and over, I hollered, "Whoa! Whoa! Whoa! Beck! Whoa! Julie!" The mules only ran faster. Dirt flew. The plow rocked and rolled under me. I wrapped my legs around the frame of the plow to keep from falling and being sheared by the sharp shovels.

Uncle George dragged along behind, panting, pleading, and screaming, "Whoa! Whoa! Whoa! Hold 'em, boy! Hold 'em!" Tall corn slapped and beat his face. Julie and Beck flew to the end of the row. There they stopped and picked grass quietly by the fence.

Uncle George walked around the plow and came up to me. He frowned and mumbled under his breath. He grabbed my arm and held it tightly. My arm ached. "Son," he said angrily, "maybe you can beat and punch Pa's old stacks-of-bones, but don't you ever lay a line on my mules again!" He pinched my arm hard. "I'll send you home this minute!" His hot breath hit my face. "Now, run back down that row and get my hat. I've a mind to send you home right now!"

I jumped off the plow and started after his hat. "Wait!" he commanded sternly. "Do you think you can drive like I tell you to?" He pulled off a shoe and shook dirt out of it.

"I—I—I'll try, Uncle George," I said trembling. "I—I'll try. I'm sorry." I sniffled as I ran for his hat. I was sure I had lost the beautiful rooster.

"Now, do you think you can drive them right, boy?" he asked as I handed him his tattered, dusty hat. He said this in his calm, slow voice.

"I'll try my best, Uncle George. Honest I will. I'll try."

"Talk mule talk to Beck and Julie like I do, easy and low."

I pulled on the lines easy-like and spoke softly, "Get up, Beck. Come on, Julie," I said quietly. They walked slowly, pulling the plow back and forth, back and forth across the field. Uncle George smiled. He concentrated on getting out all the weeds.

"Gee. Haw. Whoa. Back. Get up," I said quietly. I pulled the lines lightly. Beck and Julie understood and minded me. My work grew easy. I daydreamed. I wondered what to do with my Caruso, as I now thought him to be. "Shall I take him home to the city or leave him with Grandma's chickens?" I asked myself. I hummed and whistled tunes that I had learned in school. I watched the birds fly down from trees, grab worms, and fly away with the worms wiggling and squirming.

I did everything Uncle George asked. I ran for the cow and drove her in at milking time, fed the chickens, split kindling, and straightened covers on the beds. I would have worked through dinner and supper, too, to own Caruso. "It isn't dark yet," I pleaded when we finished plowing the hillside field.

"Let's start the flat field and plow some more before supper."

"No, son, the mules are tired, and so am I." He stopped and rested on a tree stump beside the path. "We've done enough for one day." He pointed to dark cloud banks. "If those clouds don't stir up a storm, we might finish by sundown tomorrow."

"A rain, Uncle George?" I asked in a worried voice. I feared I would not get Caruso if it rained.

"Maybe and maybe not," he said.

Late Tuesday evening, we plowed the last row of the flat field. "Caruso is mine, Uncle George. Caruso is mine." I called. I laughed and hollered, "Caruso is mine! Caruso is mine!" I said over and over.

"You earned him fair and square, son," he replied in a lifeless voice.

PART TWO
CARUSO AND ME

I hurried Beck and Julie toward the barn, where Uncle George and I unharnessed them. Then I rushed the mules into a pasture. Finally, I rushed Uncle George into the chicken shed. He talked quietly, "Here, Caruso. Here, boy. Come to me, Caruso," he coaxed. Caruso moved cautiously to a far corner. He watched with a startled look in his eye. Uncle George stooped low, on a level with Caruso, and grabbed him by both legs. Caruso squawked, "Awe! Awe! Awe!" He flapped and beat Uncle George's arms with his wings. "Awe! Awe! Awe!" he cried, fighting to free himself.

"Watch him fight! This is a strong rooster, boy!" Uncle George held him firmly and stroked his back. Caruso settled himself and blinked his sparkling eyes. "Look at those golden red feathers. See these dark, green ones on his neck? This is a royal rooster, son! He's a champion!"

Uncle George pulled a cord from his pocket and tied it around Caruso's legs. "I hate to do this to you, Caruso, but you'll have a good master." He held the beautiful rooster out to me. I took him into my arms. I stroked his glowing feathers. "Caruso, Caruso, my Caruso," I said humbly.

I carried Caruso into the yard. I was ready to leave. "Be careful the foxes or hawks don't get Caruso now, son," Uncle George warned with a serious look on his bony face. "Or maybe a mink. Minks catch chickens, too," he said, walking me toward the gate.

"I'll take good care of him, Uncle George. I wouldn't take a thousand dollars for Caruso!" He held the gate shut. I fidgeted nervously. "Thank you for letting me have Caruso, Uncle George," I said, moving up to the gate.

Uncle George patted me on the back. "Be kind to Caruso, son." He stroked Caruso's feathers tenderly once more. "He's the grandest chicken Fanny and I ever raised. You are a good little worker, son. Come back sometime when I'm not busy and we'll go fishing."

"I will, Uncle George." I put my hand beside his on the gate and opened it slightly.

He opened the gate wider. "Now, be careful about the varmints. They'll catch Caruso if you don't watch out for him."

"I'll take care of him, Uncle George," I promised. He stood watching as I trotted down the lane. Caruso nestled in my arms. He held his head high, watchfully.

Dark shadows fell over Caruso and me. Light filtered through openings of moving objects. "A cloud," I thought, "is covering the sky. No, it moves close and low." I heard harsh sounds. They seemed to be calling, "Haw—Haw—Haw—" Objects floated low above us. "Haw — Haw — Haw — " They squawked and cried loudly close above my head.

"Hawks! Hawks, Caruso, that's what they are. What shall we do?" I ran toward the woods to shelter him. "Faster, Caruso, faster," I cried tiredly, as I hid in the darkness of the woods.

"Haw — Haw — Haw — " The hawks screamed at us. They followed us into the woods. I listened breathlessly as the big birds flew into the trees and continued their horrid "Haw — Haw — Haw —." I  knew they must be collecting in great numbers to swoop down and snatch Caruso from me. I tucked him under my arm and crept silently into a narrow, hidden dark path, watching and hiding from the birds. My heart thumped and pounded. I panted and puffed.

I leaned my body forward and crept under a low-growing bush. I waited quietly until more darkness came. Then I tiptoed softly through dead leaves and limbs. A dry twig shattered loudly under my foot. I froze with fright. Caruso moved close to my body. He made no sound. The earth was deathly silent around us.

A dark figure appeared at the left of our dimly lit path. I sidled away into more low-growing shrubs and huddled against a decayed tree trunk to avoid the creature.

A bear? A wildcat? Or a ghost? "Haw — Haw — Haw — Haw — " now screamed at us from low-hanging limbs. The dark object remained still, blocking our way, ready to snatch Caruso from my arms as we passed — or maybe to grab both of us. I hunkered down on my knees and elbows, turning my back to the birds, shielding Caruso with my body. We would steal away from the bear, wildcat, or ghost when I caught my breath. The "Haw — Haw — Haw — " became slow, softly rhythmic, faintly dying away.

The darkening woods around us became still, except for the breathing of Caruso and me. I cried and whimpered as full darkness crept slowly over the woods. My tired legs ached. My chest pained and heaved. I held Caruso firmly and sank in the bedded leaves to rest. Tears filled my eyes. I felt that we would be swallowed by the monster, that Grandma and Grandpa would never get to see my beautiful rooster.

The ghostly crescent moon slipped quietly through fluffy clouds and half lighted our path. I held Caruso near my body and made ready to sneak past the scary creature, unseen. The earth around us remained deathly still other. than the quiet "hu — hu — hu — " of Caruso's breathing. He seemed to share my feeling of danger. Through tears, I searched for the dark figure that had blocked our path. It was no longer there. In the direction of where it had crouched, near Caruso and me, the outline of an animal with fire-like eyes stared at us. The piercing eyes moved stealthily toward Caruso.

I screamed! Caruso squalled! The birds above and around us cried loudly, "Haw! Haw! Haw!" One directly over us flipped and flopped, beating its wings against limbs and leaves. It fluttered noisily to the ground within inches of Caruso, crying and squalling, "Haw! Haw! Haw!" I jumped to my feet and held Caruso in my arms. The monster with the fiery eyes slunk slowly into the darkness. Quickly, I found our path and ran toward Grandpa's until I was out of breath. Now the woods lay far behind us!

Soon, we saw the light from Grandpa's window. I sighed happily, "We made it, Caruso! We made it."

Old Jack met us in the yard. He wagged his tail and licked my hand. I felt safe and secure. I pulled the latch on the kitchen door and called bravely, "I'm home, Grandpa! I'm home!"

"Come in, boy! We've been looking for you!" he answered, cheerfully.

"Look what I bought from Uncle George! He's mine!" I puffed and panted, holding Caruso up to Grandma in full light.

"What a beautiful rooster!" she said, stroking his wide back. "He's a nice one and just what we need —a rooster. I haven't had one with my hens for some time."

"I love Caruso, Grandma. Aunt Fanny named him before she died." I untied the cord from his legs and rubbed them. "What will we do with him tonight, Grandma? Could he sleep by my bed? We can turn him out with the hens tomorrow."

"Oh, no! A rooster wants to be with his hens." I could see that Grandma liked Caruso. "Just take him to the chicken house and set him on the roost beside one of the domernicker hens."

"A hundred or a thousand old black hawks tried to snatch Caruso out of my arms and carry him away, Grandpa. They flew right down over us and hollered 'Haw — Haw — Haw.' And a wildcat, a bear, or ghost tried to get us, too."

Grandpa smiled, "I don't know about the wildcat and the ghost, son. It was probably a hungry fox. There is nothing a fox likes more than a fine chicken. And those birds were not hawks. They were crows. Hawks are brownish, and they usually fly alone. Crows are black and they say, 'Caw — Caw — Caw.'"

Grandpa took Caruso into his hands and examined the muscles of the rooster's back and the tendons of his strong legs. "Ten crows couldn't whip your rooster, son. This is a fighting cock!" He held Caruso close. "Feel those sharp spurs! He'd tussle a hawk unless the hawk swooped down and caught him napping!"

"No hawk will catch Caruso napping, Grandpa.

No, sir. He's always up and crowing before daylight. A hawk won't find him asleep."

Grandma rose and started toward the kitchen. "I'll set your supper on the table while you put Caruso on the roost for the night." She hugged me as she passed. "A growing boy has to eat," she said.

I lit the lantern, carried Caruso to the henhouse, and set him on the roost beside a large hen. Then I walked back to the door, opening and closing it quietly. The small door through which Grandma's chickens went in and out was left open. As I walked along the path toward the house, I heard Caruso squawk loudly as he had when he saw the hawk. I supposed he was having a bad dream.

I went to bed happy, and I dreamed of *my* beautiful rooster. At the height of my dream, Grandpa shook me gently. "Get up, son, it's time to see about your rooster," he said. I jumped out of bed, pulled on my overalls, and dashed to the henhouse.

Grandma's hens were clucking noisily, picking at bugs and worms. I looked for Caruso. I listened for his "Cock-a-doodle-doo-o!" I ran into and around the chicken shed. I looked in the barn and the field around it. There was no sign of my beautiful Caruso!

I ran to the house. "Grandma, Grandma! My rooster is gone! My rooster is gone!" I cried. "My beautiful Caruso is gone! What shall we do, Grandpa?" I sobbed with disappointment.

"Calm yourself, son, calm yourself," he said, trying to console me. "We'll take Old Jack to the woods after breakfast and find that rooster. He's probably gone back to George's. We'll find him for you. Jack will follow his trail. We'll find him."

I ate hurriedly. After what I thought was an eternally long breakfast, we took the old dog to the edge of the woods and ordered him, "Sic 'im, Jack! Go get 'im, Jack! Go find the rooster." We commanded him over and over. We coaxed and scolded, but Jack didn't budge.

"Could your rooster fly, son?" Grandpa asked.

"Oh, yes. He flew on high posts and crowed at Uncle George's."

"Then he's flown through the trees leaving Jack no trail to follow. Let's go to George's. That's where we'll find him."

We hurried to Uncle George's. "No," said Uncle George, "Caruso hasn't shown himself here!" He scowled, "Ma should have known better than turn Caruso loose so soon." He bit his lip and dug the toe of his shoe into the dirt. "Poor Caruso," he said, sadly. "Fanny's Caruso is a goner."

We looked around the chicken house, in the barn, through the fields and woods. We saw other chickens, but not the beautiful Caruso.

Uncle George said mournfully, "The varmints, maybe a fox or a hawk, caught Caruso. That's what's happened to him!" He pointed to a lone, large bird sailing overhead. "One of those long-tailed, copper-colored hawks swooped right down here in the chicken yard and caught one of my fat hens."

"No hawk got him, George. He was in the woods. If anything, a fox has carried him to his den," Grandpa said.

"Caruso is still alive, and I'll find him," I insisted. It was only midsummer. I had another month to stay in the country.

Each morning I went into the woods and fields, seeking my Caruso. "Chick, chick, chick. Here, Caruso. Here, Caruso. Here, boy. Come to me, Caruso," I would call.

Grandma and Grandpa tried to console me. "We'll go to George's and get the finest young rooster he has and have it here for you when you come back next summer," they promised.

"But I want Caruso. He was the best rooster in the whole wide world," I protested. "I only want Caruso."

The thought of a varmint killing and eating my Caruso made me furious. "Let's go kill all the foxes and hawks. If we don't hurry, they'll be sure to catch Caruso," I pleaded. "Let's go!"

"No, son," Grandpa said. "I need them. If it weren't for the foxes and hawks, other animals — like rats, mice, and rabbits — would eat up every grain of corn, every head of cabbage, and every blade of grass on the farm. We need some varmints to catch other harmful pests."

"I see," I said. "But we don't need the ones that are after Caruso," I argued. I wanted to agree with Grandpa. Yet I felt he had deserted me and was no longer interested in finding my rooster. I went to the barn, climbed up into the hayloft, and cried until Grandma rang the bell for supper. Old Jack waited for me and wagged his tail when I climbed down. He was the only friend I had left, I felt.

It was the last week that I was to stay in the country. "So you haven't seen feather nor spur of Caruso?" Uncle George asked on his regular Sunday visits. "You might as well give up and forget Caruso, son. He's a goner for sure. One of those big copper-colored hawks caught him."

But none of their talk defeated me. I would continue to look for my Caruso.

The afternoon before I was to leave, I called Old Jack. "Let's go to Johnson's Meadow over beyond the woods, Jack. Maybe Caruso went in the wrong direction. Maybe he left before daylight and got lost."

Jack seemed to understand. He ran on ahead. He sniffed along zigzagging trails through tall grass and high weeds. We crossed the stream that fed our swimming hole. We climbed a low fence. We walked through thick, dark woods and out into the open pasture.

"Caruso must be gone forever, Jack. We better go, too," I said. Then, something seemed to say to me, "Over that rise — over that rise."

I felt myself being pulled and lifted toward a little hill.

I called, "Come on, Jack! Let's go!" Jack followed me as I ran toward the top of the low hill. I just about flew the last few yards near the summit. I stopped and looked down. I saw a dark object. I knew that I had found Caruso, my beautiful rooster.  There, among the bright purple and yellow feathers from his wings and breast, was a sweeping golden green one from his tail. I ran to it. I picked it up. "Oh," I cried. "My Caruso. My poor Caruso. My beautiful Caruso." My eyes filled. I blubbered, "Caruso, Caruso, Caruso."

I held the feather tenderly and stroked it as I had stroked his strong body. It curved like a beautiful rainbow. I stood fascinated. I turned to leave. Then I saw feathers that did not come from Caruso. They were strewn over an area larger than where his feathers had been. They were long, copper-colored ones from the tail of more than one hawk.

"You didn't swoop down and find *my* Caruso napping, old hawks," I said, shaking my fist at the shadow of a lone large bird passing overhead. "It took more than one of you to catch my Caruso," I bragged. I hurried home.

"Look, Grandpa! Look!" I shouted. "I found Caruso!" I held the beautiful feather high. "Those old copper-colored hawks caught him, but he gave them a good tussle. See? See these feathers?" I pulled two long copper-colored feathers from my pocket. I threw the hateful hawk feathers into the trash pile. "There! There!" I said angrily. "Caruso flogged and fought you, too."

Grandma came from the kitchen. I ran to her. "See? See, Grandma?" I whimpered. "Those old hawks caught him." I burst into tears.

Grandma pulled me close. "Now, now, everything will be all right," she said, soothingly. "Everything will be all right, son."

I placed the beautiful feather in her hand. "Give it to Uncle George, Grandma. It will help him remember Aunt Fanny's Caruso. Caruso was never really mine." I sobbed and cried quietly.

A little while later, Grandpa placed his arm around my shoulders. Together we walked out the door toward our swimming hole under the railroad trestle.

"I'll always remember Caruso, Grandpa."

"Yes," said Grandpa. "I know. I know."

When Clouds Cry

Imagine that you have just heard a weather report. The reporter might have said, "It rained today." But suppose the reporter had said, "The clouds cried today." That kind of report would seem very unusual. You know that clouds don't cry. Only people cry. The unusual report had talked about clouds as though they were people. The reporter had used personification to describe the weather.

Personification is a way of using language that makes a thing seem like a person. In personification, a thing is described as acting or speaking like a person.

Writers use personification for special reasons. They may want to paint an interesting picture in the reader's mind. They may want to describe something in a new and different way. The use of personification often makes writing stronger and more interesting that it would be otherwise.

There are examples of personification in the story "My Caruso." One sentence reads: "Tall corn slapped and beat his face." In this sentence, the corn is described as though it were an angry person hitting someone. By using personification, the writer has created a very clear picture of the way the boy felt as he moved through the rows of corn.

ACTIVITY A   Read the sentence that is an example of personification. Then read the three sentences that follow. Choose the sentence that correctly explains the meaning of the personification example. Write that sentence on your paper.

1. The maple tree wears its new leaves proudly.
   a. The tree is like a person laughing loudly.
   b. The tree is like a person dressed in new clothes.
   c. The tree is like a person running away.

2. The wind races furiously to the sea.
   a. The wind is like an angry person running.
   b. The wind is like a person who feels ill.
   c. The wind is like a person singing sadly.

3. The walls of the office hear many sad tales.
   a. The walls are like a person talking softly.
   b. The walls are like a person writing a note.
   c. The walls are like a person who hears unhappy stories.

ACTIVITY B   Read each sentence that is an example of personification. Decide what kind of person you think of when you read the sentence. Use this form to write your answer on your paper: The ____ is like a person ____ .

1. The thunder shouts in anger to the ground below.
2. The moon hides shyly behind a row of clouds.
3. The morning sun awakens and yawns in the sky.

HAPPENINGS

Everything that happens to you helps make you the special person you are. In "Happenings," you read about the experiences of several different characters and how each character changed in some way. Perhaps you've learned a few things from reading about these happenings. Perhaps you've begun to realize that we can learn and grow from our experiences.

Thinking About "Happenings"

1. What is one important thing that Wilbur learns from Charlotte?
2. Why did Rudy Soto finally let the hawk go?
3. What things happened to Wufu that helped her to grow up?
4. What are some things that the boys in "My Caruso" and "Hawk, I'm Your Brother" learned from their experiences with their pets?
5. Which story did you like best? Why?
6. If you were the author of "My Caruso" how would you end the story? Write a paragraph describing your ending.

Glossary

This glossary will help you to pronounce and to understand the meanings of some of the unusual or difficult words in this book.

The pronunciation of each word is printed beside the word in this way: **o·pen** (ō′pən). The letters, signs, and key words in the list below will help you read the pronunciation respelling. When an entry word has more than one syllable, a dark accent mark (′) is placed after the syllable that has the heaviest stress. In some words, a light accent mark (′) is placed after the syllable that receives a less heavy stress.

The pronunciation key, syllable breaks, accent mark placements, and phonetic respellings in this glossary are adapted from the Macmillan *School Dictionary* (1981) and the Macmillan *Dictionary* (1981). Other dictionaries may use other pronunciation symbols.

Pronunciation Key

a bad	**hw** white	**ô** off	**th** that	**ə** *stands for*
ā cake	**i** it	**oo** wood	**u** cup	a *as in* ago
ä father	**ī** ice	**o͞o** food	**ur** turn	e *as in* taken
b bat	**j** joke	**oi** oil	**yo͞o** music	i *as in* pencil
ch chin	**k** kit	**ou** out	**v** very	o *as in* lemon
d dog	**l** lid	**p** pail	**w** wet	u *as in* helpful
e pet	**m** man	**r** ride	**y** yes	
ē me	**n** not	**s** sit	**z** zoo	
f five	**ng** sing	**sh** ship	**zh** treasure	
g game	**o** hot	**t** tall		
h hit	**ō** open	**th** thin		

A

ab · so · lute · ly (ab′sə l⊙̄ot′lē, ab′sə l⊙̄ot′lē) *adv.*   completely.

ac · cus · tom (ə kus′təm) *v.*   to make familiar by use, custom, or habit. **accustomed to.** used to; in the habit of.

ac · knowl · edge (ak nol′ij) *v.*   to admit the truth or fact of.

ac · ro · bat (ak′rə bat′) *n.*   a person skilled in performing feats or stunts that require a great deal of physical strength or control, such as walking on a tightrope.

ac · ro · bat · ics (ak′rə bat′iks) *n. pl.* feats or acts done by an acrobat.

ac · tiv · i · ty (ak tiv′ə tē) *n.*   the state of being active; movement.

ad · mis · sion (ad mish′ən) *n.*   the price that a person has to pay to enter a place.

aer · i · al (er′ē əl) *adj.*   of or in the air.

aisle (īl) *n.*   the space between two rows or sections, as in a theatre.

al · ma · nac (ôl′mə nak′) *n.*   a book that contains many facts and figures on many different subjects. Most almanacs are published every year.

al · ter · na · tive (ôl tur′nə tiv) *n.*   one of two or more possibilities from which to choose.

am · a · teur (am′ə chər, am′ə tər) *n.*   **1.** a person who does something for pleasure, rather than for money. **2.** a person who does something without experience.

a · maze · ment (ə māz′mənt) *n.*   overwhelming wonder or surprise;

an · cient (ān′shənt) *adj.*   having to do with times very long ago; very old.

an · gle (ang′gəl) *n.*   **1.** the figure formed by two lines coming from the same point. **2.** the space between these lines.

an · gle · worm (ang′gəl wurm′) *n.*   an earthworm.

an · nounce (ə nouns′) *v.*   to make something known.

an · noy (ə noi′) *v.*   to bother or disturb.

an · nu · al (an′yⓄ əl) *adj.*   happening or done once a year; yearly.

ant · eat · er (ant′ē′tər) *n.*   a toothless animal with a long, narrow head, a long, sticky tongue, and strong front claws. It claws into ant hills and uses its tongue to capture ants and other insects for food.

anteater

an · te · lope (ant′əl ōp) *n.*   a slender swift animal that has long horns. Antelopes look like deer, but they are related to goats.

an · ten · na (an ten′ə) *n. pl.,* **an · ten · nae** (an ten′ē).   one of a pair of feelers on the head of an insect or other animal.

an · tique (an tēk′) *n.*   something made very long ago that is valued for its age, especially something that is more than one hundred years old.

ap · pe · tite (ap′ə tīt′) *n.*   a desire for food.

ap · prov · al (ə prⓄ′vəl) *n.*   good opinion; acceptance.

ar · gu · ment (är′gyə mənt) *n.*   a discussion of something by people who do not agree.

ar · mor (är′mər) *n.*   any protective covering.

as · cend (ə send′) *v.*   to move upward; rise.

as · phalt (as′fôlt) *n.*   a black or brown tarlike substance used for paving roads.

as · sem · bly (ə sem′blē) *n.* people gathered together for some purpose.

as · tron · o · mer (əs tron′ə mər) *n.* a scientist who studies the stars and planets by looking at them through a telescope.

ath · lete (ath′lēt) *n.* a person who is trained in activities that require physical strength or skill.

at · tach (ə tach′) *v.* **1.** to fasten to or on; join; connect. **2.** to add at the end.

at · tach · ment (ə tach′mənt) *n.* a part or device that is connected to a larger thing.

at · ten · dant (ə ten′dənt) *n.* a person who takes care of or waits on another.

at · tract (ə trakt′) *v.* to draw or pull.

at · trac · tion (ə trak′shən) *n.* a person or thing that attracts.

aud · i · ence (ô′dē əns) *n.* a group of people gathered to hear or see something.

Au · guste (ō gōōst′)

auk (ôk) *n.* a diving sea bird that lives along northern sea-coasts.

av · er · age (av′rij, av′ər ij) *adj.* ordinary.

awk · ward · ly (ôk′wərd lē) *adv.* in a clumsy manner; not gracefully.

auk

ax · le (ak′ səl) *n.* a bar or shaft on which a wheel or pair of wheels turn.

B

back · woods (bak′woodz′) *n. pl.* an area with many trees and few people, far from towns or cities.

baf · fle (baf′əl) *v.* to be too confusing to understand.

ba · king pow · der (bā′king pou′dər) a powder used in baking to make dough or batter rise.

bal · ance (bal′əns) *n.* the ability to keep one's body in a steady, upright position. — *v.* to keep in a steady condition or position.

bal · le · ri · na (bal′ə rē′nə) *n.* a woman or girl who dances ballet.

bal · let (ba lā′, bal′ā) *n.* **1.** a form of dancing, usually with formal steps and positions. **2.** a theatrical presentation of such dancing.

bar · be · cue (bär′bə kyoo′) *v.* to cook a meal outdoors over an open fire.

Bar · num, Phi · ne · as Tay · lor (bär nəm, fin′ē əs tā′lər)

ba · sin (bā′sin) *n.* **1.** a shallow, round container with sloping sides. **2.** a bowl or sink for washing.

bask (bask) *v.* to lie in and enjoy a pleasant warmth.

bat · ter · y (bat′ər ē) *n.* a device that produces an electric current by chemical changes in the materials inside.

bead · y (bē′dē) *adj.* small, round, and glittering.

bear · hound (bār′hound′) *n.* a dog trained to hunt and chase bears.

beech · nut (bēch′nut′) *n.* the nut of the beech tree, used to make cooking oil and flavoring.

Bee · tho · ven (bā′tō′vən) a German composer.

a bad, ā cake, ä father; e pet, ē me; i it, ī ice; o hot, ō open, ô off; oo wood, ōō food; oi oil, ou out; th thin, th that; u cup, ur turn, yōō music; zh treasure; ə ago, taken, pencil, lemon, helpful

be · gin · ner (bi gin′ər) *n.* a person who is just beginning to do or learn something.

be · seech (bi sēch′) *v.* to ask someone in a pleading way; beg.

bil · low (bil′ō) *n.* a great wave or swell.

bin (bin) *n.* a closed place or box for holding something.

bi · ol · o · gist (bī ol′ə jist) *n.* a scientist who studies plants and animals.

bi · ol · o · gy (bī ol′ə jē) *n.* the study of plants and animals.

bi · o · med · i · cal (bī′ō med′i kəl) *adj.* having to do with the relationships among medicine, body chemistry and body function.

bird's nest soup (burdz′ nest′ sōōp′) a Chinese soup made from edible bird nests or substitutes.

birth · place (burth′plās′) *n.* the place where a person was born.

blame (blām) *n.* the responsibility for something wrong or bad. — *v.* to find fault with.

blu · et (blōō′it) *n.* a plant with bluish flowers and tufted stems.

bluff (bluf) *n.* a high, steep bank or cliff.

blu · ish (blōō′ish) *adj.* somewhat blue.

blur · ry (blur′ē) *adj.* dim; hard to see; not distinct.

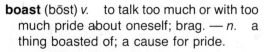

bluet

boast (bōst) *v.* to talk too much or with too much pride about oneself; brag. — *n.* a thing boasted of; a cause for pride.

bod · y con · tact (bod′ē kon′takt) the touching of one person by another.

bog (bog) *n.* wet, spongy ground; marsh; swamp.

bolt (bōlt) *n.* a rod used to hold things together.

bolt up · right (bōlt up′rīt′) stiffly straight; erect.

bough (bou) *n.* a branch of a tree, especially a large or main branch.

bound (bound) *adj.* certain; determined.

brand (brand) *n.* **1.** a certain kind, quality, or make of product. **2.** a mark burned on the skin of cattle or other livestock to show who owns them. — *v.* to mark with a brand.

breast (brest) *n.* the front part of the body.

brin · y (brī′nē) *adj.* like brine; salty.

bronze (bronz) *n.* a reddish-brown metal made by melting together copper and tin.

Breu · ghel, Pie · ter (broo′gəl, pyā′tər)

bulb (bulb) *n.* a round, underground part of a plant. Plants such as tulips, onions, and lilies grow from bulbs.

bull · doz · er (bool′dō′zər) *n.* a tractor with a powerful motor.

bul · ly (bool′ē) *v.* to frighten into doing something.

bu · reau (byoor′ō) *n.* a department, agency, or office.

bur · row (bur′ō) *v.* to dig a hole in the ground.

C

cac · tus (kak′təs) *n.* a plant that has a thick stem covered with spines instead of ieaves.

cac · tus wren (kak′təs ren′) a small songbird that makes its nest in a cactus.

cal · a · bash (kal′ə bash′) *n.* the dried, hollow shell of a gourd, used as a bowl, pipe, or the like.

calf (kaf) *n.* the young of such animals as cows, elephants, whales, and seals.

ca · nal (kə nal′) *n.* a tube-like passage in the body of an animal or plant.

can · vas (kan′vəs) *n.* a strong, heavy cloth made of cotton, flax, or hemp.

can · yon (kan′yən) *n.* a deep valley with steep sides, usually with a stream running through it.

Car · dan · o, Ge · ron · i · mo (kär dä′nō, jə ron′ə mō)

carp (kärp) *n.* a fish that lives in fresh water and is used as food.

Car · ri · llo, Gra · ci · el · a (kə rē′yō, grä sē el′ä)

car · touche (kär to͞osh′) *n.* an oval figure on Egyptian monuments that contains the name or title of a ruler.

Ca · ru · so (kə ro͞o′ sō)

cat · tail (kat′tāl′) *n.* a tall plant that grows in marshes. Cattails have long, furry brown tips.

cau · tious · ly (kô′ shəs lē) *adv.* very carefully.

Ca · vat · i · ca (kə vat′ə kə)

cel · e · bra · tion (sel′ ə brā′shən) *n.* the ceremonies or festivities carried on to celebrate something.

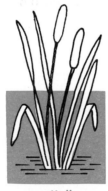
cattail

cen · ti · pede (sen′tə pēd′) *n.* any of a group of small animals that resemble worms.

cen · tu · ry (sen′chər ē) *n.* a period of one hundred years.

chal · lenge (chal′ənj) *n.* something that calls for work, effort, and the use of one's talents.

Cham · pig · ny, Joe (cham pig′nē)

cham · pi · on (cham′pē ən) *n.* a person or thing that is the winner in a contest or game.

cham · pi · on · ship (cham′pē ən ship′) *n.* the position or honor of being a champion.

char · ac · ter (kar′ik tər) *n.* a person who is different, funny, or strange.

charge (chärj) *n.* care or responsibility. **in charge of.** responsible for.

char · i · ot (char′ē ət) *n.* a two-wheeled carriage pulled by two, three, or four horses.

charm (chärm) *n.* an act, saying, or thing that is supposed to have magic powers.

chem · ist (kem′ist) *n.* a person who knows a great deal about chemistry.

chem · is · try (kem′is trē) *n.* the science that studies all kinds of substances to learn what they are made of, what they are like, and what kinds of changes happen when they are mixed.

Chi · ca · go (shə kä′gō) a city in Illinois.

chimp (chimp) *n.Informal.* a chimpanzee.

chim · pan · zee (chim′ pan zē′, chim pan′zē) *n.* a small African ape that has brownish-black hair.

a bad, ā cake, ä father; e pet, ē me; i it, ī ice; o hot, ō open, ô off; oo wood, o͞o food; oi oil, ou out; th thin, th that; u cup, ur turn, yo͞o music; zh treasure; ə ago, taken, pencil, lemon, helpful

Chi · na · town (chī′nə toun′)   a Chinese section of any city outside China, as in San Francisco or New York City.

chir · rup (chēr′əp, chur′əp) *v.*   to chirp continuously.

choc · o · late (chô′kə lit, chok′ə lit) *n.*   a food product made from cacao beans. — *adj.*   made of or flavored with chocolate.

chop · sticks (chop′stiks′) *n. pl.*   a pair of long, slender sticks, usually wood or ivory, that are used for eating.

cho · rus (kôr′əs) *n.*   a group of people who sing or dance together.

chuck · le (chuk′əl) *v.*   to laugh in a quiet way.

cit · a · del (sit′ ə del) *n.*   a fortress that overlooks a city.

claw (klô) *n.*   a nail on the foot of a bird or other animal.

clear · ing (klēr′ing) *n.*   a piece of land, especially within a thickly wooded area, that is free of trees and brush.

clev · er · ness (klev′ər nes) *n.*   mental sharpness; alertness; shrewdness.

cli · max (klī′maks) *n.*   the highest point.

clime (klīm) *n.*   an old-fashioned word for country, region, or climate.

clo · ver (klō′vər) *n.*   a plant having leaves made up of three leaflets and rounded, fragrant flower heads of white, red, or purple flowers.

clus · ter (klus′tər) *n.*   a number of things of the same kind that grow or are grouped together.

coat of arms (kōt ov ärms)   a design, often on a shield, that is the emblem of a person, family, or institution.

coax (kōks) *v.*   to try to persuade by pleasant manners, or soft, gentle speech.

cob · ble · stone (kob′əl stōn′) *n.*   a round stone.

co · coon (kə kōōn′) *n.*   the silky case that a caterpillar spins around itself.

col · o · nist (kol′ ə nist) *n.*   a person born or living in a colony.

col · o · ny (kol′ ə nē) *n. pl.,* **col · o · nies.** a territory that is under the control of another, usually distant, country.

comb (kōm) *n.*   a thick, fleshy crest on the head of roosters and other fowl.

com · men · ta · tor (kom′ən tā′tər) *n.*   a person who explains, describes, or criticizes something.

com · merce (kom′ərs) *n.*   the buying and selling of goods; trade; business.

com · mons (kom′ənz) *n. pl.*   a plot of land, such as a pasture or park, that is owned or used by the public.

com · mon sense (kom′ən sens)   ordinary good judgment. A person learns common sense from experience.

com · mun · i · cate (kə myōō′ ni kāt′) *v.*   to make known or understood; give knowledge or information.

com · pass (kum′pəs) *n.*   an instrument for showing directions. A compass has a needle that points north.

com · pe · ti · tion (kom′ pə tish′ ən) *n.* **1.** the act of striving against one or more persons. **2.** a contest.

compass

com · plete (kəm plēt′) *adj.*   having all its parts; whole; entire.

com · pli · ment (kom′plə mənt) *n.*   an expression of admiration or praise.

com · pose (kəm pōz′) *v.*   **1.** to make up. **2.** to put together; create.

com · pos · er (kəm pō′zər) *n.*   a person who composes, especially one who composes a musical work.

con · cert (kon'sərt) *n.*   a performance of music by a number of musicians.

con · duct (kən dukt') *v.*   to direct or lead.

con · duc · tor (kən duk'tər) *n.*   a person who conducts.

con · quer (kong'kər) *v.*   to get possession of by force.

con · quer · or (kong'kər ər) *n.*   a person who overcomes or defeats another person or other persons.

con · sole (kən sōl') *v.*   to comfort.

con · struc · tion (kən struk'shən) *n.*   the act of constructing something; building.

con · ti · nent (kont'ən ənt) *n.*   one of the seven great land areas of the earth. The continents are Asia, Africa, North America, South America, Antarctica, Europe, and Australia.

con · tin · u · ous (kən tin'yoo əs) *adj.*   going on without a break; unbroken.

con · tri · bu · tion (kon'trə byoo'shən) *n.*   something given or contributed.

con · ven · ient · ly (kən vēn'yənt lē) *adv.*   easily and comfortably.

con · ver · sa · tion (kon'vər sā'shən) *n.*   a friendly and informal talk.

co · op · er · ate (kō op'ə rāt') *v.*   to work or act with one or more persons for the same purpose or goal.

corn · crib (kôrn'krib') *n.*   a bin or small building for storing cobs of corn, built with slats that are spaced for ventilation.

Cor · tez (kôr tez')

court · ship (kôrt'ship') *n.*   a courting; wooing.

cox · a (kok'sə) *n.*   the first segment of the leg of an insect.

cray · fish (krā'fish') *n.*   a small freshwater animal that looks something like a lobster.

cre · ate (krē āt') *v.*   to cause something new to exist or happen.

cres · cent (kres'ənt) *adj.*   shaped like the moon when it appears thin and curved.

crescent

crew (kroo) *n.*   a group of people who work together to make something run.

crime (krīm) *n.*   something that is against the law.

crin · kle (kring'kəl) *v.*   to form wrinkles or ripples; wrinkle.

criss · cross (kris'krôs') *v.*   to mark with crossing lines; to cross repeatedly.

croc · o · dile (krok'ə dīl') *n.*   a large lizard-like animal that has thick skin, a long, narrow snout, strong jaws, and long rows of teeth.

cross-leg · ged (krôs'leg'id, krôs'legd') *adv.*   with the ankles crossed and the knees out.

crouch (krouch) *v.*   to stoop or bend low with the knees bent.

crust (krust) *n.*   any hard outside part.

cu · ri · o (kyoor'ē ō') *n.*   an object valued as a curiosity.

cu · ri · os · i · ty (kyoor'ē os'ə tē) *n.*   something that is interesting because it is strange, rare, or unusual.

cur · lew (kur'loo) *n.*   a wading bird of arctic and temperate regions.

a bad, ā cake, ä father; e pet, ē me; i it, ī ice; o hot, ō open, ô off; oo wood, oo food; oi oil, ou out; th thin, th that; u cup, ur turn, yoo music; zh treasure; ə ago, taken, pencil, lemon, helpful

cush · ion (koosh'ən) *n.*   anything that softens a blow or protects against harm.

cy · cle (sī'kəl) *n.*   a series of events that happen one after another in the same order, over and over again.

D

dan · gle (dang'gəl) *v.*   to hang or swing loosely.

dawdle (dôd'əl) *v.*   to waste time; linger.

dawn (dôn) *n.*   the first light that appears in the morning; daybreak.

day · break (dā'brāk') *n.*   the time each morning when light first appears; dawn.

daz · zling (daz'ling) *adj.*   dazing or making almost blind by too much light.

DDT   a powdery compound that is poisonous to humans and animals. It was once widely used to kill insects.

de · cal (dē'kal, di kal') *n.*   a design or picture on specially treated paper, that can be transferred to glass, wood, or other surfaces.

de · cay (di kā') *v.*   to rot slowly.

de · code (dē kōd') *v.*   to change secret writing into ordinary language.

de Cou · ber · tin, Pi · erre (də koo'bär tin', pē ār')

de · feat (di fēt') *v.*   to win a victory over; overcome in a contest of any kind.

def · i · nite · ly (def'ə nit lē) *adv.*   without question.

de · lec · ta · ble (di lek'tə bəl) *adj.*   highly pleasing, especially to the taste.

del · i · cate (del'i kit) *adj.*   fine or dainty in structure, quality, texture, or form.

de · light · ful (di līt'fəl) *adj.*   highly pleasing; giving delight.

de · liv · er · y room (di liv'ər ē room') a hospital room where babies are born.

de · pot (dē'pō) *n.*   a railroad or bus station.

Der Chung (där' chung')

Der Wai Lee (där' wā' lē')

de · scent (di sent') *n.*   ancestry or birth.

de · scrip · tion (di skrip'shən) *n.*   **1.** picture in words. **2.** a statement or account that describes.

des · per · ate (des'pər it) *adj.*   ready or willing to take any risk.

de · stroy (di stroi') *v.*   to ruin completely; wreck.

de Va · ro · na, Donna (də və rō'nə)

de · vel · op (di vel'əp) *v.*   **1.** to bring into being or activity. **2.** to change gradually. **3.** to put to use.

dew (doo, dyoo) *n.*   moisture from the air that forms drops on cool surfaces.

di · al (dī'əl, dīl) *v.*   to call by means of a telephone dial.

di · a · lect (dī'ə lekt') *n.*   a form of a language that is spoken in a particular area or by a particular group of people and that differs from other forms of the same language in grammar, pronunciation, vocabulary, or idioms.

di · am · e · ter (dī am'ə tər) *n.*   a straight line passing through the center of a circle or other round object from one side to the other.

dia · mond (dī'mənd, dī'ə mənd) *n.*   a mineral that is usually colorless, used as a jewel; the hardest natural substance known.

diamond

di · a · ry (dī'ər ē) *n.*   a written record of the things that one does each day.

dil · i · gence (dil'ə jəns) *n.*   careful attention and effort.

din · o · saur (dī′nə sôr′) *n.* one of a large group of extinct reptiles that lived millions of years ago.

dinosaur

dis · ap · point · ment (dis′ə point′mənt) *n.* the state of being unhappy by failure of one's hopes or expectations.

dis · card (dis kärd′) *v.* to throw aside or give up as useless or worthless.

dis · cus (dis′kəs) *n.* a heavy round plate used in athletic contests.

dis · mal (diz′məl) *adj.* causing gloom or sadness; dreary; miserable.

dis · pute (dis pyo͞ot′) *n.* argument, disagreement.

do · do (dō′dō) *n.* a large bird that no longer exists.

dog · wood (dog′wood′) *n.* a tree that has flowers with a greenish-yellow center and pink or white leaves that look like petals.

Do Na · ci · men · to, Ed · son A · ran · tes (dō nash′ə men′tō, ed′sən ə ran′tez)

doze (dōz) *v.* to sleep lightly or for a short time.

drag · line (drag′līn′) *n.* a dragrope or guide rope.

dress · ing gown (dres′ing goun′) a robe, especially a long, loose one, usually worn before or while dressing or for resting.

du · pli · cate (do͞o′pli kāt′, dyo͞o′pli kāt′) *v.* to make an exact copy of something; to reproduce.

dwell · ing (dwel′ing) *n.* a place where a person lives.

E

ear ca · nal (ēr′kə nal′) a tube-like passage that leads from the outer ear to the inside of the head.

earth · en (ur′thən) *adj.* made of earth.

ed · u · ca · tion (ej′ə kā′shən) *n.* the act or process of teaching or training.

ee · rie (ēr′ē) *adj.* strange in a scary way; making people frightened or nervous.

egg roll (eg′ rōl′) a fried egg-dough casing filled with minced vegetables.

e · lab · o · rate (i lab′ər it) *adj.* worked out or made with great care and in great detail.

e · las · tic (i las′tik) *adj.* able to go back to the same shape soon after being stretched, squeezed, or pressed.

eld · est (el′dist) *adj.* born earliest; oldest.

e · lec · tric · i · ty (i lek tris′ə tē) *n.* one of the basic forms of energy.

em · bar · rass · ment (em bar′əs mənt) *n.* the feeling of being uncomfortable or ashamed.

em · broider (em broi′dər) *v.* to decorate cloth with designs sewn on with thread.

e · mo · tion (i mō′shən) *n.* a strong feeling.

em · per · or (em′pər ər) *n.* the male ruler of an empire.

emp · ti · ness (emp′tē nis) *n.* the state of being empty or containing nothing.

en · chant (en chant′) *v.* **1.** to charm. **2.** to bewitch.

---

a bad, ā cake, ä father; e pet, ē me; i it, ī ice; o hot, ō open, ô off; oo wood, o͞o food; oi oil, ou out; th thin, <u>th</u> that; u cup, ur turn, yo͞o music; zh treasure; ə ago, taken, pencil, lemon, helpful

en · dan · gered (en dān'jərd) *adj.*   put in danger.

en · e · my (en'ə mē) *n.*   a person, animal or thing that is dangerous or harmful.

en · grav · ing (en grā'ving) *n.*   **1.** the art or process of creating a design, inscription, or picture by cutting letters or lines into a metal plate, stone, wood, or other material. **2.** the design, inscription, or picture engraved in this way.

en · thu · si · asm (en thoo'zē az'əm) *n.*   a strong feeling of excitement and interest about something.

e *plu · ri · bus u · num* (ē' ploor'ə bəs oo'nəm)   out of many, one. A Latin phrase that is the motto of the U.S.

e · quip · ment (i kwip'mənt) *n.*   anything that is provided for a particular purpose or use; supplies.

es · say (es'ā) *n.*   a short written composition on a subject.

e · ter · nal · ly (i turn'ə lē) *adv.*   always; for all time; without stopping.

E · thi · o · pi · a (ē'thē ō'pē ə)   a country in eastern Africa, once known as Abyssinia.

ex · ag · ger · ate (eg zaj'ə rāt') *v.*   to make something seem larger or greater; overstate.

ex · am · ine (eg zam'in) *v.*   to look at closely and carefully; check.

ex · haus · tion (eg zôs'chən) *n.*   extreme tiredness; the state of being drained of energy and strength.

ex · hib · it (eg zib'it) *n.*   something shown.

ex · ist (eg zist') *v.*   **1.** to be real; have reality. **2.** to be present or found; occur.

ex · pe · ri · ence (eks pēr'ē əns) *n.*   knowledge, skill, or wisdom gained over a period of time.

ex · pla · na · tion (eks'plə nā'shən) *n.*   **1.** a reason or meaning. **2.** the act of making something plain or clear.

ex · press train (eks pres' trān')   a train that is fast and makes few stops.

ex · tend (eks tend') *v.*   **1.** to make or be longer; stretch out. **2.** to offer to give.

ex · tinct (ek stingkt') *adj.*   no longer existing.

eye · drop · per (i'drop'ər) *n.*   a dropper for applying medicine to the eye.

F

fa · cial (fā'shəl) *adj.*   of or for the face.

fair · y shrimp (fār'ē shrimp')   a freshwater shrimp that is transparent.

fame (fām) *n.*   widespread reputation, especially for something outstanding.

fa · mil · i · ar · i · ty (fə mil'ē ar'ə tē) *n.*   the condition of knowing something well.

farm · hand (färm'hand') *n.*   a person who works on a farm.

fas · ci · nate (fas'ə nāt') *v.*   to attract and hold the interest of; charm.

fas · ci · na · tion (fas'ə nā'shən) *n.*   strong attraction; charm.

fe · mur (fē'mər) *n.*   the long bone of the upper leg; thigh bone.

fern (furn) *n.*   a plant that has large feathery leaves (called fronds) and no flowers.

fern

fes · ti · val (fes'tə vəl) *n.*   a celebration or holiday.

fes · tive (fes'tiv) *adj.*   relating to or suitable for a festival; gay.

fidg · et (fij'it) *v.*   to be nervous or uneasy; to make restless movements.

fier · y (fīr'ē, fī'ə rē) *adj.*   like fire; flashing.

fil · ter (fil'tər) *v.*   to go through slowly.

fire · fly (fīr'flī') *n.*   a small beetle that gives off short flashes of light.

fleece (flēs) *n.*   the coat of wool covering a sheep or other animal.

flick (flik) *v.*   to hit or remove with a quick, light snap.

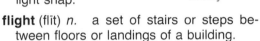

firefly

flight (flīt) *n.*   a set of stairs or steps between floors or landings of a building.

flit (flit) *v.* **flit · ted, flit · ting.**   to move quickly and lightly.

flog (flog) *v.* **flogged, flog · ging.**   to beat or whip severely.

flut · ter (flut'ər) *v.*   to move or fly with quick, light movements.

foot · man (foot'mən) *n.*   a male servant who assists a butler with various jobs.

foot · rest (foot'rest') *n.*   something, such as a small stool or platform, on which the feet may be rested.

fore · arm (fôr'ärm') *n.*   the part of the arm between the elbow and the wrist.

fore · cast · ing (fôr'kast ing) *n.*   telling what will or may happen; predicting.

fore · paw (fôr'pô') *n.*   an animal's front paw.

fos · ter (fôs'tər) *v.*   to help the growth or development of.

foun · da · tion (foun dā'shən) *n.*   something that serves as a base or support.

fran · tic (fran'tik) *adj.*   wildly excited by worry, anger, or fear.

fresh · wa · ter (fresh'wô'tər) *adj.*   living in fresh water.

Fres · no (frez'nō)   a city in California.

fret (fret) *v.*   to be upset, or worried.

frond (frond) *n.*   the leaf of a fern.

froth · y (frôth'ē) *adj.*   foamy.

fu · el (fyoo'əl) *n.*   something that is burned to provide heat or power. Coal, wood, and oil are fuels.

fur · ther · more (fur'thər môr') *adv.*   in addition; moreover, besides.

fu · ry (fyoor'ē) *n.*   violent, uncontrollable anger.

fuzz (fuz) *n.*   fine, loose particles, hair or fibers.

G

gash (gash) *n. pl.,* **gash · es.**   a long, deep cut or wound.

ga · zelle (gə zel') *n.*   a small, graceful antelope that has a fawn-colored coat with black and white markings, curving horns, and large eyes.

Geb · el-Wil · liams, Gun · ther (geb'əl wil'yemz, goon'tər)

ge · fil · te · fish (ge fil'tə fish')   chopped fish mixed with chopped onion, egg and seasoning that is put into a casing of the skin and boiled, often with vegetables.

gen · tle (jen'təl) *adj.*   mild and kind.

a bad, ā cake, ä father; e pet, ē me; i it, ī ice; o hot, ō open, ô off; oo wood, ōo food; oi oil, ou out; th thin, <u>th</u> that; u cup, ur turn, yōo music; zh treasure; ə ago, taken, pencil, lemon, helpful

ge·ra·ni·um (jə rā′nē əm) *n.* a plant with bright red, pink, or white flowers.

get·a·way (get′ə wā′) *n.* **1.** the start of a race. **2.** escape.

gin·ger (jin′jər) *n.* a spice that is ground from the roots of a tropical plant, used in cooking and medicine.

geranium

giz·mo (giz′mō) *n. Slang.* an object or thing.

giz·zard (giz′ərd) *n.* the muscular second part of the stomach of a bird, in which partially digested food from the first part of the stomach is finely ground.

glass count·er (glas′koun′tər) a long table, as in a store or restaurant, with a top and sides made of glass. Items for sale are displayed in glass counters.

gloom·i·ly (gloom′ə lē) *adv.* in a sad or dreary way.

glo·ri·ous (glôr′ē əs) *adj.* magnificent; splendid.

glum (glum) *adj.* gloomy.

gnat (nat) *n.* a small fly.

goal (gōl) *n.* an area or an object into or through which players in certain games try to get a ball or puck in order to score.

goal·ie (gō′lē) *n.* goalkeeper.

goal·keep·er (gōl′kē′pər) *n.* the player who defends the goal in certain games, such as hockey and soccer.

Gon·zal·es, Cir·i·cao (gon zä′lez, sēr′ə kä′ō)

gorge (gôrj) *n.* a deep, narrow valley between steep, rocky sides of a mountain.

gos·ling (goz′ling) *n.* a young goose.

gourd (gôrd) *n.* a rounded fruit related to the pumpkin and squash.

gour·met (goor′mā′, goor mā′) *n.* a person who is an expert in choosing and judging fine food and drink.

gov·ern·ment (guv′ərn mənt, guv′ər mənt) *n.* an organization that rules, controls, or directs a city, state, nation, or other political unit.

grace·ful·ly (grās′fə lē) *adv.* in a graceful or harmonious manner.

gra·cious (grā′shəs) *adj.* having or showing kindness and courtesy.

gra·cious·ly (grā′shəs lē) *adv.* in a graceful and charming manner.

grad·u·a·tion (graj′oo ā′shən) *n.* receiving a diploma or degree for completing a course of study.

gram·mar (gram′ər) *n.* a system of arranging words in sentences so that the meaning of what is said is clear.

gram·o·phone (gram′ə fōn′) *n.* a phonograph.

Gri·mal·di, Joseph (grə mäl′dē)

grit·ty (grit′ē) *adj.* made up of or like very small bits of sand or stone.

gro·tesque (grō tesk′) *adj.* strange, ugly, or not natural.

ground bee·tle (ground′ bēt′əl) a shiny black or metallic beetle with long antennae. Ground beetles often destroy harmful insects.

grove (grōv) *n.* a group of trees.

grub (grub) *n.* a beetle or other insect in any early stage of growth, when it looks like a worm.

gulp (gulp) *n.* the act of swallowing greedily or rapidly in large amounts.

H

half hitch (haf′hich′) a knot made by passing the end of a rope around the rope and then through the loop thus made.

hand · i · crafts (han'dē krafts') *n. pl.* articles or objects made by hand.

han · dle · bars (hand' əl bärz) *n. pl.* the part of a cycle that the rider holds and steers by.

hard · ship (hard'ship') *n.* something that causes difficulty, pain, or suffering.

har · mo · ny (här'mə nē) *n.* agreement; goodwill; accord.

har · ness (här'nis) *n.* the straps, bands, or other fastenings used to attach something to a person or animal.

hawk (hôk) *n.* a bird of prey. A hawk has a sharp, hooked beak, long claws, and short rounded wings.

hay · fork (hā'fôrk') *n.* a pitchfork.

hay · loft (hā'lôft') *n.* a loft, or upper story, in a barn or stable for storing hay.

ha · zy (hā'zē) *adj.* full of or blurred by smoke, mist, or dust.

hawk

head · ache (hed'āk') *n.* a pain in the head.

head · phone (hed'fōn') *n.* a radio or telephone receiver held against the ears. It is held in place by a band that fits over the head.

health · y (hel'thē) *adj.* having, showing, or giving good health.

hear · ing aid (hēr' ing ād') a small device that makes sounds louder. It is worn in or near the ear to make poor hearing better.

her · it · age (her' ə tij) *n.* something that is handed down from previous generations or from the past; tradition.

her · mit thrush (hur'mit thrush') a bird with a brown body, a spotted breast, and a reddish-brown tail.

he · ro (hēr'ō) *n.* a man or boy who is looked up to by others because he has done something brave or outstanding.

hes · i · tate (hez' ə tāt) *v.* to wait or stop for a moment; to pause briefly.

hi · ber · na · tion (hī'bər nā'shən) *n.* spending the winter in a dormant or inactive state, as do many animals, such as bears, squirrels, and snakes.

high wire (hī'wīr') a tightly stretched wire, cable, or rope placed high above the ground; tightrope.

hilt (hilt) *n.* the handle of a sword or dagger.

His · pan · ic (his pan'ik) *adj.* of or relating to Spain or Spanish America.

hob · by · horse (hob'ē hôrs') *n.* an early form of the bicycle.

hod (hod) *n.* a long-handled tool used for carrying bricks and mortar.

ho · gan (hō' gän) *n.* a dwelling used by the Navaho, usually made of logs and branches covered with earth.

home ec · o · nom · ics (hōm ek'ə nom' iks) the science and art of homemaking. Home economics includes nutrition, clothing, budgeting, and child care.

hoof · beat (hoof'bēt, hōof'bēt) *n.* the sound made by a hoofed animal when it walks, trots, or runs.

---

a bad, ā cake, ä father; e pet, ē me; i it, ī ice; o hot, ō open, ô off; oo wood, ōō food; oi oil, ou out; th thin, th that; u cup, ur turn, yōō music; zh treasure; ə ago, taken, pencil, lemon, helpful

ho · ri · zon (hə rī'zən) *n.* the line where the sky and the ground or the sea seem to meet.

hor · i · zon · tal (hor'ə zont'əl) *adj.* flat and straight across; parallel to or level with the horizon.

hor · net (hôr'nit) *n.* a large wasp that can give a very painful sting.

hos · pit · al (hos'pit əl) *n.* a place where doctors and nurses take care of people who are sick or hurt.

hornet

hum · bly (hum'blē) *adv.* in a way that is not proud.

hum · bug (hum'bug') *n.* one who tries to trick others.

hum · ming · bird (hum'ing burd') *n.* a small bird with brightly colored feathers and a long, narrow bill. Its wings beat so fast that they make a humming sound.

hun · ker (hun'kər) *v.* to squat.

Hwei Ming (hwā' ming')

I

i · den · ti · fi · ca · tion (ī den'tə fi kā'shən) *n.* anything by which a person or thing can be identified.

im · pe · ri · al (im pēr'ē əl) *adj.* having to do with an empire or an emperor or empress.

im · pres · sion (im presh'ən) *n.* an effect on the mind or feelings.

im · pres · sion · ism (im presh'ə niz'əm) *n.* a style of painting developed in the late nineteenth century by French painters such as Monet and Renoir.

im · pres · sion · is · tic (im presh'ə nis'tik) *adj.* of, relating to, or characteristic of impressionism.

in · ex · pen · sive (in'iks pen'siv) *adj.* not costing much; cheap.

in · for · ma · tion (in'fər mā'shən) *n.* **1.** knowledge or facts about something. **2.** a service that gives facts.

i · ni · tial (i nish'əl) *n.* the first letter of a word or name.

in · ju · ry (in'jə rē) *n.* damage or harm done to a person or thing.

inn (in) *n.* a small hotel, usually in the country.

in · sti · tute (in'stə tōōt', in'stə tyōōt') *n.* a school or other organization that is set up for a special purpose.

in · struc · tion (in struk'shən) *n.* the act of teaching or providing knowledge.

in · teg · ri · ty (in teg'rə tē) *n.* honesty.

in · ter · na · tion · al (in'tər nash'ə nəl) *adj.* having to do with or made up of two or more countries.

in · ter · rupt (in'tə rupt') *v.* to break in upon or stop a person who is acting or speaking.

in · ter · sec · tion (in'tər sek' shən, in' tər sek' shən) *n.* the place where two or more lines, roads, or streets meet and cross.

in · ter · view (in'tər vyōō') *n.* a meeting for a specific purpose.

in · volve (in volv') *v.* to have as a necessary part; include.

is · sue (ish'ōō) *n.* something that is sent or given out.

i · vo · ry (ī'və rē, īv'rē) *n.* a smooth, hard, white substance that forms the tusks of elephants, walruses, and certain other animals.

J

jas · mine (jaz′min) *n.* a fragrant bell-shaped flower growing in yellow, white, or pink clusters.

jave · lin (jav′lin, jav′ə lin) *n.* a light spear, used especially in athletic contests in which the object is to see who can throw it the farthest.

jasmine

jel · ly · fish (jel′ē fish′) *n.* a sea animal with a body that is soft and firm like jelly.

jest · er (jes′tər) *n.* a person who makes others laugh, especially a clown.

jew · el (jōō′əl) *n.* a precious stone; gem.

jig (jig) *n.* a fast lively dance.

jo · ey (jō′ē) *n.* a clown who uses white make-up to paint his or her face.

jour · ney (jur′nē) *n.* a long trip.

jug · gle (jug′əl) *v.* to keep two or more balls or other objects in continuous motion from the hands into the air by skillfully tossing and catching them.

jug · gler (jug′lər) *n.* a performer whose work is juggling.

junk · yard (jungk′yärd′) *n.* a place where junk is collected, stored, or sold.

Ju · ra (joor′ə)

K

Kam · ba (käm′bə)

Ken · ya (ken′yə, kēn′yə) *n.* a country in Africa.

ker · chief (kur′chif) *n.* a piece of cloth worn over the head or around the neck.

ki · mo · no (ki mō′nə) *n.* a loose robe or gown that is tied with a sash.

kind · ling (kind′ling) *n.* material for starting a fire, especially small pieces of wood.

Kin · tar · o (kin tär′ō)

kneel (nēl) *v.* **knelt, kneel · ing.** to go down on a bent knee or knees.

knelt (nelt) *v.* see *kneel.*

knife (nīf) *n. pl.,* **knives.** a tool that is used for cutting. A knife has a sharp blade attached to a handle.

knob (nob) *n.* a rounded lump.

knot (not) *n.* a fastening made by tying string, cord, rope. —*v.* **knot · ted, knot · ting.** to tie or fasten with a knot.

know-how (nō′hou′) *n.* the knowledge of how to do something; practical skill.

Kwa · ku A · nan · si (kwä′kōō än än′sē)

Kwa · ni (kwä′nē)

L

lack (lak) *n.* the state of being without or having too little.

lac · y (lā′sē) *adj.* of or resembling lace.

la · dy · bird (lā′dē burd′) *n.* a lady-bug; a small round insect that is red or orange with black spots.

lair (lār) *n.* a place where a wild animal lives or nests; den.

ladybird

lan · tern (lan′tərn) *n.* a case or container for a light, usually made to be carried.

a bad, ā cake, ä father; e pet, ē me; i it, ī ice; o hot, ō open, ô off; oo wood, ōō food; oi oil, ou out; th thin, th that; u cup, ur turn, yōō music; zh treasure; ə ago, taken, pencil, lemon, helpful

lar · va (lär′və) *n. pl.,* **lar · vae** (lär′vē)   the form of an insect in which it looks like a worm. The caterpillar is the larva of a moth beetle.

las · so (las′ō, la sōō′) *n.*   a long rope with a loop at one end, used especially to catch horses and cattle.

Lat · in (lat′in) *n.*   the language of the ancient Romans.

Lat · in A · mer · i · can (lat′in ə mer′i kən)   a person from one of the countries in the Western Hemisphere south of the United States in which the languages, such as Spanish or Portuguese, are of Latin origin.—*adj.* of or relating to Latin America.

leath · er · y (le<u>th</u>′ər ē) *adj.*   like leather; tough and hardened.

lec · ture (lek′chər) *v.*   to give a talk to an audience.

ledge (lej) *n.*   a narrow, flat surface jutting out from the side of a mountain or hill.

leg · end (lej′ənd) *n.*   a story passed down through the years that many people believe, but that is not entirely true.

length · wise (lengkth′wīz′, length′wīz′) *adj.*   in the direction of the length.

leop · ard (lep′ərd) *n.*   a large member of the cat family, found in Africa and Asia.

le · o · tard (lē′ə tärd′) *n.*   a stretchable, close-fitting piece of clothing, often worn while exercising or dancing.

let · tuce (let′is) *n.*   a plant with large green leaves.

li · brar · y (lī′brer′ē) *n.*   a room or a building for a collection of books and magazines.

li · chen (lī′kən) *n.*   a tiny plant without flowers that grows on tree trunks, rocks or the ground.

like · ness (līk′nis) *n.*   a being alike; resemblance.

lil · y pad (lil′ē pad′)   one of the large, flat, floating leaves of the water lily.

lin · en (lin′ən) *n.*   **1.** a strong cloth woven from flax fibers. **2.** articles or garments such as sheets, towels, and tablecloths, made of or once made of linen.

liv · er · wort (liv′ər wurt′) *n.*   a simple plant that looks something like moss.

liv · er · y (liv′ər ē) *n.*   a stable where horses are cared for and rented out.

loam (lōm) *n.*   soil that is a mixture of sand, clay, and silt.

lob · by (lob′ē) *n.*   an entrance hall.

lock · et (lok′it) *n.*   a small case for holding a picture of someone. It is usually worn on a chain around the neck.

lone · li · ness (lōn′lē nəs) *n.*   the state or quality of being lonely.

loom (lōōm) *n.*   a machine for weaving thread into cloth.

lug (lug) *v.* **lugged, lug · ging.**   to carry or drag with much trouble or effort.

lunge (lunj) *v.*   to move forward suddenly.

M

ma · gi · cian (mə jish′ən)   **1.** a person who entertains people by doing magic tricks. **2.** a man who has magical powers; wizard.

mag · nif · i · cent (mag nif′ə sənt) *adj.* splendid; exceptional; outstanding.

Ma · li · ki (mä lē′kē)

mam · mal (mam′əl) *n.*   a kind of animal that is warm-blooded and has a backbone. Most mammals are covered with fur or have some hair. Female mammals have glands that produce milk, which they feed to their young. People, cattle, dogs, and whales are mammals.

Ma · net (mä nā′)   a French impressionist painter.

ma · neu · ver (mə nōō′vər) *v.* to move or plan skillfully or cleverly.

man · ure (mə noor′, mə nyoor′) *n.* waste matter from animals that is used to fertilize land.

mar · a · thon (mar′ə thon′) *n.* **1.** a foot race of 26 miles and 385 yards that is run over an open course. **2.** any long race or contest to test endurance.

ma · rine (mə rēn′) *adj.* having to do with or living in the sea.

ma · rine bi · ol · o · gist (mə rēn′ bī ol′ə jist) a scientist who studies plants and animals that live in the sea.

marsh · y bog (märsh′ē bog′) low, wet, soft land covered with grasses and reeds.

Ma · sa · mu · ne (mä′sä′mōō nə)

mate (māt) *v.* to join in a pair for breeding.

math · e · mat · ics (math′ə mat′iks) *n. pl.* the study of numbers, quantities, measurements, and shapes, and how they relate to each other.

Mc Gui · gan, Frank (mə gwi′gən)

Mchung · wa (chung′wä′)

meas · ure (mezh′ər) *n.* an instrument or device used for measuring. — *v.* to find or show the size, weight, or amount of something.

meas · ure · ment (mezh′ər mənt) *n.* something found by measuring; the size, height, or amount of something.

me · chan · i · cal (mi kan′i kəl) *adj.* produced or operated by a machine.

med · al (med′əl) *n.* a flat piece of metal bearing a design or inscription.

med · i · cine man (med′i sin man′) Indian tribesman thought to have magical powers.

mel · o · dy (mel′ə dē) *n.* a series of musical notes; a tune.

mel · on (mel′ən) *n.* a large fruit that grows on a vine. Melons have a sweet, soft pulp that can be eaten.

mem · brane (mem′brān) *n.* a thin layer of skin or tissue.

mem · o · rize

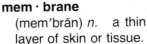

melon

(mem′ə rīz′) *v.* to learn by heart; fix in the memory.

Men · dez, Con · sue · lo (men′dez, con swä′lō)

met · a · tar · sus (met′ə tär′səs) *n.* the part of the foot between the ankle and the toes, consisting of five bones.

me · te · or · ol · o · gist (mē′tē ə rol′ə jist) *n.* a person who studies meteorology or who knows a great deal about meteorology.

me · te · or · ol · o · gy (mē′tē ə rol′ə jē) *n.* the science that studies the earth's atmosphere and the changes that take place within it. One branch of meteorology is the study of the weather.

mim · ic (mim′ik) *v.* **mim · icked, mim · ick · ing.** to imitate; copy movement or sound.

a bad, ā cake, ä father; e pet, ē me; i it, ī ice; o hot, ō open, ô off; oo wood, ōō food; oi oil, ou out; th thin, th that; u cup, ur turn, yōō music; zh treasure; ə ago, taken, pencil, lemon, helpful

mi · nor · i · ty (mə nôr′ə tē, mī nôr′ə tē) *n.* a group of people that is thought of as different from the larger group of which it is a part because of race, religion, politics, or nationality.

mix · ture (miks′chər) *n.* something made up of different things that are put together.

Mmo · bor · o (mə bôr′ō)

mod · er · ate (mod′ər it) *adj.* not too much or too little; not extreme.

mod · ern (mod′ərn) *adj.* relating to the present or recent time.

moist (moist) *adj.* slightly wet; damp.

mole crick · et (mōl′ krik′it) an insect with large front legs used for digging in moist soil.

mon · arch (mon′ərk) *n.* a person, such as a king or queen, who rules a country.

Mo · net (mō nā′) a French impressionist painter.

monk (mungk) *n.* a man who has joined a religious order, lives in a monastery, and is bound by religious vows.

mon · key · shine (mung′kē shīn′) *n.* a playful trick, joke, or prank.

mon · o · gram (mon′ə gram′) *n.* a design made by combining two or more letters, especially the initials of one's name.

mon · u · ment (mon′yə ment) *n.* a building, statue, or other object that is made to honor a person or event.

mor · sel (môr′səl) *n.* a small bite of food or piece of something.

mos · qui · to (mə skē′tō) *n. pl.,* **mos · qui · toes** or **mos · qui · tos.** a small insect with two wings. The female gives a sharp sting or bite that itches.

moth (môth) *n.* an insect that looks like a butterfly, but that flies mostly at night. The larvae of some moths eat holes in wool and other fabrics.

mound (mound) *n.* **1.** any heap or pile of earth, stone, garbage, and so on. **2.** a small hill.

moun · tain li · on (mount′ən lī′ən) a large wildcat found mainly in North America, also known as a cougar or a puma.

mountain lion

moun · tain · side (mount′ən sīd′) *n.* the side or slope of a mountain.

mount · ing (moun′ting) *n.* a support or setting.

mourn · ful · ly (môrn′fə lē) *adv.* in a manner expressing sorrow.

mouth harp (mouth härp) a musical wind instrument consisting of a small slotted case that contains a series of metal reeds. It is played by inhaling and exhaling through the slots; harmonica.

move · ment (mōōv′mənt) *n.* one of the main divisions or sections of a musical composition.

mu · ral (myoor′əl) *n.* a picture painted on a wall or ceiling.

mus · tard greens (mus′tərd grēnz′) the edible green leaves of any of several plants, such as broccoli, cabbage, and turnips, belonging to the mustard family.

mus · ty (mus′tē) *adj.* moldy; stale.

mut · ter (mut′ər) *v.* to speak in a low, unclear way with the mouth almost closed.

mys · ter · y (mis′tə rē) *n.* something that is not or cannot be known, explained, or understood.

N

nar · cis · sus (när sis′əs) *n.* a showy yellow or white flower.

nar · ra · tor (nar′āt ər) *n.*   a person who tells or relates something. A narrator often reads descriptive passages between the speeches or scenes of a play.

nat · u · ral sci · ence (nach′ər əl sī′əns) any of the sciences concerned with nature. The natural sciences include bio - logy, physics, chemistry and geology.

Nav · a · ho (nav′ə hō, näv′ə hō)   a member of a tribe of North American Indians living in New Mexico, Arizona, and Utah.

nerv · ous · ly (nur′vəs lē) *adv.*   uneasily; anxiously.

nes · tle (nes′əl) *v.*   to press or lie close; snuggle; cuddle.

nick · name (nik′nām′) *n.*   **1.** a word or phrase, especially a descriptive one, used in addition to or instead of a name. **2.** a familiar, usually shortened form of a name.

night · in · gale (nīt ən gāl′, nī′ ting gāl′) *n.* a small bird with reddish-brown feathers and a whitish breast.

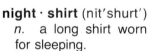

night · shirt (nīt′shurt′) *n.* a long shirt worn for sleeping.

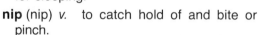

nightingale

nip (nip) *v.*   to catch hold of and bite or pinch.

no · ble (nō′bəl) *adj.*   having high rank or title.

No · mu · ra, Danny (nō mōō′rə)

non · sense (non′sens) *n.*   a way of talking or acting that is silly and makes no sense.

non · stop (non′stop′) *adj.*   not making any stops; without stops.

nook (nook) *n.*   **1.** any small recess or corner. **2.** a secluded place.

nurs · er · y (nur′sə rē) *n.*   a baby's bedroom.

Ny · a · me (nī ä′mē)

o

ob · lige (ə blīj′) *v.*   to make thankful for a service or a favor.

ob · ser · va · tion (ob′zer vā′shən) *n.*   the act or power of noticing.

oc · ca · sion · al · ly (ə kā′zhən ə lē) *adv.*   once in a while; at times.

o · dor (ō′dər) *n.*   smell; scent.

of · fi · cial (ə fish′əl) *n.*   a person who holds a certain office or position.

old-fashioned (ōld′fash′ənd) *adj.*   of or having to do with former times; out-of-date.

O · lym · pic Games (ō lim′pik gāmz′)   **1.** a festival in ancient Greece consisting of a series of competitions in athletics, poetry, music, and oratory. **2.** modern international athletic contests held every four years in a different country.

O · ni · ni (ō nē′nē)

op · er · a · tor (op′ə rā′tər) *n.*   a person who operates a machine or other device.

o · pin · ion (ə pin′yən) *n.*   a belief or conclusion based on a person's judgment rather than on what is proven or known to be true.

---

a bad, ā cake, ä father; e pet, ē me; i it, ī ice; o hot, ō open, ô off; oo wood, o͞o food; oi oil, ou out; th thin, <u>th</u> that; u cup, ur turn, yo͞o music; zh treasure; ə ago, taken, pencil, lemon, helpful

o·pos·sum (ə pos'əm) *n.* a small furry animal that lives in trees and carries its young in a pouch.

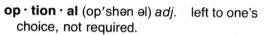

opossum

op·po·nent (ə pō'nənt) *n.* a person who opposes, fights, or competes with another.

op·tion·al (op'shən əl) *adj.* left to one's choice, not required.

o·ral (ôr'əl) *adj.* not written; using speech; spoken.

or·ches·tra (ôr'kis trə) *n.* a group of musicians playing together on various instruments.

or·di·nar·y (ôrd'ən er'ē) *adj.* commonly used; habitual or regular; usual.

o·ryx (ôr'iks) *n.* an antelope found in desert regions of Africa and Arabia.

O·se·bo (o sē'bō)

os·trich (os'trich, ô'strich) *n. pl.,* **os·trich·es.** a large, two-toed bird that has a long neck, long strong legs, and a small flat head. The ostrich is the largest of all living birds.

o·ver·grown (ō vər grōn') *adj.* covered with weeds, vines, or other growth.

o·ver·look (ō'vər look') *v.* to not see, notice, or think of.

oys·ter (ois'tər) *n.* an animal that has a soft body and a rough, hinged shell.

P

Pan-A·mer·i·ca (pan'ə mer'i kə) North, Central, and South America.

par·a·chute (par'ə shōōt') *n.* a large device made of fabric that is shaped like an umbrella. A parachute is attached to something to slow it down as it falls through the air.

par·a·sol (par'ə sôl') *n.* a small, lightweight umbrella usually used as a protection from the sun.

par·tic·u·lar (pər tik'yə lər) *adj.* very careful; special.

pas·sen·ger (pas'ən jər) *n.* a person who travels in an automobile, bus, train, airplane, or boat.

Pass·o·ver (pas'ō'vər) *n.* a Jewish holiday that celebrates the escape of the Jews from slavery in Egypt long ago.

pa·tel·la (pə tel'ə) *n.* the kneecap.

pat·ent (pat'ənt) *n.* a piece of paper given to a person or company by the government. It gives someone the right to be the only one to make, use, or sell a new invention.

pa·tience (pā'shəns) *n.* the ability to put up with hardship, pain, trouble, or delay without getting angry or upset.

pa·tient (pā'shənt) *adj.* being able to put up with hardship, pain, trouble, or delay without getting angry or upset.

Pav·lo·va, An·na (päv'lō və, än'ə) a Russian ballet dancer.

peb·ble (peb'əl) *n.* a small stone that is usually round and smooth.

ped·al (ped'əl) *n.* a lever worked by the foot.

peer (pēr) *v.* to look closely or searchingly.

peg (peg) *n.* a piece of wood, metal, or other hard substance that can be fitted or driven into a surface to fasten parts together or to serve as a marker.

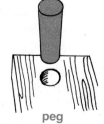

peg

Pe·king (pē'king') the capital of the Chinese People's Republic.

pel · let (pel'it) *n.* a small hard piece of something that is shaped like a bullet or ball.

per · cent (pər sent') *n.* the number of parts in or to every hundred.

Pe · rez, Irene (pä rez')

per · fec · tion (pər fek'shən) *n.* the condition of being perfect or without fault.

per · form (pər fôrm') *v.* **1.** to carry out; do. **2.** to sing, act, or do something in public that requires skill.

per · for · mance (pər fôr'məns) *n.* a public presentation of a play, musical program, or other entertainment.

perk up (purk' up') to recover one's liveliness and vigor.

per · suade (pər swād') *v.* to cause to do or believe something by argument; convince.

pest (pest) *n.* a person or thing that is troublesome or annoying; nuisance.

phil · har · mon · ic (fil'här mon'ik) *adj.* of, relating to, or presented by a musical society or an orchestra, especially a symphony orchestra.

phos · pho · res · cent (fos'fə res'ənt) *adj.* giving off of light from a substance that has absorbed radiant energy, continuing after the source of energy is removed.

phys · i · cal (fiz'i kəl) *adj.* of or relating to the body.

phy · si · cian (fə zish'ən) *n.* a doctor.

pi · an · ist (pē an'ist, pē'ə nist) *n.* a person who plays the piano.

pierc · ing (pēr'sing) *adj.* sharp and shrill.

Pi · er · rot (pē'ər ō', pē'ə rō')

pil · low · case (pil'ō kās') *n.* a removable cloth cover for a pillow.

pin · cush · ion moss (pin'koosh'ən môs') a kind of moss that grows in clumps that resemble pincushions.

pin · point (pin'point') *n.* **1.** the point of a pin. **2.** something very small or unimportant.

pip · er (pī'pər) *n.* a person who plays on a pipe, especially a bagpipe.

pit (pit) *n.* **1.** a hole in the ground that is natural or made by people. **2.** a hollow place in the surface of anything.

plead (plēd) *v.* to request; beg.

pli · ers (plī'ərz) *n. pl.* a tool made for gripping or bending things. Some pliers can also cut wire.

plo · ver (pluv'ər, plō'vər) *n.* a bird with a straight, pointed bill.

po · et · ry (pō'i trē) *n.* poems.

poi · son · ous (poi'zə nəs) *adj.* causing sickness or death by poison.

poi · son-tipped (poi'zən tipt') *adj.* having the tip covered with a substance that causes sickness or death.

po · lar bear (pō'lər bār') a large white bear that lives in the Arctic.

por · ce · lain (pôr'sə lin) *n.* a fine baked clay material that is hard and white.

polar bear

por · ridge (pôr'ij, por'ij) *n.* a soft food made by cooking oatmeal or other cereals in water or milk.

---

a **b**a**d**, ā **c**a**ke**, ä **f**a**ther**; e **pet**, ē **me**; i **it**, ī **ice**; o **hot**, ō **open**, ô **off**; oo **wood**, ōō **food**; oi **oil**, ou **out**; th **thin**, <u>th</u> **that**; u **cup**, ur **turn**, yōō **music**; zh **treasure**; ə **ago**, tak**e**n, penc**i**l, lem**o**n, helpf**u**l

por · trait (pôr′trit, pôr′trāt) *n.* a picture of someone.

pos · ses · sion (pə zesh′ən) *n.* something owned.

pos · si · bil · i · ty (pos′ə bil′ə tē) *n. pl.,* **pos · si · bil · i · ites.** something that is possible.

pos · sum (pos′əm) *n.* a small furry animal. The female carries its young in a pouch on its stomach. This animal is usually called an *opossum.*

po · tion (pō′shən) *n.* a drink, especially one believed to have magic powers.

pounce (pouns) *v.* to come down on suddenly and take hold of; leap on and attack suddenly.

prai · rie (prār′ē) *n.* flat or rolling land covered with grass.

prayer wheel (prer′hwēl′) a revolving drum containing written prayers used by Buddhists of Tibet.

pre · cious (presh′əs) *adj.* of great cost or value.

prey (prā) *n.* an animal that is hunted by another animal for food.

pri · ma bal · le · ri · na (prē′mə bal′ə rē′nə) the leading female dancer in a ballet company.

probe (prōb) *v.* to investigate or explore thoroughly.

pro · ces · sion (prə sesh′ən) *n.* a group of people moving forward in a line or in order.

pro · fes · sion · al (prə fesh′ə nəl) *adj.* **1.** of or relating to a profession or a person in a profession. **2.** working for money in an activity or occupation not usually pursued for gain, especially a sport. — *n.* a person skilled or expert in a particular activity or occupation.

pro · gress (prog′res) *n.* a forward movement; advancement.

prop (prop) *n.* a moveable thing, except scenery and costumes, used in a play or other theatrical entertainment. The word *prop* is short for *property.*

pro · test (prə test′) *v.* to object to or disapprove of.

pug nose (pug′ nōz) a short, broad, turned-up nose.

pul · let (pool′it) *n.* a young hen less than a year old.

pu · pa (pyōō′pə) *n. pl.,* **pu · pae** (pyōō′pē). an insect at the stage after it is a larva and before it is an adult. A caterpillar in its cocoon is a pupa.

pur · ti · est (pur′tē ist) *adj.* dialect for *prettiest.*

py · thon (pī′thon′) *n.* a large snake that coils around its prey and crushes or suffocates it.

Q

quaint (kwānt) *adj.* pleasant or attractive in an old-fashioned or amusing way.

qual · i · ty (kwol′ə tē) *n.* something that makes a person or thing what it is.

quan · ti · ty (kwon′tə tē) *n. pl.,* **quan · ti · ties.** a number or amount.

queen ant (kwēn′ ant′) the fully developed reproductive female ant.

Queens · bor · o Bridge (kwēnz′bər ō) a bridge in New York City over the East River, connecting the borough of Manhattan to the borough of Queens.

ques · tion · ing · ly (kwes′chə ning lē) *adv.* in the manner of one who questions.

qui · pu (kē′pōō, kwip′ōō) *n. pl.,* **qui · pus.** an arrangement of knotted strings used by the Indians of Peru to keep records and send messages.

quo · ta · tion (kwō tā′shən) *n.* a person's words repeated exactly by another person.

quote (kwōt) *v.*   to repeat the exact words.

R

rac·coon (ra'kōōn') *n.*   a small animal with brownish-gray fur. It has a pointed face with black mask-like markings and a long, bushy tail marked with black rings.

raccoon

raft·er (raf'tər) *n.*   one of the sloping beams that support a roof.

rail·road tie (rāl'rōd' tī')   a wooden beam to which the rails are fastened.

rail·road tres·tle (rāl'rōd' tres'əl)   a framework used to support a railroad bridge.

re·al·is·tic (rē'ə lis'tik) *adj.*   showing people, things, or events as they actually are in everyday life.

reb·el (ri bel') *v.*   **re·belled, re·bel·ling.**   to refuse to obey laws or authority.

re·build (rē bild') *v.*   **re·built, re·build·ing. 1.** to build again. **2.** to make changes in, repair, or remodel.

re·call (ri kôl') *v.*   to remember; bring back to mind.

reed (rēd) *n.*   a tall grass having long, narrow leaves and jointed stems.

re·flec·tor (ri flek'tər) *n.*   something that turns or throws back light, heat, or sound.

reg·is·ter (rej'is tər) *v.*   to write in a list or record.

reg·u·lar (reg'yə lər) *adj.*   **1.** customary; expected; usual; normal. **2.** unvarying; steady.

reg·u·la·tion (reg' yə lā'shən) *n.*   a law, rule, or order.

re·la·tion·ship (ri lā'shən ship') *n.*   link; connection.

rel·a·tive (rel'ə tiv) *n.*   a person connected with another by blood or marriage.

re·li·gion (ri lij'ən) *n.*   **1.** belief in or worship of God or a god or gods. **2.** a particular system of belief and worship.

re·mark·a·ble (ri mär'kə bəl) *adj.*   worthy of being noticed; not ordinary, unusual.

Re·noir (ren wär')   a French painter.

re·peal (ri pēl') *v.*   to take back; cancel; do away with something.

re·pre·sent (rep'ri zent') *v.*   to stand for; symbolize.

re·quest (ri kwest') *v.*   to ask or ask for.

re·quire (ri kwīr') *v.*   **1.** to have need of. **2.** to have as a duty.

res·o·lu·tion (rez'ə lōō'shən) *n.*   something decided upon; vow.

re·spect (ri spekt') *v.*   to have or show consideration or respect.

re·sult (ri zult') *n.*   something that occurs or is brought about.

rhyth·mic (rith'mic) *adj.*   having a regular or orderly repetition of sounds or movement.

rick·et·y (rik'ə tē) *adj.*   shaky; about to fall apart or break down.

ring·mas·ter (ring'mas'tər) *n.*   a person who introduces the acts in a circus.

rip · ple (rip′əl) *v.* to form or cause to form waves or wavelike ridges.

Rod · ri · guez, Patricia (rod rē′ gez)

Ro · man (rō′man) *adj.* of or relating to Rome. — *n.* a person who lived in ancient Rome.

roost (rōōst) *n.* a perch on which birds rest or sleep.

round up (round′up′) to drive or herd something together, such as cattle or horses.

rouse (rouz) *v.* **1.** to awaken from sleep or rest. **2.** to stir up; excite.

roy · al · ty (roi′əl tē) *n.* a royal person or persons. Kings, queens, princes, and princesses are royalty.

ruf · fled (ruf′əld) *adj.* gathered, pleated, or folded.

S

sal · a · man · der (sal′ə man′dər) *n.* an animal that looks like a small lizard. Salamanders live in or near fresh water.

salamander

sam · u · rai (sam′oo rī′) *n.* in feudal Japan, a member of the warrior class.

San Fran · cis · co (san′ frən sis′kō) a port city in western California on the Pacific Ocean.

sash (sash) *n.* a broad band of cloth or ribbon worn around the waist or over one shoulder.

scab · bard (skab′ərd) *n.* a case or sheath for the blade of a sword, bayonet, or similar weapon.

scal · lop (skol′əp, skal′əp) *v.* to shape or make with a series of curves.

scar · let fe · ver (skär′ lit fē′vər) a disease occurring most often in children, marked by a scarlet rash, high fever, and a sore throat.

scen · er · y (sē′nə rē) *n.* the general appearance of a place.

Sche · nec · ta · dy (skə nek′tə dē) a city in eastern New York.

schol · ar (skol′ər) *n.* a person having much knowledge and an interest in learning and study.

schol · ar · ship (skol′ər ship′) *n.* a grant of financial aid given to help a student continue studies.

scorn (skôrn) *n.* a feeling of hatred for someone or something.

scowl (skoul) *n.* an angry frown.

scram · ble (skram′bəl) *v.* to move or climb quickly.

scrim · shaw (skrim′shô′) *n.* the art of carving or engraving designs on whalebone, ivory, or shells.

scur · ry (skur′ē) *v.* **scur · ried, scur · ry · ing.** to go or move in a hurry.

scut · tle (skut′əl) *v.* to move with short, rapid steps.

seal · ing wax (sēl′ing waks′) a mixture usually made of shellac and turpentine that is used to seal letters, packages, and jars.

sec · ond · hand (sek′ənd hand′) *adj.* once owned or used by someone else.

sec · tion boss (sek′shən bôs) the person who watches over and plans the work of the crew who maintain a railroad section.

sed · en · tar · y (sed′ən ter′ē) *adj.* remaining in one place, not moving about.

se · lec · tion (si lek′shən) *n.* a person or thing that is chosen.

sen · ior (sēn′yər) *adj.* higher in rank, longer in service, or older in age. — *n.* a person who is older than another or higher in rank than another.

sen · si · tive (sen′sə tiv) *adj.* capable of receiving signals through the senses.

se · ries (sēr′ēz) *n.* a number of similar things coming one after another.

ser · pent (sur′pənt) *n.* **1.** a snake, especially a large or poisonous one. **2.** a kind of fireworks that resembles a snake when it explodes.

shal · low (shal′ō) *adj.* not deep.

shear (shēr) *v.* to cut off; remove.

sheer (shēr) *adj.* total; utter.

shield (shēld) *n.* a piece of armor used in olden times. It was carried on the arm to protect the body during battle.

shil · ling (shil′ing) *n.* a coin that was once used in Great Britain and other countries.

shoe · shine chair (shoo′shīn chār′) a chair on which to sit while having one's shoes shined.

shov · el (shuv′əl) *n.* a tool with a broad scoop.

shriv · el (shriv′əl) *v.* to become smaller and wrinkled or curled.

Si · a · mese (sī′ ə mēz′) *adj.* from, of, or relating to Siam, a country in Southeast Asia now known as Thailand.

shovel

si · dle (sīd′əl) *v.* to move sideways, especially in a sly manner.

sight · less (sīt′lis) *adj.* unable to see; blind.

sil · hou · ette (sil′oo et′) *n.* a picture or drawing showing the outline of a figure or object filled in with black or another solid color.

silk · en (sil′kən) *adj.* like silk; silky.

sim · i · lar (sim′ə lər) *adj.* much the same; alike.

sim · i · le (sim′ə lē) *n.* a figure of speech in which one object or idea is compared with another in order to suggest that they are alike.

siz · zle (siz′əl) *v.* to make a hissing sound.

sketch (skech) *v.* to draw roughly and quickly.

skill · ful (skil′fəl) *adj.* having, showing, or involving the power or ability to do something.

skit · ter (skit′ər) *v.* to glide or skim lightly and quickly over a surface.

sky blue (skī bloo) warm, light blue, like the color of the clear sky.

slave (slāv) *n.* a person who is the property of another person.

slav · er · y (slā′və rē, slāv′rē) *n.* the practice of owning slaves.

slice (slīs) *n.* a thin, flat piece cut from something larger.

slight · est (slī′tist) *n.* smallest in quantity, degree, or strength.—*adj.* of smallest importance.

slit (slit) *n.* a long, narrow cut or opening.

slith · er (slith′ ər) *n.* a sliding or gliding motion.

---

a bad, ā cake, ä father; e pet, ē me; i it, ī ice; o hot, ō open, ô off; oo wood, ōō food; oi oil, ou out; th thin, th that; u cup, ur turn, yōō music; zh treasure; ə ago, taken, pencil, lemon, helpful

sloop (slo͞op) *n.* a sailboat with one mast and sails that run from front to rear.

slump (slump) *v.* to fall or sink suddenly or heavily.

snag (snag) *v.* to catch by a quick action.

snail (snāl) *n.* a kind of animal that is found in water and on land. Snails have soft bodies that are protected by a spiral-shaped shell.

snap · ping tur · tle (snap'ing tur'təl) a large freshwater tur-tle of the eastern and southern United States. It has power-ful jaws that snap with great force.

snapping turtle

snare (snār) *v.* to catch.

snif · fle (snif'əl) *v.* to breathe through the nose or sniff again and again.

snort (snôrt) *v.* to force air violently and noisily through the nose.

sod (sod) *n.* the top layer of soil that has grass growing on it.

sol · emn (sol'əm) *adj.* very serious; grave.

sol · i · tar · y (sol' i ter' ē) *adj.* **1.** alone. **2.** single.

so · lu · tion (sə lo͞o'shən) *n.* the answer to a problem.

sow bug (sou' bug') a small animal re-lated to crabs and shrimp that lives on the ground in damp places.

spare · ribs (spār' ribz') *n. pl.* a cut of pork consisting of the thin end of the ribs with most of the meat trimmed off.

spec · ta · cles (spek'tə kəls) *n. pl.* a pair of eyeglasses.

spec · tac · u · lar (spek tak'yə lər) *adj.* of or resembling a spectacle.—*n.* an elaborate show.

spec · ta · tor (spek'tā'tər) *n.* a person who watches but does not take part.

spi · der · y (spī'də rē) *adj.* resembling a spider or a spider's web; long and thin or delicate.

spin · ner · et (spin'ə ret') *n.* an organ by which various animals, such as spiders, spin silken threads.

sponge (spunj) *n.* a water animal that lives attached to rocks. Sponges have bodies that are full of holes and absorb water eas-ily.

sponge

spook · y (spo͞o'kē) *adj.* scary.

sprint (sprint) *v.* to run at full speed, espe-cially for a short distance.

spur (spur) *n.* a spine-like projection on the legs of certain birds.

squall (skwôl) *v.* to cry or scream loudly and harshly.

squash · y (skwosh'ē) *adj.* soft and wet.

squirm (skwurm) *v.* to turn or twist the body; wriggle.

sta · di · um (stā'dē əm) *n.* a large, usu-ally unroofed structure surrounding an open area that is used for athletic events or other purposes.

stag · ger (stag'ər) *v.* to move or cause to move with a swaying motion.

stale (stāl) *adj.* **1.** not fresh. **2.** not new or interesting.

starch (stärch) *n.* any substance used to stiffen cloth.

star · flow · er (stär'flou'ər) *n.* a plant with white or pink flowers having five petals in the shape of a star.

starve (stärv) *v.* to suffer from or die of hunger.

state · ment (stāt′ mənt) *n.* something said.

sta · tion · mas · ter (stā′shən mas′tər) *n.* a person in charge of a railroad station or a bus station.

steal · thi · ly (stel′thə lē) *adv.* in a secret manner.

steam · shov · el (stēm′shuv′əl) *n.* a large machine that is used for digging. It has a large bucket or scoop on the end of a long beam.

stee · ple (stē′pəl) *n.* a high tower with a top part that narrows to a point. Steeples are often built on the roofs of churches.

steer (stēr) *n.* a bull, especially one raised for beef.

Steg · o · sau · rus (steg′ə sôr′əs) *n.* a large dinosaur with a spiked tail and two rows of bony plates along its back.

stern (sturn) *adj.* strict; harsh.

sting (sting) *v.* **stung, sting · ing.** to cause or have a sharp, burning pain or hurt.

stone fly (stōn′ flī′) an insect with two pairs of thin wings.

store · keep · er (stôr′ kē′pər) *n.* a person who owns or runs a store.

straight · for · ward (strāt′fôr′wərd) *adj.* direct; sincere.

strand (strand) *n.* one of the threads or wires twisted together to form a rope, cord, cable, or yarn.

stroll (strōl) *v.* to walk in a slow, relaxed way.

stud (stud) *v.* **stud · ded, stud · ding.** to set or ornament with.

stum · ble (stum′bəl) *v.* to lose one's balance; trip.

stunt (stunt) *n.* a special feat or performance that is done to attract attention.

stur · dy (stur′dē) *adj.* strong; hardy.

style (stīl) *n.* a particular way of doing things, especially in painting and in other arts.

sub · ject (sub′jikt) *n.* a person under the control or authority of another.

sub · stance (sub′stəns) *n.* material; matter.

sub · urb (sub′urb) *n.* a residential area close to or on the edge of a city.

sub · way (sub′wā′) *n.* a railroad under the ground.

su · ki · ya · ki (sōō′kē yä′kē, skē yä′kē) *n.* a Japanese dish made of thin strips of meat and vegetables cooked quickly in butter or oil.

sulk · i · ly (sul′kə lē) *adv.* in a silent or withdrawn manner that is a sign of anger or a bad humor.

sum · mit (sum′it) *n.* the highest point.

sum · mon (sum′ən) *v.* to send for or request the presence of.

sun · beam (sun′bēm′) *n.* a ray of sunlight.

sun · down (sun′ doun′) *n.* the setting of the sun.

su · per · mar · ket (sōō′ pər mär′ kit) *n.* a large store that sells food and household goods.

sup · port (sə pôrt′) *n.* a person or thing that supports or holds up something.

---

a bad, ā cake, ä father; e pet, ē me; i it, ī ice; o hot, ō open, ô off; oo wood, ōō food; oi oil, ou out; th thin, th that; u cup, ur turn, yōō music; zh treasure; ə ago, taken, pencil, lemon, helpful

sur · face (sur′fis) *n.* the outside or top part of a thing.

swal · low (swol′ō) *n.* a small bird with long wings and a forked tail.

swear (swār) *v.* **swore, sworn, swear · ing.** to make a solemn statement; vow.

swerve (swurv) *v.* to turn aside suddenly.

swoop (swo͞op) *v.* to rush or come down with a sudden, sweeping movement.

swore (swôr) *v.* see *swear.*

syc · a · more (sik′ə môr′) *n.* a kind of tree that has smooth, brown bark that flakes off in thin layers, leaving patches on the trunk.

sycamore

sym · bol (sim′bəl) *n.* something that stands for or represents something else.

sym · pa · thize (sim′pə thīz′) *v.* to agree with the feelings, ideas, or aims of.

sym · pho · ny (sim′fə nē) *n.* **1.** a long musical composition written for an orchestra. A symphony usually has four parts. **2.** A large orchestra that plays symphonies.

T

Ta · glio · ni, Ma · rie (tǟl yō′nē) a nineteenth century ballerina.

tal · ent (tal′ənt) *n.* a natural ability or skill.

tan · ge · rine (tan′jə rēn′) *n.* a sweet, juicy, reddish-orange citrus fruit.

tar · di · ness (tär′dē nəs) *n.* lateness.

tar · sus (tär′səs) *n.* the seven small bones making up the ankle.

task (task) *n.* a piece of work to be done.

tas · sel (tas′əl) *n.* a hanging group of threads or cords that are tied together at one end.

tat · tered (tat′ərd) *adj.* torn or hanging in shreds.

tax (taks) *n. pl.,* **tax · es.** money paid by people for the support of the government.

tel · e · cast (tel′ə kast′) *n.* a program broadcast over television.

tel · e · type (tel′ə tīp′) *n.* equipment by which a message typed on one teletypewriter is sent over an electric circuit to another typewriter, which types out the message.

tem · per · a · ture (tem′pər ə chər) *n.* the degree of heat or coldness.

tempt · ing (temp′ting) *adj.* attractive; appealing.

ten · ant (ten′ənt) *n.* a person who pays money to use a house, apartment, office or land.

ter · ri · fy (ter′ə fī′) *v.* **ter · ri · fied, ter · ri · fy · ing.** to fill with terror.

ter · ri · to · ry (ter′ə tôr′ ē) *n.* a large area of land; region.

tex · ture (teks′chər) *n.* the look or feel of something.

the · a · ter (thē′ ə tər) *n.* a building or other place where plays or motion pictures are presented.

thigh (thī) *n.* the part of the leg between the hip and the knee.

thor · ough · ly (thur′ə lē) *adv.* in a careful and complete manner.

thrash (thrash) *v.* to make wild movements; toss violently.

threat · en (thret′ən) *v.* **1.** to express an intent to do harm or injury. **2.** to give signs or warnings of.

thrush (thrush) *n.* one of many kinds of birds known for their song.

thrush

tib · i · a (tib′ē ə) *n.* the inner and thicker of the two bones of the leg, extending from the knee to the ankle; shinbone.

tight · rope walk · er (tīt′rōp′ wô′ kər) a performer who does tricks on a tightly stretched wire, high above the ground.

tin · gle (tin′gəl) *v.* to have a slight stinging feeling.

to · bac · co (tə bak′ō) *n.* plant leaves that are used for smoking and chewing.

ton (tun) *n.* a measure of weight equal to 2000 pounds in the United States.

torch (tôrch) *n.* a flaming light, usually consisting of some material soaked in a substance that will burn when wound around the end of a stick.

to · tem (tō′təm) *n.* an animal, plant, or other object that is the symbol of a family of North American Indians. The Indians carved these symbols on poles that stood outside their homes.

tour · ist (toor′ist) *n.* a person who travels on a vacation.

tour · na · ment (toor′nə mənt, tur′nə mənt) *n.* a series of contests involving two or more persons or teams.

trace (trās) *v.* to follow the trail, course, or path of someone or something.

trade · mark (trād′märk′) *n.* a picture, word, or mark that a manufacturer uses to show that it made a product.

trad · ing post (trād′ing pōst′) a store or station set up by a trader or trading company in a frontier region, where the local people can obtain goods, often in exchange for local products.

tra · di · tion (trə dish′ən) *n.* customs, beliefs, or other knowledge that is passed down from parents to their children.

trans · con · ti · nen · tal (trans′kon tə nent′əl) *adj.* crossing a continent.

tra · peze (tra pēz′, trə pēz′) *n.* a short, swinging horizontal bar hung high above the ground by ropes.

trem · ble (trem′bəl) *v.* to shake with cold, fear, weakness, or anger.

Tri · cer · a · tops (trī ser′ə tops′) *n.* a plant-eating dinosaur that had one long horn over each eye, a shorter horn on the snout, and a bony shield over the back of the neck.

trick · le (trik′ əl) *v.* to flow or fall drop by drop or in a thin stream.

tri · col · or (trī′ kul′ ər) *adj.* having three colors.

trill (tril) *n.* a quavering, trembling, usually high-pitched sound.

Tri · na (trē′ nə)

tri · um · phant (trī um′fənt) *adj.* victorious; successful.

tro · chan · ter (trō kan′tər) *n.* any of several jutting processes at the upper end of the thighbone.

trop · i · cal (trop′ i kəl) *adj.* having to do with or found in the tropics.

a bad, ā cake, ä father; e pet, ē me; i it, ī ice; o hot, ō open, ô off; oo wood, ōō food; oi oil, ou out; th thin, th that; u cup, ur turn, yōō music; zh treasure; ə ago, taken, pencil, lemon, helpful

trough (trôf) *n.* a long, deep, narrow box or other container. Farmers use troughs to hold food and water for animals.

trou · sers (trou′zərz) *n. pl.* a piece of clothing worn over the lower part of the body that covers each leg.

trow · el (trou′əl) n. a hand tool with a narrow, curved, pointed blade used in gardening to scoop or dig.

trowel

trudge (truj) *v.* to walk slowly and with an effort.

truf · fle (truf′əl) *n.* a mushroom shaped like a potato that grows underground.

tun · nel (tun′əl) *v.* to make a long passageway under or through something.

tur · quoise (tur′kwoiz, tur′koiz) n. a greenish-blue stone.

tusk (tusk) *n.* a long, pointed tooth that sticks out of the side of the mouth of certain animals. Elephants, walruses, and wild boars have tusks.

tus · sle (tus′əl) *v.* to engage in a disorderly fight.

tweez · ers (twē′zərz) *n. pl.* small pincers for plucking out hairs or for picking up small objects.

twitch (twich) *v.* to move or pull with a sudden jerk or tug.

twitch · e · ty (twich′ə tē) *adj.* moving with sudden jerks.

U

un · der · brush (un′dər brush′) *n.* bushes, shrubs, or other plants growing beneath large trees in a forest or woods.

un · ex · pect · ed (un′iks pek′tid) *adj.* unforeseen; coming or happening without warning.

un · har · ness (un här′nis) *v.* to take the harness or gear from.

u · ni · ver · si · ty (yōō′ nə vur′ si tē) *n.* a school of higher learning. It is usually made up of one or more colleges.

us · age (yōō′sij, yōō′zij) *n.* use.

Ut · kin, Josef (ōōt′ kən, jō′zəf)

V

va · cant (vā′kənt) *adj.* empty; containing nothing; unoccupied.

vague · ly (vāg′lē) *adv.* not in a clear or definite manner.

vain (vān) *adj.* conceited; overly concerned with or proud of one's appearance, abilities, or accomplishments.

var · mint (vär′mint) *n.* a troublesome or objectionable animal or person.

ve · hi · cle (vē′ə kəl) *n.* a device, such as a car, sled, or carriage, used for carrying goods and people.

vel · vet (vel′vit) *n.* a fabric with soft, thick pile.

Ven · e · zue · la (ven′ i zwā′lə) a country in northern South America, on the Caribbean Sea.

ves · sel (ves′əl) *n.* a tube that carries a body fluid.

vet · er · an (vet′ər ən) *n.* a person who has had a great deal of experience.

vi · bra · tion (vī brā′ shən) *n.* rapid movement back and forth or up and down.

vic · to · ry (vik′tər ē) *n.* the defeat of an opponent or enemy.

vin · e · gar (vin′ə gər) *n.* a sour liquid that is made by fermenting cider, wine, or other liquids. Vinegar is used in salad dressings and to flavor and preserve food.

vi · sion (vizh′ən) *n.* something that is imagined or dreamed.

wack · y (wak′ē) *adj.* *Slang.* strange, crazy, silly.

wal · rus (wôl′rəs, wol′rəs) *n.* a large sea animal that lives in arctic regions.

wam · pum (wom′pəm, wôm′pəm) *n.* small polished beads made from shells and strung together or woven into belts, collars, and necklaces. Wampum was used by certain tribes of North American Indians as money.

walrus

wan · der (won′dər) *v.* **1.** to go or move about aimlessly; roam. **2.** to go at a slow, relaxed pace; stroll.

ward · robe mis · tress (wôrd′rōb′ mis′tris) a woman who is in charge of taking care of the costumes for a play, an opera, or a dance program.

warp (wôrp) *n.* threads running lengthwise in a woven fabric.

wa · ter · mark (wô′tər märk′) *n.* a mark or design impressed upon something, especially paper.

wat · tle (wot′əl) *n.* the fleshy, often brightly colored fold of skin hanging down from the neck or throat of certain birds.

weap · on (wep′ən) *n.* anything used in a fight to attack or defend.

wea · ry (wēr′ē) *adj.* very tired.

wedge (wej) *v.* to drive, push, or crowd.

weep (wēp) *v.* **wept, weep · ing.** to show strong emotion, such as joy or grief, by shedding tears.

weft (weft) *n.* the crosswise threads in weaving; woof.

wheel · chair (hwēl′ chār, wēl′ chār) *n.* a chair on wheels, used especially by people who cannot use their legs.

where · a · bouts (hwer′ə bouts′) *adv.* near or in what location.— *n. pl.* the location of a person or place.

whif · fle tree (hwif′əl trē′) the pivoted crossbar at the front of a wagon or carriage to which the traces of the harness are attached.

whim · per (hwim′pər, wim′pər) *v.* to cry with weak, broken sounds.

whip · poor · will (hwip′ər wil′) *n.* **1.** a plump bird of eastern North America, active at night. **2.** the call of this bird.

whirl · wind (whurl′wind′) *n.* a rapidly or violently rotating column of air.

whit · ish (hwī′tish) *adj.* somewhat white.

whit · tle (hwit′əl) *v.* to cut small bits or pieces from wood, soap, or the like with a knife.

wick (wik) *n.* a cord in an oil lamp, candle, or cigarette lighter that soaks up the fuel and burns when it is lit.

wild · cat (wīld′kat′) *n.* a wild animal of the cat family, such as the bobcat and the lynx.

win · dow · pane (win′dō pān′) *n.* a single pane of glass in a window.

wildcat

---

a **b**ad, ā **c**ake, ä **f**ather; e **p**et, ē **m**e; i **i**t, ī **i**ce; o **h**ot, ō **o**pen, ô **o**ff; oo **w**ood,
ōō **f**ood; oi **o**il, ou **ou**t; th **th**in, th **th**at; u **c**up, ur **t**urn, yōō **m**usic; zh **tr**easure;
ə **a**go, tak**e**n, penc**i**l, lem**o**n, helpf**u**l

Win · ni · peg (win′ə peg′)   a city in southern Canada, the capital of Manitoba.

wisp (wisp) *n.*   a small bit or piece of something.

wit · ness (wit′nis) *v.*   to be present to see or hear something.

wob · ble (wob′əl) *v.*   to move or sway unsteadily from side to side.

wood snail (wood′ snāl′)   a small, slow moving animal with a soft body that is protected by a spiral-shaped shell.

woo · ing (wo͞o′ing) *n.*   seeking the love and affection of someone, usually with the intent to marry.

wrest · ling (res′ling) *n.*   a sport in which two opponents struggle hand to hand in an attempt to force or throw each other to the ground.

wrig · gle (rig′əl) *v.*   to twist or turn from side to side with short, quick moves.

Wu · fu (wo͞o′fo͞o)

Y

year · ling (yēr′ling) *n.*   an animal that is one year old or in its second year.

yearn (yurn) *v.*   to feel a strong and deep desire.

yolk (yōk) *n.*   the yellow part of an egg.

Z

Zie · mer (zē′mər)

zig · zag (zig′zag′) *v.*   **zig · zagged, zig · zag · ging.**   to move in a line, pattern, or course that has a series of short, sharp turns from side to side.

zo · ol · o · gist (zō ol′ə jist) *n.*   a scientist who studies animals.

zoom (zo͞om) *v.*   **1.** to move or climb suddenly and swiftly. **2.** to make or move with a loud, low-pitched humming sound.